Female Novelists of Modern Africa

Oladele Taiwo

ST. MARTIN'S PRESS   New York

All rights reserved. For imformation, write:
St. Martin's Press, Inc., 175 Fifth Avenue, New York, NY 10010

Printed in Hong Kong

Published in the United Kingdom by Macmillan Publishers Ltd
First published in the United States of America in 1985

ISBN 0-312-28738-0

Library of Congress Cataloging in Publication Data
Taiwo, Oladele.
  Female novelists of modern Africa.
  Bibliography: p.
  Includes index.
  1. African fiction (English)–Women authors–History
and criticism.   2. African fiction (English)–20th century–
History and criticism.   3. Women in literature–Africa.
4. Women–Africa.
  I. Title.
  PR9344.T34   1985   823'.009'9287   84-22310
ISBN 0-312-28738-0

For
Micere Mugo
Grace Ogot
Buchi Emecheta
Bessie Head
and all others
who by their
literary activities
have glorified
African womanhood.

Contents

Acknowledgements

The author and publishers wish to thank the following who have kindly given permission for the use of copyright material:

Allison & Busby Ltd. for extracts from Buchi Emecheta's books *In the Ditch, Second-Class Citizen, The Bride Price, The Slave Girl, The Joys of Motherhood,* and *Destination Biafra*.

East African Publishing House Ltd. for extracts from *Daughter of Mumbi* by Charity Waciuma, *Honeymoon for Three* by Jane Bakaluba, *Black Night of Quiloa* by Hazel Mugot, *The Promised Land* and *Land Without Thunder* by Grace Ogot, *Your Heart is my Altar* and *The Eighth Wife* by Miriam Were.

Fontana Paperbacks for extracts from *The Man from Sagamu* by Adaora Lily Ulasi.

Heinemann Educational Books for extracts from *The Collector of Treasures* and *Serowe: Village of the Rain Wind* by Bessie Head; from *Ripples in the Pool* by Rebeka Njau; from *Efuru* and *Idu* by Flora Nwapa; from *Time of the Butcherbird* by Alex la Guma; from *God's Bits of Wood* by Sembène Ousmane, originally published as *Les Bouts de Bois de Dieu* by Les Presses de la Cité, and from *So Long a Letter* by Mariama Ba originally published by Les Nouvelles Editions Africaines.

David Higham Associates Ltd. on behalf of Kofi Awooner for an extract from "Tradition and Continuity in African Literature" in *Exile and Tradition* edited by Rowland Smith.

Longman Group Ltd. for an extract from *Our Sister Killjoy* by Ama Ata Aidoo, and for extracts from *Muriel at the Metropolitan* by Miriam Tlali.

Thomas Nelson & Sons Ltd. for an extract from *An Introduction to West African Literature* by Oladele Taiwo.

Nwamife Publishers Limited for extracts from *Never Again* by Flora Nwapa.

Ohio University Press for an extract from *Mazungumzo — Interviews with East African Writers, Publishers, Editors and Scholars* edited by Bernth Lindfors, Papers in International Studies, Africa Series No. 41.

Oxford University Press for extracts from *The Moonlight Bride* by Buchi Emecheta.

Oxford University Press, Nairobi, for extracts from *The Boy in Between* and *High School Gent* by Miriam Were.

The Punch Newspaper for an extract from the interview with Buchi Emecheta, "A Worshipper from Afar" by Tunde Obadina, May 17, 1979.

Ravan Press (Pty) Ltd. for extracts from *Amandla* by Miriam Tlali.

The Royal African Society for an extract by F W Welbourne in *African Affairs*, April 1970.

Societé Nouvelle Présence Africaine, for an extract from "Three Female Writers in Modern Africa: Flora Nwapa, Ama Ata Aidoo and Grace Ogot" by Maryse Conde in *Présence Africaine*, Paris, No. 82, 1972.

Adaora Lily Ulasi for extracts from *Many Thing You No Understand* and *Many Thing Begin for Change*.

University of California, African Studies Center, for Delyna Diop's review of *La Grève des Battu* in UFAHAMU, Vol. II. No. 2, 1981, copyright of the Regents of the University of California.

Uzima Press Limited for extracts from *The Graduate* and *The Island of Tears* by Grace Ogot.

A P Watt Ltd. on behalf of Bessie Head for extracts from *When Rain Clouds Gather* and *Maru*.

West Africa magazine for extracts from article "Women and Development" by Victoria Fleming, December 1981.

Every effort has been made to trace all the copyright holders but if any have been inadvertently overlooked the publishers will be pleased to make the necessary arrangements at the first opportunity.

Preface

This book is a celebration of the literary activities of female novelists of modern Africa. For the first time a whole volume is devoted to their attempt to present past and contemporary African society in a way generally favourable to the standpoint of the woman. Forty-one works of fourteen female novelists are considered. These writers come from different parts of Africa and represent different points of view, orientation and temperament. Some are more popular than others. Many of them, like Bessie Head, Buchi Emecheta, Grace Ogot, Flora Nwapa and Ama Ata Aidoo, are established writers who are perhaps just as well-known as any other African novelists. Others, like Charity Waciuma, Hazel Mugot, Jane Bakaluba and Miriam Tlali, may be receiving serious critical attention for the first time. The value of this work lies in the fact that it presents for critical consideration and assessment so many works from such a variety of novelists, old and new, accomplished or newly-fledged. Each writer exploits her own immediate environment in order to dramatise those aspects of modern and traditional life she considers important. It is against such a background and motivation that each work or novelist is judged.

The approach of the book is to assess a novelist's output against the concept of the changing role of women in traditional and modern society. For this reason it has been necessary to give at the beginning some extensive consideration to the role of women in literature and society. Their economic and literary contributions, and their important functions in home and family life, are compared with their present preoccupations as novelists to see what transfer of knowledge and skill has taken place. Further consideration reveals that the circumstances in which women worked and lived in the old days are vastly different from those in which the novelists under focus now seek to display their artistic talents. The world has become so painfully competitive, and only the very best artists survive and gain popular acclaim. The amount of recognition given each novelist in this work is indicated more or less by the space devoted to the writer, and this has depended somewhat on her total output. Where a chapter is devoted to a writer, it has been possible to undertake detailed discussion of each work, observe trends, note influences on the writer, highlight techniques and assess what particular contribution the writer has made to any evolving literary tradition or experiment.

In a work of this kind it is not always possible to include all novelists, partly because of the limitation of space, and partly because of the need for the work to maintain an internal coherence of its own. The title of the book has been deliberately chosen to take care of such exclusions, if any. The express intention is to concentrate on novelists of 'modern Africa', either writing in English, or whose works have been translated into English, like Mariama Ba. 'Modern Africa' is defined as Africa south of the Sahara during the second half of the twentieth century. This is, in fact, the period usually encompassed by modern African Literature. The work is also limited to indigenous African novelists, who cannot but have some sentimental and emotional attachment to the continent. The love of Africa is the common bond which holds these writers together. Even where they are critical of the social order, and some of them are bitterly satirical, the aim is to call attention to abuses in order to achieve social reform.

This volume must be regarded as the work of a pioneer in a new field. The book will be useful to all those interested in women's studies, especially the evolution of female literary tradition, in and outside Africa: college and university students, their lecturers and professors, writers and other artists, literary critics and the general reader. The work does not provide any final answers or give the last word about any of the novelists or works treated. The field is wide and developing. One expects that more critics will take an interest in this new and exciting area of study, and produce books which will do credit to the attempt of women to establish themselves in the literary field, as in other fields of human endeavour. There is, for example, the need to produce comprehensive single volumes on the more important writers like Buchi Emecheta, Grace Ogot and Bessie Head. The task ahead is to have so many of such materials in Literature and other areas that it will soon be possible to establish Departments or Centres of Women's Studies in many African universities. It is in this context that the present attempt achieves its greatest significance.

The research study for this book reached its climax during a sabbatical year. I would like to thank the authorities of the University of Lagos for granting me leave and providing necessary logistic support for my work. I also thank my colleagues in the various universities I visited for their help and encouragement. Particular thanks go to my friends in these universities – Christopher Heywood at Sheffield, Professor Micere Mugo at Nairobi and Professor John Povey at Los Angeles – for giving me so much of their time. I am grateful to my publishers for providing needed material and academic support. I am especially grateful to my wife who acted as my secretary throughout my sabbatical leave and diligently produced the final version of the script.

Oladele Taiwo
University of Lagos, Akoka
October, 1982.

CHAPTER ONE

The Role of African Women in Literature and Society

Pre-literate African women contributed a great deal to education and literature. Their art was verbal and their purpose didactic. Through the appropriate use of stories, speeches, songs, satires, praises and abuses, they not only helped the young members of the society with the process of enculturation, but also made a notable contribution to oral literature which has largely provided the material for modern African Literature.[1]

However, for social and economic reasons, it has not been possible readily to transfer this distinguished role of African women in traditional literature to the art of novel writing. There are many difficulties in the way. Buchi Emecheta mentions some of them.

> To be a good novelist the writer must operate within a conducive atmosphere. She must have time and space to reflect and indulge in introspective thinking. For many potential writers in this country neither the time nor the space is available. In addition to family drawbacks, the government seems not to appreciate the value of home-produced works. It seems to be doing very little to encourage writers, financially.[2]

These difficulties relate to all novelists, men and women. But they seem to have completely overwhelmed the women and sapped their creative energy, at least initially. The result is that the men, as in many other facets of African life, have dominated the field and successfully pushed the women to the background. Furthermore, the male novelists have created in their fiction an image of the African woman which needs to be closely re-examined against the background of her traditional role

1

and the social and economic realities of the present. For, as Maryse Conde has pointed out,

> the personality and the inner reality of African women have been hidden under such a heap of myths, so-called ethnological theories, rapid generalizations and patent untruths that it might be interesting to study what they have to say for themselves when they decide to speak.[3]

But before going into these matters in detail it might be useful to start with a consideration of the contribution of women to literature and society in the urban and rural settings of Africa.

In most parts of Africa the whole of a girl's life is one long preparation for the useful role she is expected to play in society. This role pertains mainly to marriage and child-bearing. Several writers have alluded to the hardship a girl encounters as part of her preparation for life.[4] She is put under rigid observation for a long time by members of her family. When she is bethrothed to a man his relations expect her to conform to certain traditions and norms of their family. Everybody takes an interest in how she sits, speaks, laughs, acts and reacts to situations. Every detail of her manners is noted, especially by members of the family of her prospective husband. The final decision to carry on with the marriage proposal is based on the result of such an observation carried on for a reasonable length of time. This undoubtedly puts pressure on the girl to behave well, although it may also have the effect of restricting her freedom of action. If she is found acceptable and gets married, her immediate hope will be to have children. In this lies her security. For a childless marriage has no place in African traditional life. Much attention is paid to the training of a girl so that she may be well brought up to transmit the cultural norms of the society to her children. In this way she helps to maintain the continuity of the ethnic group and the race.

It is because of the importance traditional society attaches to the girl's future role that she is not allowed on her own to choose a future husband for herself. It is the responsibility of her family, working in collaboration with relations of her prospective husband. She becomes in this transaction little more than an object whose price is negotiated. If the negotiations succeed and she gets married, she is expected to play the role of a subordinate, submissive housewife. If she is lucky enough to have children of her own, society expects that she will devote most of her time to bringing them up properly. There are conventions and cautionary riddles, proverbs and folktales to make her accept these roles. Of course, there have been instances of girls rejecting assigned roles. African literature is full of examples where a girl either refuses the

2

husband chosen for her by the family or accepts the choice and yet remains childless. The case of Agom in Onuora Nzekwu's *Highlife for Lizards* is a sad example of childlessness in marriage and its dreadful consequences. Where the girl is headstrong, clings to her desires, sets aside societal norms and marries a man of her choice, everybody expects the marriage to come to grief.

This is the basis of the conception of the Complete Gentleman in folklore and literature, which is current in many folklores of the world.[5] The girl becomes so choosy about her future husband that she rejects all suitors. Then she meets a stranger in the community and is immediately attracted to him because of his beauty or strangeness. The result is invariably disastrous. For, according to Ebun Clark,

> She usually lives, within the fable to regret her action, for the man whom she thinks is 'complete', perfect or ideal, invariably turns out to be something vile or horrifying: a beast, serpent, boa or a skull. Beneath the veneer of sophistication and perfection lies an animal or a savage.[6]

Conformity is an important aspect of traditional life. Any girl who tries to upset societal values does so at her own risk. Some female writers believe that this kind of set-up is designed primarily for male comfort. They therefore write to show that the male position is not unassailable and try to correct certain fallacies which have gained currency in a male-oriented society. One of these is the attitude of mind which automatically blames childlessness in marriage on the woman. As highly educated people themselves, female novelists do not feel that women should accept the roles carved out for them by men and society.

Economic Contribution

The contribution of African women to literature and society has been largely connected with their roles as wives, mothers and partners in the home. Their contribution to the economic well-being of society is enormous, much greater than they have ever been given credit for. While the men are busy on the farm, the women are gainfully employed at home on such activities as wine-brewing, pot-making, dyeing, and removing the coverings from melon seeds and beans. Some women work on the farms and plant cassava while their husbands plant yams. The women are largely responsible for the harvesting of all crops. Victoria Fleming is unhappy that little or no recognition is given to the economic output of women to whom she attributes 60 to 80 per cent of all agricultural work.[7] She argues her point with the hypothetical case of Fatu.

Consider, for example, Fatu, a farmer in Mali, West Africa. She gets up at 4.45 a.m. then walks to the fields where she works mainly on the cash crop, but also on her vegetable garden. At 3 p.m. she collects a heavy load of firewood, which she carries home, where she pounds and grinds corn until 5.30 p.m. Then she walks to the stream to fetch water, which she has to carry two miles on her head before she reaches home. After this she cooks, feeds and washes the children, and is asleep by 9.30 p.m.[8]

Not only is the African woman hardworking, she is also an economic asset to her husband and family. Without the money she makes from her petty trading, fishing and farming her husband will hardly be able to cope with all the needs of the children. This vital point is missed even at the level of the U.N.O., and it leads the various kinds of difficulties.

For example, one aid agency in West Africa perceived men to be the main producers and heads of household, and so it aimed its programmes towards them. One of its activities was to provide the men with ploughs, with which they were very pleased, and ploughed much larger acreages of land than ever before. However, the agency over-looked the fact that it was the women who harvested the rice, and provided with only their traditional hand blades they had great difficulty in completing the larger harvest.[9]

Literary Contribution

The contribution of women to oral literature starts with the use of nursery rhymes in the upbringing of children. In certain cultures the mother moves her legs to prevent the child on her back from waking. These rudimentary steps, being rhythmic, form the basis of sophisticated dance steps. Rhythm, for the purpose of nursery rhymes, is produced through different mediums – the human voice, the talking drum and the pounding of the pestles, as when girls pound corn or yam flour. If the girls are happy with their work, the pounding is brisk and the rhythm is tuneful. But when the work is done grudgingly the rhythm becomes irregular, slow and unpleasant because it lacks harmony. Each culture has its own set of nursery rhymes, made up of lullabies, limericks, enchanted nonsense, children's songs and games, nature and didactic poems. Their value may be purely aesthetic, educative or moralistic. Yorùbá lullabies, for example, try to achieve their purpose by the predominance of certain stylistic features in the structural arrangement of the rhyme. Only a few examples need be given in a work of this kind.[10]

4

Ta ń bá mi lọmọ wí?	Who scolded my child?
Adedekún deé kún.	Adedekún deé kún.
Ìyá rè ló baá wí.	Its mother scolded it.
Adedekún deé kún	Adedekún deé kún.
Ó gb'ọmú ro'ko,	Carrying breasts to the farm,
Ó gb'ọmu ro'do,	Carrying breasts to the brook,
Kò gb'ọmú wá'lé mọ́.	She won't bring the breasts home.

The rhyme begins with a question pertinent to the problem of the child's crying. When the question is answered it does not end at that. The manner in which the rhyme is related to the needs of the crying child is interesting.

In this piece of enchanted nonsense the repetition of certain sounds like 'o', and particular words and lines have only one purpose; that of lulling a child to sleep. The rhyme relies on its sound effect alone for its meaning.

O o to o,	Hush, hush,
O to to o	Hush, hush, hush,
Da kẹ o,	Stop, stop,
Da kẹ kẹ,	Stop, stop, stop,
Ng o p'ọpọlọ	I'll kill you a toad
Bo fun o	On my way back
Loko wa o.	From our farm.
O o to o,	Hush, hush,
O to to o,	Hush, hush, hush,
Da kẹ o,	Stop, stop,
Da kẹ kẹ o.	Stop, stop, stop.

The rhyme consists predominantly of sounds that have a soothing effect on the nerves. The repetition of 'to to to' is like water dropping in trickles, a sound which evokes sleep or a drowsy feeling because of its monotony.

Not all lullabies are of light vein. In some the tone is apprehensive. This is understandable. With the infant mortality rate so high, a mother's fears about the chances of her baby's survival are very real.

Ọmọ mi ò	Oh my baby
Alápá bebekúbe,	With the well formed arms,
Ọmọ mi ò	Oh my baby
Ẹlésẹ̀ bebekùbe	With the well shaped legs,
Ọmọ booku o	Baby if you don't die
Ng o ra'ṣọ fun ọ.	I'll buy you clothes.
Ọmọ b'o ba yee	Baby if you survive
Ng o r'ẹwu ẹtu.	I'll buy ẹtu garment

Ewu ẹtu	Ẹtu garment
Ma i kọ ọ lọrun.	I'll hang on your neck.
Ẹru meje	Seven slaves
Ni yoo sin ọ d'ode.	Will escort you out.
Iwọfa mẹfa	Six pawns
Ni yo fa ọ kalẹ,	Will help you to your seat,
Ni yo fa ọ kalẹ.	Will help you to your seat.

Many Nature poems provide suitable material for nursery rhymes:

Pẹpẹyẹ oru gbangudu,	A duck is swollen gbangudu,
O bi'mọ,	It gave birth to children,
Ko r'ẹhin pọn'mọ.	It had no back on which to carry them.

Here the rhyme is terse. There is economy in the use of words and this is effective as each word carries an appropriate meaning. The descriptive words 'oru gbangudu' in line one are ideophones portraying the shape of the duck.

The rhythm of the next poem is quite different. The tempo is fast, suggestive of some eagerness to achieve results:

Lekeleke	Cattle egret
Ta le mi.	Mark me.
Ta le mi.	Mark me.
Ta le mi.	Mark me.
Mu dudu lọọ,	Take away the black,
Mu funfun bọ wa'le.	Bring home the white.
Ṣe m'boo ti ṣ'ọmọ'ya ẹ.	Treat me like your mother's child.
Ṣe m'boo ti ṣ'ọmọ'ya ẹ.	Treat me like your mother's child.
Ṣe m'boo ti ṣ'ọmọ'ya ẹ.	Treat me like your mother's child.

One of the most popular rhymes among school children is this one that promises a white collar job and every material comfort to pupils who study hard.

Bata mi a dun	My shoes will sound
Ko, ko, ka,	Ko, ko, ka,
Bata mi a dun	My shoes will sound
Ko, ko, ka.	Ko, ko, ka.
Bi mo ba ṣiṣe,	If I do my work,
Bata mi a dun	My shoes will sound
Ko, ko, ka.	Ko, ko, ka.
Bata rẹ a dun	Your shoes will sound
Kẹ rẹ rẹ ni'lẹ	Kẹ rẹ rẹ on the floor,
Bata rẹ a dun	Your shoes will sound
Kẹ rẹ rẹ ni'le	Kẹ rẹ rẹ on the floor,

Bi o ba ṣọ ọlẹ	If you are lazy
Bata rẹ a dun	Your shoes will sound
Kẹ rẹ re ni'lẹ	Kẹ rẹ rẹ on the floor.

High heeled shoes sound 'ko ko ka' while the shuffling of sandals sound 'kẹ rẹ rẹ' on the ground. This implies that only children who are hard-working will pass their examinations and succeed in life. They will be able to afford expensive things like shoes whereas the lazy ones will only have money to buy sandals or slippers. This rhyme aptly epitomises the values of a generation which is becoming increasingly materialistic.

So we find that nursery rhymes derive from various situations and incidents in the home and community. They are used to keep the child amused or contented. They show the mother's ability to improvise and fire the child's imagination from an early age.

Women have the primary responsibility of bringing up children. It is true that the father is available to provide logistic and psychological support of a kind that gives the child comfort and security. But it is the mother who has the child under her prolonged and detailed care, moulds its character and ensures that her offspring conforms to societal norms. If the child fails, it is the mother who is generally considered to have failed. So she tries hard to ensure that the child grows not only physically but also spiritually. Through the judicious application of the sayings of the elders which embody the wisdom of several generations the child is introduced to the ways of the world. This is what Laye's mother does in *The African Child*. She brings her child up strictly according to the customs of her people and ensures that he is properly introduced to the society. In *The Promised Land* Achola, in the interest of her husband and children, remains faithful to her family gods, even in a foreign land, and regards the safety and the proper upbringing of her children as her main concern. When this is no longer possible in Tanzania she insists that all members of the family should return to Kenya.

The use of riddles, proverbs, folktales, songs and nuptial chants in the inculcation of morals is widespread. This is another area in which women play a dominant role by virtue of their close attachment to the child. They use these literary forms to impart knowledge and pleasure to their wards and children. Fortunately these forms are attractive in themselves. Riddles reflect the basic concerns and interest of a people and are usually rich in imagery. Proverbs are the stock-in-trade of old people who use them to convey moral lessons, warnings and advice. These literary forms are common modes of speech in traditional society and are therefore an appropriate means of enculturation. They make greater impact on the mind than ordinary words in the way they arrest attention. It is usually an essential part of the child's training for him to be able to provide answers to riddles and unravel the meanings of proverbs. Each woman is expected to work hard to interest the children under her care in these cultural modes of expression.

The folktale is used in a more dramatic manner to initiate children and adolescents into their cultural heritage. The folktale is an intrinsically interesting form and its presentation is made even more interesting by the active participation of all involved. The performance structure is rooted in indigenous culture and makes use of riddles and proverbs in its introductory parts. The leader of performance may be a man or woman. But it is often the woman who plays the part because she is not as tired after the day's work as the man. The content of the tale is moralistic and the purpose of the presentation is didactic. So the storyteller puts a lot of life into the narration which is often accompanied by dramatic and musical performances. This is the only way to keep the childen fully awake and make sure the purpose of the storytelling event has been achieved. For, as has been said elsewhere,

> The effectiveness of the story-teller's performance is measured by the influence of his stories on the behaviour of the young. They are expected to derive knowledge and wisdom from his stories and through these stories to become acquainted with the customs, traditions and religion of the people. Unless children gain these things from their story-telling sessions with him a story-teller is not considered successful.[11]

Nuptial chants play a significant role in the proper upbringing of girls. It is essential that girls are brought up in a highly disciplined manner so that they may become useful wives, mothers and nation-builders. They are expected, for example, to be virgins at marriage. Only then can they qualify to sing nuptial songs. These songs are composed and compiled by experienced women in society who transmit them from one generation to another. Girls learn these songs from an early age as part of their preparation for marriage. The songs achieve special significance on the eve of a girl's wedding which is the last day of spinsterhood. After that day she is traditionally no longer qualified to sing these songs. They are particularly meaningful in the context in which they are used and help to keep a girl on the path of moral rectitude until she is publicly sanctioned to go to bed with her chosen man. A girl who loses her virginity before marriage is disqualified from chanting nuptial songs and is considered a social disgrace to her age group, family and community. Three of such songs are provided to give an idea of the content of nuptial chants.[12]

In the first chant the girl is already looking forward to what will happen to her the next day. Her man will have carnal knowledge of her for the first time. She will not enjoy it, but she will endure the pain because of her expectations for a child, which is a duty she owes her ancestral god and people. The content accords with Yoruba philosophy of life and repeats popular sentiments.

Woyi ọla ọkọ a forii mi tiganna	By this time tomorrow my husband will rest my head against the wall
A a fẹṣẹ mejeeji mi ṣerọkun	He will use my legs as a pillow
A a fagbede mejii mi ṣe ijokoo	He will use my midribs as stool
Ololufẹ a maa mu faaji ọmọ	My lover will enjoy the process of producing a child
Iboosi orii mi n ke	I'll start shouting my head off
Ori apere o gbe mi de yaraa mi.	The god of head will follow me to my room.
Ori apere o gbe mi de yaraa mi.	The god of head will follow me to my room.

The second is a different kind of chant. The chant now comes from other girls as an admonition to the bride. They make her realise she is entering a new world and advise her on how to behave in her new home. The need to prepare delicious meals for her husband is stressed because in traditional society this is one sure way of sustaining marriages.

Ma ma ja	Don't fight
Ma ma ta	Don't quarrel
O ko ni l'ọta	You will thus have no enemies
Ile ọkọ ki iṣe ayunlọ	Husband's house is only one way
Ile ọkọ kiise ayunbọ.	Husband's house is not a return trip.
A diro iyawo gbọdọ duro gbọningbọnin.	The wife's hearth must be in use constantly.

In the third chant an elderly woman advises the bride on the general mode of conduct in her new situation, what ideals to embrace and how to avoid disaster.

Iwọ too n'rele ọkọ	You that you are getting married
Ma ma ta a a ro lọla	Do not discountenance the hearth

Ma fi ile Ọkọ sere alẹ	Do not make jest of marriage institution
Obitun o	Bride
Ma se ọran ija nile Ọkọ	Do not cause trouble in the husband's house
Ma sọrọ o pa nile ọkọ ati nibikibi	Do not behave in the way that you will be flogged in your husband's house or any where.
Obitun pẹlẹ o. Obitun	Bride greeting bride.
Ma fi sọrọ ijọngbọnni ile ọkọ	Don't cause trouble in your husband's house
Bi o ti mi lọ ma gba gbe, Obitun.	As you are going, bride please do not forget your duties.

So we see that these chants not only provide entertainment, they are also a means of enforcing morals and discipline.

Home and Family Life

Whether in a rural or urban setting it is the business of the woman to introduce the child to clean and acceptable social habits. The father has an assigned role to play, but the mother's part is crucial if the child is to survive socially as an adult. The atmosphere of the home in which the child is brought up influences his conception of the world. 'The family constitutes the first world of the child; . . . by continuous, intimate, numerous, and varied associations it becomes a major source of education and behaviour determination;' says Hayes.[13] The home is the first agency of education. Unless it plays its part well, all the other agencies – the School, Community and State – will have no strong foundation upon which to build. To the extent that the woman helps to lay this foundation for every child, she is directly contributing to national greatness. She should from an early age teach the child how to eat, dress, talk and laugh decently. As he grows up he should learn simple acts of consideration and courtesy to others. He should be introduced to the rudiments of speech and good manners and cultivate a healthy daily routine.

When school age is reached, the mother's role grows in importance. The first few months in school are crucial for the child. Whether he settles down quickly in school or not depends on how he is handled at this initial stage. His parents, especially his mother, must take an interest in his problems of adjustment. The ability to read is basic to all education. Reading easily becomes important in the curriculum at an early stage. Unless the child can read well, he will not be able to acquire knowledge in other subject areas, and his progress in school will be retarded. For this reason,

> the home should provide the opportunity for the child to show his interest and ability by providing an environment intellectually stimulating to the child. There should be newspapers, periodicals, magazines and books around the home from which the child can make his choice. In fact, if the child has a say in what newspapers and magazines are kept in the home, he feels all the more important and interested to read. Most families will ensure that at least one magazine chosen by the child is kept in the house.[14]

A happy and stable family life is essential for the child's ultimate success. His future happiness depends to a large extent on the kind of environment provided for him as a child by his parents. Every occasion should be exploited for the benefit of his education – family dinners, visitors to the family, important family outings and festivities, and family holidays. The child should be encouraged to become a firm believer in democratic ideals and the rights of individuals. If the correct attitude is fostered at home, in school and the community, the child has no difficulty in interacting with people and serving his nation loyally as an adult. It is only then that the mother can claim she has successfully carried out the more important obligation of parenthood which is the proper upbringing of children.

Image in African Literature

This then briefly is the contribution which traditional and modern women have made to society and oral literature. How is this reflected in modern African literature? What image of the woman emerges from African writings? What stereotypes have been created and what is being done to correct any wrong impressions? What should be the role of a female novelist in modern Africa and how successfully is she playing her role? These are some of the issues raised in this book as each novelist is discussed in detail.

However, it may be helpful to stress at this point that because male writers were early in the field they have projected an image of the woman which female writers have found rather distasteful. It is not always that male writers have been biased; they have merely presented the female social situation as it is. This is why for the most part a woman occupies a position of inferiority since the writer is anxious to be faithful to the realities of the world he portrays. This, however, hardly explains the representation of a woman as a sex symbol such as we have in Cyprian Ekwensi's *Jagua Nana* or as the morally chaotic person she is portrayed to be in David Rubadiri's *No Bride Price*. Onitsha market literature, for example, is full of instances which exaggerate the moral and psychological handicaps of women.[15]

The picture has been generally bleak and unedifying. But there have been a few important exceptions. Two examples will suffice. In *God's Bits of Wood* Sembene Ousmane highlights the important role played by women in the struggle for economic and social survival.[16] As the railway workers on the Dakar – Niger line go out on strike in order to obtain justice the women take up the challenge to cater for the material well-being of members of their families. Ousmane questions traditional male chauvinism and succeeds in enlarging the political and social base of his women. They resolutely challenge the forces of law and act independently to get the law-enforcement agencies to see reason. They act in a way to compel the attention and respect of all.

> A few minutes later a murmur of excitement rippled across the crowd, as the women of Thies came in through the main entrance gate. Their long journey together had been an effective training school; they marched in well-ordered ranks, ten abreast, and without any masculine escort now. They carried banners and pennants printed with slogans, some of them reading, EVEN BULLETS COULD NOT STOP US, and others, WE DEMAND FAMILY ALLOWANCES. (p.290)

Here Ousmane accords women a superb organisation and qualities of bravery and endurance usually considered exclusive to men.

A more radical example of women's liberation and independent action is provided by Alex la Guma in *Time of the Butcherbird* where Mma-Tau is built into a monumental figure and made the symbol of black resistance to racial oppression in South Africa.[17] She is 'the she-lion, as ferocious as ever . . . a terrifying woman'. (p.46). She keeps up the momentum of the resistance at a time her brother, Hlangeni, is demoralised because he has recently been deprived of his chieftaincy title. Her analysis of the situation in South Africa shows her deep psychological insight into the problems of her people, especially the heavy burden placed on them by the whites.

> They exist in a false happiness of guns and laws, they exist with false laughter, for the laughter is not really theirs. Do they know the meaning of their laws and their false happiness and their undignified laughter? The meaning is this: that men are of two kinds, the poor who toil and create the riches of the earth; and the rich who do not

toil but devour it. The meaning is this: that the people demand their share of the fruits of the earth, and their rulers, of whom the white man is a lackey, a servant, refuse them a fair portion. And it is this: that the people insist, the rulers deprive them of work, drive them from their homes, and if they still resist, send their lackeys to shoot them down with guns. (p.47).

Mma-Tau succeeds. She becomes the embodiment of collective justice and enjoys widespread support. She is able at the height of her popularity to halt government forces, an experience which stuns a police sergeant. Even those who are at first cynical about her prospect of success finally acknowledge that she is making a significant contribution to the liberation of the black people in South Africa. In this instance a woman succeeds where a man has failed.

This provides a brief description of the literary background against which female novelists in modern Africa write. As will soon become obvious, they react differently to this situation. Some write in total rejection of the image of women projected by male writers. Others try to glorify the role played by women in society and thereby help to raise their status. How successful female novelists have been in these endeavours is the main preoccupation of the rest of this book.

Notes

1 For a recent study of this subject, see Adewoye, S.A. 'The Role of the African Women in Traditional Literature,' paper presented at the first annual conference of the Literary Society of Nigeria in Benin, September 17-21, 1980.

2 See 'A Worshipper from Afar', interview with Buchi Emecheta by Tunde Obadina in *Punch*, May 17, 1979.

3 Maryse Conde, 'Three Female Writers in Modern Africa: Flora Nwapa, Ama Ata Aidoo and Grace Ogot', *Presence Africaine*, no.82 2e trimestre 1972, p.132.

4 See, for example, Sylvia Leith-Ross, *African Women* (1939) (London, Routledge & Kegan Paul, 1965) or V.C. Uchendu, *The Igbo of Southeast Nigeria* (New York, Holt, Rinehart and Winston, 1965).

5 For a recent discussion of this folklore, see Ebun Clark, 'Othello The Complete Gentleman: An African Folkloric Interpretation', Departmental Seminar Paper, Department of English, University of Lagos, February, 1982.

6 Ebun Clark, op. cit., p.2.

7 Victoria Fleming, 'Women and Development', *West Africa*, 7 December, 1981, p.2921.

8 Ibid.

9 Ibid.

10 These examples were previously used by me in 'Junior Poetry in English – Orientation, Content, Language and Methodology', in *Junior Literature in English*, S.O. Unoh, editor (AUP, 1981) Pp.61-79.

11 Oladele Taiwo, *An Introduction to West African Literature* (London, Thomas Nelson & Sons Ltd., 1967) 1981 Reprint. p.15.

12 The three nuptial chants are taken from Adewoye, op. cit.

13 Hayes, Waland S. 'The Family and Education' *Encyclopedia of Educational Research*, pp.433-5 quoted in Ralph C. Staiger, *Roads to Reading* (Paris, UNESCO, 1979), Pp.21-2.

14 Oladele Taiwo, *Agencies of Education* (London, Macmillan, 1966), p.14.

15 For a detailed treatment of this subject, see, for example, Emmanuel Obiechina, *An African Popular Literature* (C.U.P. 1973).

16 Sembene Ousmane, *God's Bits of Wood* (London, Heinemann, 1970). Page references are to this edition.

17 Alex la Guma, *Time of the Butcherbird* (London, Heinemann, 1979). Page references are to this edition.

CHAPTER TWO

The Woman as a Novelist in Modern Africa

A female novelist in modern Africa is a rare personality. She is invariably a member of the elite class, or at least on her way to becoming one. Because she operates in a literate medium, she is likely to be highly educated. She is a professional woman who often has benefited from university education. Her background may be lower middle or working class, but she has worked so hard that she is now accepted as an honoured member of the society. She is active in social organisations, especially those connected with the improvement of the quality of home and family life. She is particularly concerned with the role of women in local, national and international affairs, and writes mostly to highlight these roles. She ensures that women play crucial roles in her novels and are put in situations where they can prove their mettle, show initiative and contribute maximally to the development of enduring social values in the community. The female novelist not only glorifies womanhood in her writing; she also shows concern for the material and spiritual well-being of the society of which women form only a part.

Many influences have helped to shape the consciousness of the female novelist. These factors are essentially the same as those which inspired the men to start writing. After all, both groups of novelists grew up in the same society. The circumstances which encouraged Africans to write have been discussed by a number of critics.[1] So all that is required here is a brief discussion, with special reference to how these factors have affected female novelists in particular. The slave trade, slavery and colonialism may appear remote influences. But they are strong enough to provide the inspiration for some novels. Buchi Emecheta's *The Slave Girl* relies for its effect on the inhuman conditions of slavery. Adaora

Ulasi writes colonial novels which bring vividly before the reader the big gulf which usually separates the people and the Administration in a colonial relationship. The crudest form of relationship between peoples of different races is embodied in the obnoxious system of apartheid. The blacks in South Africa have been the greatest sufferers under a system which treats them as second-class citizens. The dehumanising effect of apartheid provides most of the material for Bessie Head's writings. Ama Ata Aidoo and other novelists allude freely in their works to the slave trade and colonialism, especially the adverse effect these have had on African development.

Other influences are discernible, but they affect the consciousness of the various writers differently. The image of Africa as a 'Dark Continent', as projected by European explorers and in early European fiction, the literary exploits of early African novelists like D.T. Niane and Thomas Mofolo, and the abundant supply all over Africa of traditions and customs which provide the material for a written literature, are potent factors. So also are the growth of literacy, the spread of the mass media, the gradual development of a reading public and the recent phenomenal increase in the provision of educational facilities. Once the awareness of the importance of reading is created, writers feel encouraged to produce more books which will help sustain the effort at mass education. This partly explains why many of the female novelists considered here who started writing with full-length novels now write children's books as well. The intention is to contribute constructively to the readership promotion campaigns initiated by several African governments and to make available reading materials appropriate to age, circumstance and level of education.

The influence of African male writers on female novelists has been mentioned. Many women write in direct reply to men and to keep the records straight. An equally important influence may well derive from happenings outside Africa, especially the role women are playing in the international community. Women have held highly-esteemed posts in the UNO and other world organisations, and have performed creditably. Only recently a woman was appointed the Under Secretary-General of the UNO. Women are senior members of the bench and bar of various countries, have served with distinction in the diplomatic service, successfully held the post of heads of government, and made significant contributions in welfare and voluntary organisations at the local, national and international levels. This is naturally a source of pride to other women, some of whom may feel that it is in the area of writing that they too can make a unique contribution.

The influence of one female writer on another cannot be easily quantified. But there can be little doubt that female novelists in modern

Africa have been influenced by literary women in other parts of the world. They would have come across at one time or another the writings of some of the women who have contributed in a significant manner to several literary traditions, for example, Katherine Porter, Mary Shelley, Christiana Stead, Gertrude Stein, Harriet Stowe, Flora Tristan. They almost certainly would have read with pleasure and admiration the works of distinguished female writers like Virginia Woolf, Jane Austen, Charlotte Bronte, Emily Bronte, George Eliot (Mary Ann Evans), among others.[2] From this they would have realised the enormous contribution which women have made in the intellectual field over a long period. Women's contribution has become indispensable for a rational study of any of the literary forms. This phenomenon, it must be admitted, is 'something new, something distinctive of modernity itself, that the written word in its most memorable form, starting in the eighteenth century, became increasingly and steadily the work of women'.[3] This glorious trend must have affected the consciousness of the African female novelists. They would prefer not to be left far behind by other intellectuals. They are therefore now making a spectacular contribution to literature. More importantly, they have by their totally different orientation provided a new dimension to the intellectual ferment required to sustain the feminist movement.

What then is the end-product of these influences? What do African female novelists write about? What is their particular method of approach? What impact have they made on the reading public and how effective have they been as instruments of social change? The rest of the book will be devoted to a detailed consideration of these questions. In this chapter an attempt is made to give a panoramic view of what material is available and how versatile the novelists have been in their treatment of topics and situations in different parts of the continent. Six novels taken from West, East and Southern Africa, and dealing with various topics, are used as samples.

Mariama Ba, *So Long a Letter*

So Long a Letter is a radical novel which adopts the form of a long letter.[4] Through a series of reminiscences Ramatoulaye shows how she is able to retain her sanity and dignity in the difficult situation created by the death of her husband. She records her loneliness, grief, display of courage in the face of great odds, her internal striving for a more secure life, her social inadequacies and achievements. The novelist skilfully puts together a rambling collection of episodes built around matters of national and universal significance. Through this she mobilises public opinion in favour of women's liberation, freedom of action for the individual and a total rejection of all unprogressive ideas and attitudes.

At the centre of the work is a consideration of the place of the woman in a Muslim society. Two cases are used as examples – the marriage between Modou and Ramatoulaye and that between Mawdo and Aissatou. Each ends in disaster mainly because the man takes a second wife; Binetou in the case of Modou, Nabou in the case of Mawdo. Ramatoulaye and Aissatou consider themselves unable to accept the indignity of living with a second wife. At the height of her own crisis, Aissatou writes to Mawdo to terminate the relationship between them.

> I cannot accept what you are offering me today in place of the happiness we once had. You want to draw a line between heartfelt love and physical love. I say that there can be no union of bodies without the heart's acceptance, however little that may be . . .
>
> I am stripping myself of your love, your name. Clothed in my dignity, the only worthy garment, I go my way. (pp.31-32)

Ramatoulaye, on the other hand, decides to remain with Modou for as long as it is possible. She too is annoyed that 'for the sake of "variety", men are unfaithful to their wives'. (p.34) Even so, she remains loyal to Modou after he has deserted her. Her social problems multiply after his death when she assumes responsibility for the children. She struggles very hard not to have to abandon her marital home and shows a grim determination not to succumb to the wishes of those who want her to quit.

> 'There is a saying that discord here may be luck elsewhere. Why are you afraid to make the break? A woman is like a ball; once a ball is thrown, no one can predict where it will bounce. You have no control over where it rolls, and even less over who gets it. Often it is grabbed by an unexpected hand . . . .' (p.40)

It is a great tribute to Ramatoulaye's sterling qualities that she is able to cope with the problems posed by the upbringing of her children in a society in a state of transition, where borrowed and inherited ideas battle for supremacy.

But why is Ramatoulaye so resolutely opposed to polygamous life? She is a fervent Muslim who accepts the teaching of Islam. She makes loud protestations of her faith at several stages in the novel.

> My heart concurs with the demands of religion. Reared since childhood on their strict precepts, I expect not to fail. (p.8)

> No, I would not give in to pressure. My mind and my faith rejected supernatural power. (p.49)

So her objection to her husband marrying Binetou can only be on social grounds since Islam accepts polygamy as a way of life. She is concerned with the rights of women and the need for each woman to retain her individuality and establish an acceptable personal code of conduct. She sets the example in her own life. She accepts all vicissitudes with equanimity and successfully wards off all kinds of social pressures put on her by groups and individuals after the death of Modou. For example, she rejects Daouda Dieng as a suitor and tells off Tamsir who wants to inherit her.

> You forget that I have a heart, a mind, that I am not an object to be passed from hand to hand. You don't know what marriage means to me: it is an act of faith and of love, the total surrender of oneself to the person one has chosen and who has chosen you. (p.58)

She is concerned with the dignity of man, the need to keep the human mind and body inviolate and to conceive of love more as a metaphysical than a physical activity. Only in such a situation can the rights of women in marriage be preserved. Only then can they accomplish in honour and dignity the role assigned to them by nature and society.

Ramatoulaye is an embodiment of all that is noble and dignified in a woman. As an activist she is endowed with a lot of physical and mental energy which she puts to good use. She finds herself taking on different kinds of responsibilities and she performs admirably. On her own she solves all the problems that confront her, even though these weigh her down occasionally. That she remains so mentally alert and accomplishes so much in the unhappy situation in which she finds herself is no mean achievement. She is meant to be an attractive example of how brilliantly a woman can perform when the use of her talent and ability is not obstructed by restrictions and taboos. It is by such constructive achievements, rather than by empty sloganising, that women can prove their mettle and establish a place of honour for themselves in a male-dominated world. Ramatoulaye's activities and achievements put a woman's enormous capabilities and resilience beyond doubt. She expects that her contribution will result in the glorification of womanhood.

> I am not indifferent to the irreversible currents of women's liberation that are lashing the world. This commotion that is shaking up every aspect of our lives reveals and illustrates our abilities.
>
> My heart rejoices each time a woman emerges from the shadows. I know that the field of our gains is unstable, the retention of conquests difficult: social constraints are ever-present, and male egoism resists. (p.88)

19

Although much has been accomplished, much remains to be done. Total success can only be recorded if the struggle continues relentlessly and the battle is waged with great intensity.

The novel deals with other areas of life where women have been effective or require help – education, politics, home and family life. The author is forthright in her assertions on these matters. Education is the means of achieving 'a rapid social climb' and of contributing maximally to the good of society. It is a continuing process in which teachers play a crucial role. A teacher herself, she deals at length with the nobility of the work of the teacher.

> Each profession, intellectual or manual, deserves consideration, whether it requires painful physical effort or manual dexterity, wide knowledge or the patience of an ant. Ours, like that of the doctor, does not allow for any mistake. You don't joke with life, and life is both body and mind. To warp a soul is as much a sacrilege as murder. Teachers – at kindergarten level, as at university level – form a noble army accomplishing daily feats, never praised, never decorated. An army forever on the move, forever vigilant. An army without drums, without gleaming uniforms. This army, thwarting traps and snares, everywhere plants the flag of knowledge and morality. (p.23)

Politics should not be the exclusive preserve of men. Women should be encouraged to participate in the art of government and decision-making. They help in laying a sound foundation for society in the home and are therefore eminently qualified to get involved in national affairs.

> Women should no longer be decorative accessories, objects to be moved about, companions to be flattered or calmed with promises. Women are the nation's primary, fundamental root, from which all else grows and blossoms. Women must be encouraged to take a keener interest in the destiny of the country. (pp.61-62)

On pan-African solidarity she regrets the breaking up of regional groupings like the French West Africa Organisation which provided a strong link for the Francophone peoples of the area. This 'made possible a fruitful blend of different intellects, characters, manners and customs .... We are true sisters, destined for the same mission of emancipation'. (p.15)

So it becomes obvious that Ramatoulaye uses her long letter to Aissatou only as a medium of putting forward her radical views on several issues, many of them related to the elevation of the status of women in society. Even so, she succeeds, through her style of direct narration, in retaining the intimacy which a private letter from one friend to another demands. She frequently emphasises the bond between her and her friend.

> We walked the same paths from adolescence to maturity, where the past begets the present. . . .
> Yesterday you were divorced. Today I am a widow. (p.1)

and talks of the superiority of friendship over love.

> Friendship has splendours that love knows not. It grows stronger when crossed, whereas obstacles kill love. Friendship resists time, which wearies and severs couples. It has heights unknown to love. (p.54)

Her husband may disappoint. But the friendship between her and Aissatou is reassuring. This is why she is, as it were, emptying her heart to her friend in the hope that she will get some comfort and pleasure by so doing. The novelist has thus used the letter form to carry out not only a public obligation but also a private duty. This is the unique achievement of this work.

Ama Ata Aidoo, *Our Sister Killjoy*

Our Sister Killjoy is a new thing in structure and provides a fresh approach to fiction-writing in West Africa.[5] One of the highlights of the novel is that it is written in a combination of poetry and prose. The poetry runs so naturally into narrative or dialogue that one does not always know whether to take it at face value or try to read between the lines. This does not always make the work of interpretation easy. The novel derives its complexity from the fact that, although in a few cases the literal meaning would do, for the most part a secondary meaning must be sought to get the full import of the novelist's message:

> 'Mary . . . Mary . . . Mary. Did you say in school zey call you Mary?
> 'Yes.'
> 'Like me?'
> 'Yes'
> 'Vai?'
> 'I come from a Christian family. It is the name they gave me when they baptised me. It is also good for school and work and being a lady.'
> 'Mary, Mary . . . and you an African?'
> 'Yes.'
> 'But that is a German name!' said Marija.
> . . . .

But my brother
They got
Far
Enough
Teaching among other things,
Many other things
That
For a child to grow up
to be a
Heaven-worthy individual
He had
to have
above all, a
Christian name.
And what shall it profit a native that
He should have
systems to give
A boy
A girl
Two
Three names or
More. (pp.24-26)

A passage like this introduces us, in style and content, to Ms Aidoo's complex art. Here dialogue merges easily into narrative and poetry with no strict demarcation between the various forms. The passage gives us some insight into the relationship between Sissie and Marija, a relationship which is central to the concern of the book. The differences and similarities between Africa and Germany are alluded to. As in other parts of the novel, the missionaries are rebuked for some of their activities. A case in point is their imposition of European names on Africans and the obnoxious belief that these names are intrinsically superior to African names.

Ms Aidoo takes Africa, especially West Africa, as her point of departure, and uses Sissie, her main character, to reflect on various things or react with different groups. She is the touchstone against which every person, institution or event is judged. The novelist's purpose is clearly satirical and nobody is spared – the West Africans who live abroad because foreign countries are more comfortable than home, the 'academic-pseudo-intellectual', students, politicians. The novelist comes down very heavily upon the privileged class. The rulers are considered incompetent and selfish:

From all around the Third World

You hear the same story
Rulers
Asleep to all things at
All times –
Conscious only of
Riches, which they gather in a
Coma –
Intravenously – (p.34)

and the academics are satirised for their ineffectiveness and vanity:

Dear Lord
So what can we do about
Children not going to school
When
Our representatives and interpreters
The low-achieving academics
In low profile politics
Have the time of their lives
Grinning at cocktail parties and around
Conference tables?
At least, they made it, didn't they?

No,
Man does not live by
Gari or ugali alone –
Therefore
We do not complain about
Expensive trips to
Foreign 'Varsities where
Honorary doctorate degrees
Come with afternoon teas and
Mouldy Saxon cakes from
Mouldier Saxon dames . . . (pp.57-58)

The author devotes a lot of attention to the relationship between her heroine, Sissie, and Marija. Sissie is from a middle-class home, a product of British education who speaks English very well and is fairly familiar with the British way of life. She is a member of an international group of volunteers who render selfless service to the community. It is as a member of this group that she goes to Bavaria to work at a pine nursery. All they have to do is 'to cover up the bases and stems of pine seedlings with ground turf or peat. To protect them from the coming chill of winter'. (p.35) The assignment is not a difficult one and leaves much time for leisure and sight-seeing.

It is against this background of more leisure than work that the relationship between Sissie and Marija develops. Marija invites Sissie to her home every evening and makes sure she returns to the youth hostel with paper bags full of apples, pears, tomatoes and plums. This goes on for some time in a situation where the two are always left severely alone. Little wonder the relationship soon becomes intimate and special.

> Sometimes they sat and talked . . . At other times, they just sat, each with her own thought. Occasionally, one of them would look up at the other. If their eyes met, they would smile. At the end of each day, she returned to the castle later than she had done the previous evening. (p.40)

A strong feeling of love has developed between the two women. In Africa this would have been considered an extraordinary thing to happen. Even in Bavaria the neighbours are surprised, and they gossip about what they believe is a strange relationship. Marija Sommer, 'a little housewife married to a factory hand' (p.43) is hardly the right person to show an international visitor around the village and entertain her privately. The two soon become so attached to each other that the villagers rightly suspect that a lesbian relationship has developed between them. They therefore decide to spy on Marija whenever Sissie is with her. They come into her apartment on such occasions and ask embarrassing questions. Everything they see confirms their suspicion. They can no longer hide their feelings.

> Sommer does not speak English and the African speaks no German. So who interprets for them? asked the manager of a supermarket.
> What could they be talking about? wondered an insurance broker.
> She must not take her to her house every day!
> She must be getting neurotic!
> It is perverse.
> SOMEONE MUST TELL HER HUSBAND!! (p.44)

Ms Aidoo pursues the close relationship between Sissie and Marija with great artistic efficiency and raises in her exposition several issues connected with lesbianism and its social implications. In what circumstances does an African woman become interested in this kind of strange relationship? What are the particular advantages or attractions of lesbianism over heterosexuality? What frame of mind breeds lesbianism? The author shows personal interest in these matters and sets the scene for the display of affection between Sissie and Marija as if they are man and wife. The whole problem of love is put in a realistic context and treated in a way that reveals a feminine mode of imagination. Sissie appears initially to be playing the role of the man

Once or so, at the beginning of their friendship, Sissie had thought, while they walked in the park, of what a delicious love affair she and Marija would have had if one of them had been a man.

Especially, if she, Sissie had been a man. She had imagined and savoured the tears, their anguish at knowing that their love was doomed. But they would make promises to each other which of course would not stand a chance of getting fulfilled. She could see Marija's tears . . .

That was a game. A game in which one day, she became so absorbed, she forgot who she was, and the fact that she was a woman. (p.61)

'Their love was doomed' from the beginning. But they enjoy it while it lasts. Sissie and Marija meet for longer periods each day. This gives Marija the opportunity she has been looking for. She invites Sissie to her bedroom and gives her a warm embrace and fondles her the way a woman does a man.

Sissie felt Marija's cold fingers on her breast. The fingers of Marija's hand touched the skin of Sissie's breast while her other hand groped round and round Sissie's midriff, searching for something to hold on to.

It was the left hand that woke her to the reality of Marija's embrace. The warmth of her tears on her neck. The hotness of her lips against hers . . .

It all happened within a second. Two people staring at one another. Two months wide open with disbelief. (p.64)

The love affair between the two appears sealed. Marija now considers Sissie bonded to her. That is why she is so perplexed and disconsolate when Sissie's time is up and she has to leave Bavaria. She does everything possible to keep Sissie and promises to give a banquet at which Big Adolf will be present. Sissie, who has been mostly in charge of the situation, decides to put an end to an undesirable relationship and return to her country. Marija looks 'generally disorganised' and sad, but Sissie is not moved. She appears to have lost all affection for Marija and enjoys 'herself to see the woman hurt . . . there is pleasure in hurting'. (p.76)

Is Sissie then an unwilling accomplice in her relationship with Marija? Why does she find it so easy to disengage herself from her former partner? Has Sissie not been presented as an opportunist who will exploit any situation for her own benefit? The author's treatment is so detailed that the perceptive reader has no difficulty in tracing the psychological development of Sissie in the novel, especially with regard to her relationship with Marija. Given her African background, the relationship would have appeared perfectly normal at the beginning, something like the hospitality she is used to giving foreigners at home. At this stage she thoroughly enjoys the friendship and does everything to encourage it. She becomes suspicious when it is obvious that Marija is using her to ward off her loneliness in the absence of Big Adolf. She becomes completely disenchanted with Marija's rash display of affection and lesbian passion. Sissie herself complains of this unwholesome development.

> You make friends with a woman. Any woman. And she has a child. And you visit the house. Invited by the woman certainly. Every evening for many days. And you stay many hours on each occasion but you still never see the husband and one evening the woman seizes you in her embrace, her cold fingers on your breast, warm tears on your face, hot lips on your lips, do you go back to your village in Africa and say . . . what do you say even from the beginning of your story that you met a married woman? No, it would not be easy to talk of this white woman to just anyone at home . . . (pp.64-65)

Sissie remains African to the core. She knows her people at home will not stand for lesbianism. The subject will be an anathema to them; so she will not mention it. Why then does an African female novelist glorify the close relationship between two women, one a Ghanaian, the other, a German? Is it to promote the idea of universal brotherhood or a community of interests between women all over the world? It may be the intention of the author to prove that women can do without men in their private relationships, the way Marija is gradually learning to live without Big Adolf. Marija appears initially to be able to contain the situation. But it is almost certain that she will gladly welcome her husband back when Sissie departs. Ms Aidoo is quite entitled to put women at the helm of affairs in her novel. But it is an error to think that they can live a full life without men. If such a situation is tenable in Europe, it has no chance of succeeding in Africa. This is the significance of the role Sissie is made to play in this novel.

The novelist shows a great passion for Africa in her work. At various stages she stands up for Africa and comes down heavily on the Western world for the atrocities perpetrated on Africa – slave trade, slavery, colonialism and, more recently, neo-colonialism. She considers the economic exploitation of Africa by the imperial powers unpardonable and, in a series of paradoxes, recounts 'modern versions of ancient cruelties'.

> Burning people's farms, poisoning their rivers and killing all their trees and plants as part of the effort to save them from a wicked philosophy.
> Supplying brothers with machine guns and other heavy arms

because you want to stop them from slaughtering one another.

Making dangerous weapons that can destroy all of the earth in one little minute, in order to maintain peace. (p.116)

Africans are no longer deceived by the hypocrisy of the West. The worst that can happen is for Africans to be reconciled to a position of inferiority and attempt to bask in the glory of the West. This is one of the reasons Sissie is disappointed with the situation of the Africans in Western countries. Some of them have become everlasting students in these countries. They go to Britain and America, for example, against their better judgement, ostensibly in search of higher education. As they attend school they live a sub-standard, sub-normal life. When they complete their studies they are reluctant to return to Africa. Sissie encounters many such cases on her visit to Britain. Here, again, she takes particular interest in the women. They suffer more than the men. They are more easily corrupted by society and exist for the most part to serve the pleasure of their menfolk. They are 'especially very pitiful' and cannot cope with the social demands of the society on which they have imposed themselves. The author, exercising an eye for detail and her feminine instinct, finds that the women dress in a most ridiculous and shabby manner.

Unused to the cold and thoroughly inefficient at dealing with it, they smothered their bodies in raiments of diverse lengths, hues and quality – in a desperate effort to keep warm:
A blue scarf
  to cover the head and the ears,
A brown coat lined with
Cream synthetic fibre
Some frilly blouse
  its original whiteness compromised.
A red sweater
  with a button missing.
An inch or two of black skirting
  showing under the coat.
An umbrella,
  chequered green, red and blue.
A pair of stockings that are too light for
A chocolate skin,
A pair of cheap shoes,
  Never-mind-what-colour
But
Cheap. (pp.88-89)

As part of the injustice done to Africa the novelist complains of a brain drain, of Africans 'running very fast just to remain where they are'. (p.89) There is, for example, Kunle who has been living in London for seven years. He glorifies the good Christian Doctor (Dr Christian Bernard) for his famous heart transplant on a white man with the heart of a black man. He sees this as a sign of universal brotherhood of man. To him there is nothing wrong in a black man dying to keep a white man alive. This,· he is sure, is the

> type of development that can
> solve the question of apartheid
> and rid us, 'African negroes
> and all other negroes' of the
> Colour Problem. The whole of the
> Colour Problem. (p.96)

There is the case of Uncle who has been in London for quite a while. He buys houses and lets them out to other Africans 'at moderate rates'. 'Uncle is good', the other Africans say. (p. 125) There is no hope that Uncle will ever return to Africa. There is also the case of the African who has got to the top of his profession, 'gaining recognition as one of the world's ten experts on gastric disorders . . .' (p.127). Again, there is the African research fellow who has become internationally famous in his field.

> Now, I only do research. No joke. They'll tell you I am becoming the last word in Medical Science as far as the human abdomen is concerned. No conference on the subject is any good if I am not invited. I do the Intestinal-By-Pass as a hobby. Listen, I know that lots of times white people come to me just to verify for themselves that I am indeed an African . . . My fame has spread to Russia and China. (p.128)

All these Africans have been enticed away from the continent by foreign vested interests or are reluctant to return home because of inadequate facilities. The author shows some understanding of the problems of the Africans living abroad. But she insists that the noblest role the African can play is to help develop his country in Africa. Meaningful development can only take place when a country mobilises all its material and human resources. Africans cannot make desirable progress by merely copying European models. There is need for originality and a return to ancestral roots. Only then can there be true African solidarity to replace the present differences and divisions. Africa needs to display oneness of purpose and a continental determination to succeed. The author demonstrates a considerable amount of pan-Africanist zeal and reflects extensively on the role of Africa in world politics.

The novelist shows an amazing control of language and situation. She clearly demonstrates through the efficient manner the material in this work is handled that, however frequently the locale of the events of a novel may change, that needn't affect its unity as a work of art. All that is required is an overriding passion which, in this case, seems to be the total emancipation of Africa. What we have now is no more than 'a dance of the masquerades called Independence'. (p.95) The novelist wants this to be translated to true independence – political, social and economic. She hopes for a situation in which Africans will be able to uphold their ancestral values and yet feel equal to any other race in the world. This is the noble wish, the impelling force which has led Ms Aidoo to her achievement in this novel.

Rebeka Njau, *Ripples in the Pool*

Ripples in the Pool is a mystery story in which the author dramatises various kinds of tragic relationships among people and the conflict of ideas which usually lead to such tragedies.[6]

The most tragic of such relationships, one that is crucial to the central preoccupation of the novel, is the love affair between Gikere and Selina. The two are incompatible and cannot be expected to live a happy marital life. Gikere is a simple village lad, unused to the intricacies of life in the city. He is a humble hospital attendant, content with his position in life, but vaguely hoping that one day he may be of help to his people at Kamukwa by establishing a clinic there. Selina, on the other hand, is a prostitute who has become an expert in playing on men's passions. She is, we are told, 'no ordinary girl: she was arrogant, self-centred, highly expensive and feared no man'. (p.1) She has attractive features. 'Her face was smooth, not a pimple on it. Her colour was rich and creamy and the tight-fitting gowns she wore flattered the shape of her body'. (p.1) She confesses her preference for the good life.

> I love beautiful things . . . I like to possess them, to make them my own. It's a disease with me. But I make men pay for them. If they want me, they must spend their money. (p.2)

This is the woman Gikere marries. It is not surprising that their relationship is not popular among the people right from the beginning.

> No one could explain why Gikere married Selina even in the face of the strong protests of his own mother. Nor could they understand why Selina herself chose to live with a man of Gikere's kind. The whole thing seemed somehow wrong and men talked about it everywhere in town. (p.1)

Mystery surrounds the relationship between Gikere and Selina. Nobody expects the marriage to succeed because of the differences in background and orientation to life between husband and wife. And Gikere's mother does not help matters by her harassment and open denunciation of Selina. Gikere seems attached to his wife by some mysterious bond. He does everything possible to please her and carries out her wishes. So long as Gikere is willing to play the part of 'a woman's slave' Selina feels glorified and contented. Once he decides to assert his manliness and take charge of his domestic affairs, Selina feels hurt and humiliated. She expects the man to remain eternally subjected to her whims. It is disappointing that Gikere plays the role of a fool for so long and demeans himself to satisfy a woman he ought not to have married in the first place. But for the pressures exerted on him by his mother he might have been permanently enslaved by Selina. It may be the author's intention to raise the woman's ego by getting a man to play such a submissive role.

Perhaps it is for the same reason that Selina is put right in the centre of affairs in this novel. She not only lords it over her husband, she also succeeds in sending her mother-in-law packing from the house. She is naturally not liked at Kamukwa because the villagers believe she is too sophisticated and corrupt for the community, that she is introducing the vices of the city to the village, thus polluting their rural simplicity and virtues. They find her past life disgusting and her treatment of her husband cruel in the extreme. She lays claim to extraordinary powers – 'I have power within me, a magnetic kind of power that no other woman has' (p.112) – and intends to use them to achieve her selfish aims – 'I have discovered that a woman must fight her way in this cruel man's world.' (p.114) Such thoughts lead to disaster. She becomes so domineering that she wants to rule everybody around her. As soon as she loses Gikere she falls in love with his sister, Gaciru, and does all she can to enslave her.

'Your face is so smooth, Gaciru,' she said, stroking it. 'You have no red on your lips, no powder on your cheeks, yet you are the prettiest thing on earth. You are my tomato. My fresh ripe tomato. The kind that grows along river valleys. I shall gobble you up whole.' (p.103)

To her Gaciru is no more than a toy to play with in order to soothe her nerves. So when the girl falls in love with Karuga she kills her. Later in a dreadful encounter with Karuga at the pool she murders him too. She becomes demented and wanders about like a ghost.

After three hours of aimless wandering, she felt thirsty. She needed water, a lot of water to drink and plunge herself in and cool her burning throat. She kept walking and soon she came to the path which could lead her to Itukarua if she kept long on it. Yes, there was a hiding-place there. She remembered the place among the reeds shut away from the world of man. A place where no man dared penetrate. She hurried on through plains and hills. For days she wandered looking for the world of hyenas and jackals. This was her world now. The human being in her had ceased to exist and she had become a beast lost in the wilderness. (pp.144-5)

All activities converge on the pool which is presented in this novel as the communal symbol of truth and purity. From it every event derives its character and authenticity. It is the touchstone against which every-body is judged. It embodies a mystery which needs to be unravelled by every individual for himself. Its antiquity commands respect, and nobody can defy its laws with impunity. It is an inscrutable personality which remains for ever to bring prosperity and happiness to those who do good and ruin to those who cheat their countrymen and indulge in city vices. The closer any character is to accepting the mystery connected with the pool, the better life is for him. That is why, when Karuga is uncertain of his future and is desperately looking for a spiritual anchor on which to rest his hopes of success, he is advised by Muthee to rely on the life-giving power of the pool.

Look at the pool. That is where the mystery of life is. You are at the bottom of the ladder. Dig deeper and deeper at the bottom of it. Then one day you will discover the mysteries I have been talking to you about. (p.85)

Muthee himself has come to accept the spiritual powers of the pool after undergoing a strange experience on one occasion when he stays long at the pool.

Suddenly he felt haunted; something inside him warned him to leave the pool. And when he turned to go home, a branch from the huge tree fell with a heavy thud and a noise like thunder roared from the water. He tried to move, but something tightened the muscles of his legs, and he could not lift them even one step. He fell prostrate on the ground and when he tried to call Karuga for help, this time loudly, no sound came. His throat was dry. He struggled on the ground, trying to crawl forward on his belly, but his body was heavy and limp, and he lay there helpless. What sin had he committed against the spirits of the pool? (p.21)

It would appear that many people in the novel commit sins 'against the spirits of the pool' without knowing it. These spirits demand, among other things, honesty, hard work, respect for the truth, loyalty to indigenous culture and total commitment to individual liberty. Given this yardstick, it is easy to see why Selina's life ends in disaster. The failure of people like Gikere and Munene can also be explained. Gikere marries Selina for her money and, for this reason, endures a lot of indignities from her. He deserts her when the situation becomes intolerable. He becomes an alcoholic and therefore unable to set up the clinic for which he returns to the village in the first place. Munene is a political activist who returns to the village to set up a hospital. He too fails because his motives are not genuine. We are told that 'he uses people to get what he wants . . . He is now out for himself and anything he does is always calculated.' (p.47) He has deceived the people for so long that they now begin to see through him and recognise him for what he is – a callous brute who will stop at nothing to achieve his selfish ends. The author uses him to satirise politicians as a whole.

> 'Men like Kefa Munene are ruining the country every day. What is the use of talking politics, talking of doing this and doing that for his constituency? Always talking, endless talk and never doing anything for the people! And those disciples of his, are they not supposed to be working for the people? Are they not supposed to know what suffering is? Yet, what do they do? They follow him everywhere expecting to share his wealth, expecting a position in the government! (pp.30-31)

Other characters and ideas are introduced to satisfy the author's satirical intent. Kimani, for example, is Gikere's friend and is expected to help him with work on his proposed clinic. But as soon as he is given a lot of money by Munene, he deserts his friend. For, according to him,

> 'Money is a drug, Gikere, especially to a poor man like me with debts to pay. I know Kefa Munene is wicked. I know he has drugged me with money and played tricks on me but I need money badly. I have nothing, my friend!' (p.76)

When Gikere questions him about the morality of his action, he provides a ready answer. 'Who listens to the truth these days? . . . I am not like you. You have your principles. I shall take money no matter where it comes from.' (p.82) So cynical have the villagers become that only a few of them care for principles. Most of the world has been overtaken by greed and avarice which leave little room for the display of public morality and a strong conscience. So far have people departed from the path of rectitude and the traditions of their forefathers that their lives have become socially and politically chaotic. Their troubles come 'from their own meanness, their jealousy, their lust, their greed and their lack of faith in the mysteries around them.' (p.83) Little wonder that the vision of happiness shown in the love affair between Karuga and Gaciru comes to nothing. In a situation where moral laxity and social decadence prevail, people suffer at times for public rather than personal reasons.

Fortunately all is not gloom, all is not misery and woe. There are hopeful pointers to a bright future in people like Maria who are hard-working, reliable and fair to friends and foes alike. There is also Muthee who is an embodiment of all that is culturally sound and attractive. As an old man he has acquired a vast experience in the ways of the world. This he often shares with Karuga as part of the latter's education. Through the interaction of the two the author constantly brings out the differences between the old and the young in their attitudes to life and the solution of problems. Consider, for example, their different attitudes to Njeru, the troublesome goat. Karuga wants the goat destroyed. But Muthee instinctively realises that destroying Njeru cannot provide a permanent solution to their problems. His attitude to the situation is quite appropriately philosophical.

> 'Life that is smooth is not life at all,' the old man said. 'Where is our strength if we fail to control one helpless little creature? If we destroy Njeru, is that the end of pain? What shall we do with all the other Njerus among us? Let us keep Njeru here indoors away from the other goats. He, too, must face a time of trial. He must learn to control his greed.' (p.68)

Young people like Karuga represent the nation's hope for the future. As Maina says, 'Our hope lies in the young. It is they who must wake up and realise that men like Kefa Munene . . . must be removed from the face of the earth.' (p.31) However, the most enduring symbol in the novel is the fig tree which, we are told, will 'survive the generations and the generations to come like the light, spirit and truth that live on for ever.' (p.152) These are the assurances that we have that the corruption, inefficiency and greed which dominate the present may be a passing fad. The pool may still radiate very attractive qualities which will motivate men to embrace the truth. Then they will live by standards of justice and equity which alone bring peace and happiness to individuals, peoples and nations. It is through such a vision of hope that the author raises the value of her work.

Charity Waciuma, *Daughter of Mumbi*

Daughter of Mumbi is an autobiography which presents national history in a favourable light.[7] Into the narration of childhood experiences are integrated the hopes and fears of a nation in the grip of the worst manifestations of imperialism and colonialism. Christian missionaries collude with the colonial administration to subvert the legitimate rights of the people, deny them every kind of freedom and deprive them of their land. The work devotes a lot of attention to this organised oppression of the Kikuyu and to the people's fight for justice and equality. Since every form of political association is banned, the resistance goes underground, resulting in the Mau Mau organisation and the period of Emergency which inevitably follows.

The author quite rightly concentrates on the sufferings of the individual Kikuyu. Once war is declared, his movement and personal liberty are restricted under the Emergency regulations. He is terrorised by home guards, if his loyalty to the Administration is in doubt, and by Mau Mau supporters, if he is not openly nationalistic in his attitude. When the home guards and the Mau Mau terrorists clash, it is the ordinary people who suffer. People are moved frequently from one location to another and, in the process, they experience great hardship. Children suffer more than the adults.

> When they moved from the farms, children were separated from their parents and many have never been traced to this day. In many cases they were herded into camps like cattle, men in one place, women in another and children in yet another. After 'screening' they were sent back to their district or division. Many small children did not know where they came from and were left, often at railway stations. They spent months wandering about the countryside. How they suffered is more than a tongue can tell or a pen can write. (p.117)

Land is a sore point in the dispute between the white settlers and the Kikuyu. Deprive him of his land and the Kikuyu feels deprived of life. He lives on the land which is about the only security he has. Furthermore, the land is an ancestral property which passes from one generation to another. So when the British come and appropriate Kikuyu land, herd the original owners into unattractive locations and make them work for a pittance on their own land, war is inevitable. For, as we are told,

> The labourers on the estates had little alternative for they were mainly landless people. They were allocated a one-acre plot on their master's land if they lived there. They became bitter, bitter to the roots, about the strangers who came and took their land. Before the White Man came they had the right to use part of the hundreds of acres of their clan land and now they had to beg a tiny plot as if they were strangers in the country of their forefathers. (p.52)

There is a complete breakdown of communication between the Kikuyu and their white oppressors. The Kikuyu are excluded from the process of decision-making and for a long time there is no African representation in parliament. The colonial administrators rely on warrant chiefs who are chosen because of their loyalty to the government. These chiefs are despised by the people whose interests they cannot truly represent. Added to all this is the supercilious attitude of government officials who give the impression that the British are a superior group of people who 'had been encouraged to come by the government, which in many cases paid their passages from Britain'. (p.100) They see this as a right to live in Kenya for ever if they wish. Faced with this monstrous claim and the other atrocities perpetrated against them, the people decide to take extraordinary measures to defend their inalienable right. As soon as Jomo Kenyatta appears on the scene the revolution gathers momentum.

A special feature of this work is the convincing picture it gives of the original beauty and solidity of Kikuyu culture. The reader is given enough information about the people for him to feel truly acquainted with them and their way of life. The author realistically presents many aspects of village life – belief in witchcraft and the existence of ghosts, ancestor worship, adherence to polygamous practices, the use of cattle as the currency for various transactions, the role of the council of elders, and the place of oral traditions in the life of the people. In each case the novelist gives sufficient detail for the background against which she writes to be fully realised. She achieves great success in the way she links the past with the present. Take, for example, the significance attached to names.

> In our country names are not chosen haphazardly; they are vitally bound up with being the sort of person you are. Any name includes many people who are now dead, others who are living, and those who are still not born. It binds its owner deep into Kikuyu history, beyond the oldest man with the longest memory. All our relatives to the furthest extent of the family, their actions, their lives and their children are an intrinsic part of our being alive, of being human, of being African, of being Kikuyu. (p.8)

The author undoubtedly has a fascination for this culture. But she is not sentimental in her presentation of facts. Just as there are merits, there are weaknesses. For instance, people with supernatural powers use them mostly to destroy their enemies. There are frequent inter-tribal wars, especially between the Masai and the Kikuyu, and these bring untold hardship to the people. The novelist looks at the situation from very varied points of view and at times puts these simultaneously before the reader. The aim certainly has been to present a culture that has a root in reality.

This social reality has to some extent been distorted by a conflict between the old and the new, between traditional medicine and orthodox medical practice, between the colonial administration and traditional authority. This has led to difficulties in various spheres of traditional and modern life. The work offers several examples. There is, for example, the confrontation between the witchdoctors and Waciuma, the sanitary inspector who is firmly warned by the witch-doctors, 'You must no longer tell the people that your medicine is better than ours. Otherwise we shall put a curse upon you.' (p.28) The powers of the witchdoctors have been declining as more people come to embrace medical science and attend Waciuma's dispensary regularly. There is also the mockery of oath-taking in court. With the traditional Kikuyu, oath-taking is a serious matter and it assumes various forms, each with dreadful consequences for the guilty person or party. This process has been so grossly abused with the advent of the Europeans that it is no longer effective. People do not believe in the oath they take because 'for them, the God concerned is a white man's God, not their own Mwenenyaga. That God's just a sort of joke to them'. (p.43) With the introduction of new ideas, the influx of strangers into the Kikuyu community and the contacts the Kikuyu themselves have made with the outside world during the world wars, the society is now in a state of flux. The people are in a state of confusion, socially and culturally. They are gradually drifting away from traditional authority without being given all the opportunity they require to embrace modern ideas and live in comfort and freedom. The link between tradition and modern life in this novel is a disturbing one. Not even Christianity is able to change the way of life of the people in any significant manner. The people need a spiritual stimulus to carry on with the business of life and put behind them the corruption and greed which are eating deep into the fabric of society.

You know it is by a set of laws that we are supposed to live, but the law itself is based on a code of ethics, a religion. Religion matters to the whole man. But what do we have? The people do not meaningfully follow the white man's religion, Christianity, yet, at the same time, they have turned their backs on their own traditional beliefs. With nothing behind them, they are an uneasy prey to corruption. See, our own laws are neglected, yet they are what three-quarters of the Kikuyu population believe in, even the so-called Christians like myself. (p.44)

The novel gives the impression that it is only through increased provision of educational opportunities and an energetic public enlightenment crusade that the Kikuyu can be redeemed from their superstitious beliefs and mass ignorance, and be encouraged to march forward confidently into the technological age. The author sees education as an instrument of social change. Wanjiku's case clearly illustrates how an individual, even in a period of national crisis, can achieve rapid personal development through education. She moves rapidly up the educational ladder and displays great industry and mental alertness in every institution she attends. She is meant to be a worthy representative of her people and race. She is nationalistic, conscious of her glorious Kikuyu heritage and shows maturity in her approach to personal and societal problems. Since the work is autobiographical, it is appropriate that the author devotes a lot of space to Wanjiku, her heroine. We see her move from humble beginnings in the village to achieving the status of a college student in the town, exposed to all the temptations of city life. She acquits herself creditably both academically and morally. She personifies Kenya of the future, free from superstitious ideas and ritual worship, liberated from the shackles of imperialism, restored in honour and dignity to its ancestral land, and accepted as a respectable member of the international community.

Jane Bakaluba, *Honeymoon for Three*

Honeymoon for Three thrives on the conflict between the old and the new, between traditional and modern life with emphasis on the incompatibility between the two.[8] Mukasa and his sister Sulu are made the embodiments of indigenous culture. They hold rigid views about the inherited way of life and are therefore suspicious of any outside influence, such as Christianity, which they regard as an unwarranted assault against the people's traditional beliefs. The basis of these beliefs is continually eroded by Christian education through which new and unorthodox ideas are introduced. Education for girls is a social abuse which must be discouraged, if it cannot be completely stopped. The tenets of traditional life, especially as they relate to marriage and family life, should remain unadulterated.

A woman gets married to be protected and to bear children. (p.97)

A woman finds pleasure and satisfaction in her children. (p.99)

A woman has no life of her own ... a woman cannot decide for herself ... (p.24)

To maintain the smooth surface and coherence of village life every member of the community must adhere to these laws. Any violation is regarded as an act of rebellion against society, which calls for the heaviest punishment.

Naiga finds herself unable to fulfil traditional expectations in the method of choosing her future husband. She rejects the rule that 'no girl chooses a husband for herself. It is the privilege of the father and aunties to do so'. (p.89) She rejects the man chosen for her by her father and falls in love with Nuwa. She asserts her independence and personal liberty in a way that embarrasses members of her family and the community as a whole. To have turned down a rich man like Kidza for a husband is bad enough. To choose in his place a Christian and the son of a clergyman is inconceivable. Christianity and traditional religion represent two different ways of life which are diametrically opposed to each other. As Nakato says: 'Religion and tradition are like two witch-doctors, one dispels the other.' (p.86) It is not surprising therefore that there is a strong objection to the love affair between Naiga and Nuwa from both sides. Aunt Sulu provides a strange reason for what she considers Naiga's stubbornness.

'I knew that it would come to this, the way you kept going back to school term after term. Wiser girls never stay that long. They leave school after a term or two and get married. Treachery I call it. You betray your father who sent you to school, and you betray your own people. Your father was a fool to send you to school. You should be digging in the shambas and having children like any other woman. That's the proper life for a girl; not going to school to pick up all the wrong ideas about life. Nuwa of all men! A clergyman's son! A Christian!' (pp.6-7)

The objection from Nuwa's family is equally uncompromising and is directed mainly against Naiga's background. The details are revealed in this spirited argument between Nuwa and his sister, Phoebe.

'What you forget, Nuwa, is that the girl grew up in Mukasa's home. What more can you expect of her? We are all victims of our environment and upbringing. The only way of life that girl knows is that of Mukasa and his household.'

'Which way of life is that?' asked Nuwa, a little shocked.

'Oh, Nuwa, you know. These people believe in witch-craft and indulge in heathen practices and customs.'

'But what's heathen about one's tribal customs? All people have got their own traditional customs. That is society. Are you condemning our entire society as heathen?'

'You must be losing your sense of judgement, Nuwa. What they say about love being blind must be true! Surely you know that all tribal customs are heathen, because they are based on heathen beliefs.'

'That is wrong, Phoebe. There is nothing heathen about our traditional customs.'

'Something has happened to you since you became friendly with this girl. We have told you time and again that this marriage won't work, but you won't listen. You will be the first to regret it.' (pp.67-68)

The two sides are so far apart initially that there appears to be little chance of compromise and accommodation between them.

Naiga and Nuwa are used as the means of ultimately bringing the two sides together. They go ahead with their plans to get married. There are naturally periods of doubts and uncertainties. At a stage when she is encountering much trouble and opposition, Naiga regards herself no more than 'a puppet in the hands of fate, and she had to lie low and let things take their own course'. (p.108) But later they accomplish their aim through the help of friends and well-wishers from within and outside the family. A substantial bride-price is paid, and this gladdens Mukasa's heart. Both families drop their objection to the union, attend the wedding ceremony and become friends. By showing such a mighty love and consideration for each other and displaying such a great resolve in the face of apparently insurmountable obstacles, the young couple are able to bring together traditional and modern elements in society. They demonstrate by their example of a happy, hopeful married life that differences in background between husband and wife should not constitute an impediment to marital bliss. This is their greatest achievement in this novel, a fitting reward for their steadfastness and honesty of purpose. They have quite rightly been made the focus of attention. Their fears and hopes have been used to point the way forward to the future.

In the same way the mode of life of Mukasa and Sulu is used to show what aspects of indigenous culture need to be changed. Mukasa lives like a dictator over an empire of five wives and twenty-six children. His word is law in his kingdom. He does not allow for any personal opinion or display of individualism by any members of his family. This is why Naiga's preference for Nuwa is initially brushed aside. This is also why he feels strong enough to attempt to give Naiga to Kidza after he has received a bride-price from Nuwa, an action that is clearly indefensible. His motives are often mercenary and dishonest. We are told that there are many people he has defrauded in one way or other because of his greed. Sulu is more rigid in her attitude to tradition, but she is infinitely more honest than her brother. She establishes a reign of terror over her brother's household and ensures that nothing happens without her express permission. These two behave in a way that can easily bring discredit to traditional life. They do not seem to realise the need for individuals to experience life fully and live by a code of personal conduct.

The work is steeped deep in Buganda culture, and the author takes every opportunity to acquaint readers with the various aspects of this culture. What is offered·is a picture of a polygamous society where everybody seems contented with his lot, that is, before new ideas are introduced. Emphasis is placed on respect for elders, the proper upbringing of children, preparing girls for marriage, the rewards of honesty. The witchdoctors play their part to ensure that justice is done to all. Naiga considers the role of housewives whose world for the most part consists of their husband, children and the extended family.

At least they are content with their lot, she told herself, those women who were doomed to a life of child-bearing and household drudgery. Women whose rough hands bore testimony to their hard way of living. Every day is the same to them. But they never complain. The dignity of family warmth is always maintained in their homes. They enjoy their children and their way of life, and they love their husbands. That is how it should be. That is how I would like it to be with me. (p.29)

This culture has other attractive aspects. Two examples will suffice. Take, for instance, the importance attached to virginity for a new bride. As Nuwa makes clear, 'a parent is honoured by a well-behaved child. Girls' behaviour, especially, is subject to heavy scrutiny'. (p.119) The bride must be found a virgin or else she is considered a social disgrace. Sulu understandably makes a great capital of this point and insists that the requirements of custom should be observed in respect of her niece. 'I believe Naiga is a virgin. I have no doubt about that, but it must be proved for everybody to know . . . This is our custom. It is our tradition.' (p.114) Consider also the convivial atmosphere which traditional weddings generate. The rigidity of the church wedding with its fixed rules of procedure and solemnity is avoided. In its place we have relations, colleagues and friends of the bride and bridegroom expressing their joy without inhibition. Instead of church hymns, there is music, drumming and dancing. Various performances take place in a free atmosphere to make the day a memorable one. There can be no doubt that 'the traditional wedding is less formal than the church one, and people feel more relaxed'. (p.126) It is against such a social and cultural background that the drama of Naiga and Nuwa is enacted. This is the culture that is being threatened in many of its important aspects by borrowed ideas.

An interesting aspect of this novel is the way the old gradually yields place to the new. Modern ideas triumph in the end. Naiga and Nuwa start a new, interesting life. On his death bed Mukasa is reconciled to everybody – Naiga, Nuwa, Rev Kasule, among others.

'Nuwa, can you believe that my father called your father to his death-bed and talked with him for a long time?'

'You must be joking'.

'He did. My uncle told me. He even talked about becoming a Christian.'

'Naiga.'

'Yes, Nuwa. He wanted to be a different man in the end.' (p.180)

Mukasa comes to accept many of the ideas he has rejected in the past and asks for forgiveness of his sins. His last days provide the necessary calm at the end of a stormy life and point to the acceptance of the need for change. This is the assurance we have that 'Mukasa's body will lie in peace. He made peace with himself before he died'. (p.181) Naiga, with her new orientation, will take over her father's responsibilities. She will become the new 'Auntie Sulu' to her numerous brothers and sisters and give them a new direction in life. Her task will be easy and pleasant because Nuwa has promised 'to be by her side and give her all the help she needed, to the end of their days'. (p.182) This is the picture of a peaceful social transformation which the novel presents.

Hazel Mugot, *Black Night of Quiloa*

Black Night of Quiloa concentrates on the tragic love affair between Cy and Hima.[9] Their marriage breaks up after a short time because of the social gulf which separates them. The whole affair fits perfectly into the framework of the theory of the Complete Gentleman referred to in the last chapter. Hima meets Cy and falls in love with him at first sight. She immediately abandons her arrangement to marry Abu, disappoints her parents, relations and friends, and violates the customs of her people in order to marry this stranger and follow him home to Britain. It is in Britain that the man reveals his barbaric nature and treats Hima callously. In keeping with the theory it is essential for Hima to be so completely captivated by Cy that nobody else matters to her. The adoration must be total for the process to be carried to its logical conclusion. To her he is a demi-god.

His sea-green eyes – Hima had never seen such before – held a deep magic all of their own. His speech was sometimes beyond her. His strength and physique left her breathless. His muscle-bound limbs, metal-strong. She . . . completely adored this strange god. Hima was as much in wonder of him as she was of their ruler. And as was their custom, she would have sacrificed anything for him, even her life. (p.31)

It takes her only a little time in Britain to realise that her new object of worship is a false god.

Why does the love affair between the two end so abruptly after all the sacrifices that the woman has made? The novel provides only part of the answer. When a couple side-track all the rules, circumvent laid-down procedures in order to satisfy their infatuation for each other, disaster inevitably results. Cy and Hima do not give themselves enough time to understand each other. Yet, to succeed, they require a detailed knowledge of each other's background and circumstances in life. Not only are there social differences; there are also racial barriers to overcome. Life in Britain is vastly different from that in Quiloa. Therefore when Hima gets to Britain she encounters enormous problems of adjustment. She is invited to embrace a new way of life for which she has not been prepared. She discovers to her bitter disappointment that the British are a race-conscious people who do little to make an outsider feel at ease in their midst. She feels betrayed and becomes bitter. To make matters worse Cy turns out to be a negrophobist.

> His was a deep, deep dislike. Something he himself was not completely aware of. But as natural to him as his body to vomiting foreign matter. It seemed that he was made to captivate and break everything that was alien; so he had drawn her, to destroy her, because of his nature and not any conscious intent. It seemed like an instinct almost; like a lion who had to devour, to prove its dominance. (p.49)

It is when Cy deserts Hima that she begins to feel the full weight of the loneliness of the city. As we are told, 'a slow-crushing loneliness began to weigh on Hima'. (p.34) She cannot on her own cope with the fast pace of life. The whole environment becomes strange and hostile. As the situation deteriorates, she returns to Quiloa.

Quiloa has always been deeply embedded in Hima's consciousness. She has great respect and admiration for its people and traditions. It is a place of great antiquity and beauty. The people live a full life and cherish their glorious heritage. These are some of the qualities which attract Cy to the Seychelles in the first place. Hima misses the rural pleasures, simplicity of life and warmth in interpersonal relationships. To her these factors make the British way of life decidedly inferior to that of the African. In place of the communal living she is used to, she finds herself alone in a small cold room, which is extremely depressing. No wonder she frequently remembers her native Quiloa, a centre of civilisation in its own right.

> How proud Quiloa is of her romantic past and rich background. People of different origin living together peacefully, after many wars

and rulers. The room seems to fill with the gold dust of dreams ... Their chronicles date back to Mapha pirate chiefs. Later the Persian settlers, Hassan with his six sons and seven ships, who bought Quiloa from the local tribe. Then the Moors. Soon Quiloa was known as mistress of the seas, and for her gold, so much gold, and pure ivory. (pp.82-83)

But can Hima be married to a white man and still retain Quiloa customs and live Quiloa life in Britain? This is one of the problems posed by the events of the novel. Why, for example, does Hima finds it so difficult to adjust to her new environment? Why does she consider the people so unfriendly and the whole situation so intolerable? So many Africans have survived in worse conditions in Britain. True enough, Cy's change of attitude must have come as a complete disappointment. But her own rigidity and attachment to Quiloa have not helped matters. What is required is a little flexibility on both sides. Unfortunately this is not forthcoming. There is a complete breakdown in communication which results in untold hardship for Hima.

It is the author's deliberate doing that an opportunity for a successful inter-racial marriage is lost. Why, for instance, does Cy demonstrate such a fierce loyalty to his people in utter disregard of his obligation to his wife?

Cy so loved his country, his people; he was so proud of them. If Hima said anything against them, he was hurt, even these people in the slums, vicious as some of them were. Sometimes Hima was sure he felt disloyal to have married her. (p.37)

Is the author totally against cross-cultural marriages? Or is it just that she feels on this occasion the circumstances are not right? This is difficult to say. But she does enough to show that even if Hima and Cy belong to the same culture, their marriage stands very little chance of succeeding. They hold such divergent views on life and approach marital problems so immaturely that their union cannot be expected to last for too long. Given similar circumstances with people of the same cultural background, the outcome is likely to be the same. Cultural differences, no doubt, play a significant part. But the sudden tragic end of the relationship is brought about mainly by personal faults and social inadequacies.

Literary Assessment

After that fairly extensive discussion of six novels it becomes clear that the topics treated by African female novelists are varied in content and approach. Mariama Ba uses the letter form to discuss matters of public policy, especially as they relate to the status of women in society. She advocates a dynamic approach and an assertion of the liberty of the individual. Ama Ata Aidoo is concerned with the problems of continental unity and development. She shows an admirable amount of pan-Africanist zeal and discusses the place of women in the African society. The greater part of her work is set outside Africa. She is therefore able to introduce alien concepts like lesbianism, and treat in detail the disposition of Africans in foreign countries. Rebeka Njau concentrates on social problems. She analyses the conditions which result in unsuccessful marriages, using that of Gikere and Selina as an example. Issues of great significance and universal concern like peace, justice, corruption, and inefficiency are introduced and discussed in the context of urban and rural life. It is only when people embrace the truth that they can expect to live in peace and happiness.

There is an amazing variety in the content and approach of the other novels as well. *Daughter of Mumbi* is devoted to the problems of Kenya before independence, especially the circumstances which lead to the organisation of the Mau Mau movement. The work emphasises the importance attached to land as an ancestral property and shows how the supercilious attitude of the white settlers leads to war. The people make the necessary sacrifice to ensure that the country eventually becomes independent. *Honeymoon for Three* deals with the successful love affair between Naiga and Nuwa. Initially the young couple encounter opposition from both families. They overcome this obstacle by their patience and steadfastness in the face of great odds. The novel underlines the circumstances in which love flourishes between two individuals who are determined to succeed. *Black Night of Quiloa* calls attention to an inter-racial marriage which fails because of the big social gulf which separates Hima and Cy. Their background is so different that the union has no chance of succeeding. The differences in the way of life of the people of the Seychelles and Britain are dramatised as part of the explanation for failure in this case.

Each writer has adopted the literary technique that most suits her work. Mariama Ba adopts the letter form which relies for effect on a series of reminiscences which are put together in an episodic manner. This technique is well suited to the mood in which Ramatoulaye writes and allows her to record her thoughts in the order in which they come to her. Ama Ata Aidoo bases her work on the 'reflections from a black-eyed squint'. This technique seems appropriate for a work which is devoted to a consideration of a number of topics so varied and divergent. What gives the novel its unity and coherence is that the reflections emanate from the same source. The other writers have adopted various devices to make their works attractive. Rebeka Njau concentrates all the important events of her book around the symbol of a life-giving pool for maximum effectiveness. Charity Waciuma adopts the autobiographical mode into which she successfully integrates national history. Jane Bakaluba uses the love affair between Naiga and Nuwa to illustrate the triumph of modernity over traditional life while Hazel Mugot exploits the social and racial differences between Hima and Cy to show why their love affair ends in disaster. Each of these writers has been remarkably successful with the technique and approach adopted for her work.

These novels have some attractive features common to all of them. The first is the consistent attempt of the novelists to exploit fully the background against which they write so that the reader may easily grasp all the attendant circumstances of the work. Hazel Mugot writes against the background of ancient Quiloa culture and shows her admiration for this culture. Enough is said about the culture for the reader to appreciate why Hima considers life at Quiloa as superior in every way to life in Britain. Apart from any consideration of Senegalese culture and way of life, Mariama Ba writes to portray Muslim life lived according to the tenets of Islam. It is only when *So Long a Letter* is considered against the requirements of the Islamic faith that the reader can appreciate its true significance and beauty as a work of art. Other writers as well are faithful to the social and cultural background against which they write – Jane Bakaluba brings out the attractive aspects of ancient Buganda culture while Charity Waciuma and Rebeka Njau project in their works the various facets of the glorious heritage of Kenyans.

In all these novels a woman plays a leading role. She is often in the centre of affairs and occasionally plays her part in competition with a man. For the most part she is linked with a man who, as a husband, shares the pride of place with her. This is the case with Selina and Gikere in *Ripples in the Pool*, Naiga and Nuwa in *Honeymoon for Three* and Hima and Cy in *Black Night of Quiloa*. In *Our Sister Killjoy* and *So Long a Letter* the scene is almost completely monopolised by women. In the former novel two women attempt to do away with men entirely by establishing a lesbian relationship with each other. The attempt is unsuccessful, but it shows the kind of confidence women are gradually acquiring in their dealings with one another and their new conception of their role in society. In *Daughter of Mumbi* Wanjiku dominates the scene because the whole work is about her personal development. Every other character plays a subordinate role. In this matter every female novelist tries to make a contribution to the feminist ideals and helps to lay the foundation for a female literary tradition which is yet to be fully established in Africa.

Notes

1 See, for example, Emmanuel Obiechina, *Culture, Tradition and Society in the West African Novel* (CUP, 1975); Oladele Taiwo, *Culture and the Nigerian Novel* (London, Macmillan 1976).

2 For a detailed discussion of these writers, see, for example, Ellen Moers, *Literary Women* (London, The Women's Press Ltd., 1978).

3 Ellen Moers, op. cit., p.IX.

4 Mariama Ba, *So Long a Letter* (London, Heinemann, A.W.S., 1981). Page references are to this edition.

5 Ama Ata Aidoo, *Our Sister Killjoy* (London, Longman, 1977). Page references are to this edition.

6 Rebeka Njau, *Ripples in the Pool* (London, Heinemann, A.W.S., 1978) Page references are to this edition.

7 Charity Waciuma, *Daughter of Mumbi* (Nairobi, East African Publishing House, 1969). Page references are to this edition.

8 Jane Bakaluba, *Honeymoon for Three* (Nairobi, East African Publishing House, 1975). Page references are to this edition.

9 Hazel Mugot, *Black Night of Quiloa* (Nairobi, East African Publishing House, 1971). Page references are to this edition.

CHAPTER THREE

Flora Nwapa

Flora Nwapa is the first Nigerian woman in modern times to write a full-length novel. She arrived on the literary scene at a time when it was almost completely dominated by men. She was at first received with mixed feelings. Some received her works with admiration while others considered them as an unwarranted imitation of what the men were doing. It took some time for the works to be considered on their own merit. When finally this was done, it was discovered that she was writing in depth, at least initially, on topics which were better handled by a woman, even if her methods and approaches were not significantly different from those employed by other writers. Flora Nwapa's topics have been to some extent unique to her. Her reputation as a writer rests solidly on her achievements in *Efuru* and *Idu*. In these works she concentrates on marriage, mothercare, home and family life, the status of women in traditional society, the hierarchical structure of Igbo society, the place of the gods in the maintenance of peace and order in tribal communities. She creates a self-contained world in which her villagers live a full life based on their own customs and beliefs, with only minimum influence from outside sources.

She has since written two shorter novels – *Never Again* and *One is Enough*, and also has to her credit two collections of short stories – *This is Lagos* and *Wives at War*. These latter works have benefited from her personal experiences of the Nigerian Civil War, especially as they concern her hometown, Ugwuta. She writes with insight on the ravages of war – the loss of men and property, the psychological effect on the human environment and the abrupt large-scale disruption of a way of life. She also takes a great deal of interest in the moral laxity, social

47

decadence and the craze for wealth which result from the mass movement of people from their secure home-base to the comparative
insecurity of the city. The point at issue is usually so well dramatised
that the social risks being taken by groups and individuals become
obvious for all to see. So effectively has the novelist diversified her
literary interests in recent years that her versatility as a creative artist is
no longer in doubt.

Efuru

In *Efuru* the novelist devotes her attention to the exposition of several
aspects of Igbo traditional and corporate life.[1] Efuru's experiences are
used to demonstrate the harsh realities of Igbo communal life as it
moves close to the modern age. The heroine is put in various situations
in which she interacts with a large number of people. Because she is
good it becomes easy to use her as a touchstone by which others are
judged. For example, her two husbands are different in temperament,
belief, social status and attitude to marital problems. It is therefore not
surprising that different sets of conditions result in failure in each case.
We have in Adizua a case of an essentially traditional man trying, in
spite of himself, to become modern. He is an impecunious farmer when
he meets Efuru and decides to marry her. He is unable to pay the dowry
required by tradition. Yet he encourages Efuru to break the law by
moving to his house before he fulfils all customary requirements.

> The mother of the young man went to the market; when she returned
> she was surprised to see Efuru's clothes and a few other possessions in
> her son's room. The young man was quick to explain. He told his
> mother that Efuru was his wife. 'I have no money for the dowry yet.
> Efuru herself understands this. We have agreed to be husband and
> wife and that is all that matters.' The young man's mother was
> excited for her son had indeed made a good choice.
> 'You are welcome, my daughter. But your father, what will you say
> to him?'
> 'Leave that to me, I shall settle it myself.' (p.8)

Traditional law has been violated, and the culprits, Adizua and Efuru,
cannot go unpunished. They have made light of custom by agreeing to
be husband and wife without involving the two families and the
community in their arrangement.

Judged by the way the relationship between the two develops, Efuru
has been the dominant personality. Adizua is a nonentity playing

second fiddle to his wife. Efuru virtually directs his movement and dictates his mode of life. His place as a farmer is on the farm. There he can hope to prosper. But because his wife will not go with him – 'I am not cut out for farm work. I am going to trade' (p.10) – he deserts farming. When his wife finds life in the village boring, he agrees to move to the town with her to keep her company. This relationship is unnatural in a traditional setting. Having violated tradition to start with, Efuru refuses to play the woman's traditional role. How can such a situation escape the attention of villagers who live a communal life? So they discuss the unusual case of this childless woman who lords it over her husband.

> Neighbours talked as they were bound to talk. They did not see the reason why Adizua should not marry another woman since, according to them, two men do not live together. To them Efuru was a man since she could not reproduce. (p.24)

Efuru's apparent barrenness creates a problem for husband and wife, and the community as a whole. Adizua's initial reaction is to play down the whole affair and reassure his wife of his sincerity – 'Please don't think that it makes any difference to me whether you have a baby or not. You know I will be the last person to do anything that will hurt you, my wife.' (p.26) He shows little interest in Efuru's suggestion that he should 'begin to look around for a young girl for a wife'. (p.26) He is probably at this stage already fed up with his wife and has made up his mind to escape from the oppressive situation in which he finds himself. In the meantime Efuru becomes pregnant and Ogonim is born. Even so, Adizua deserts his wife for another woman. He dramatically asserts his manliness and decides to start a new life in a modern setting far away from the drudgery of farm work and the boredom of the village.

The effect of Adizua's desertion on Efuru is devastating. She becomes subdued and humble. She conducts a little investigation into Adizua's background – what she should have done before marrying him – and discovers from her mother-in-law that the man has only taken after his father. She is not impressed by the way Ossai in her time resigned herself to her fate when she was deserted by Adizua's father. She is not willing to make an unnecessary sacrifice – 'To suffer for a truant husband, an irresponsible husband like Adizua is to debase suffering. My own suffering will be noble. When Adizua comes back, I shall leave him.' (pp.61-62) She eventually returns to her father's house. Why does Efuru's first marriage fail? What lessons does she learn from her experiences? Reference has already been made to the violation of tradition. There is also the problem of assumed childlessness which is not necessarily solved with the birth of Ogonim – Efuru has difficulty having another child. True enough, she has made a lot of money from her trade and become prosperous. But she realises her riches will avail nothing without a child.

'What is money? Can a bag of money go for an errand for you? Can a bag of money look after you in your old age? Can a bag of money mourn you when you are dead? A child is more valuable than money.' (p.37)

Faced with the reality of the situation, Efuru moderates her claims. She will not object to her husband having a second wife; she will only wish to retain her position of first among equals. 'It is only a bad woman who wants her husband all to herself.' (p.53) She accepts polygamy as a way of life and says so openly. Her sad experiences with Adizua have taught her a salutary lesson which proves useful in her next marriage. She goes to Eneberi (Gilbert) as a mature, hardworking and reliable wife anxious to work closely with her husband to make a success of their marriage.

But why does this other marriage also fail? Why does a union which starts with so much promise end in disaster? This time all necessary precautions are taken, and the customary laws are observed. Unlike Adizua, Eneberi is literate, polite and gentle. He is a Christian who displays the virtues of love and respect for a wife publicly, at times to the amusement and, even, annoyance of the villagers.

'I like them,' one woman said as Gilbert and Efuru were leaving the stream.

'When two people live like that, then the world is worth living in,' another added.

'What do you admire in the lives of those two?' Omirima asked contemptuously.

'Do you know what they went through last night? Don't be carried away by the fact that they come to the stream together and swim and play in the deep.'

'You are right,' one of the women said.

'Have they children?' another asked.

'Children? You don't pluck children from a tree you know. You don't fight for them either. Money cannot buy them. Happiness cannot give you children. Children indeed, they have no children.'

'What is he doing? Foolish man. He sits down there and refuses to do anything. He doesn't see young girls all over the place to take one as a wife. It is their business not mine.' (pp.174-175)

This dialogue is a good example of the kind of village gossip which gets down to the root of an important matter. Efuru and Eneberi are greatly in love with each other. But between them are differences in orientation which are capable of ruining their relationship. Childlessness is again at the heart of the matter – 'Happiness cannot give you children'. The village gossips consider Eneberi foolish not necessarily because he loves his wife, but because he appears to condone her barrenness. If a woman fails, as in this case, the man should take positive steps to get himself children from other sources. Ironically, at the time this dialogue takes place Eneberi already has a child by another woman, a fact yet unknown to the speakers, or Efuru. These facts are capable of widening the social gulf which has always existed between Eneberi and Efuru. Eneberi is essentially a modern man who is struggling hard not to get too deeply involved with tradition. On the other hand, Efuru is a traditionalist who finds the pace of modernism, as represented by Eneberi, too fast and unbearable. So when her husband accuses her falsely of adultery, her pride is hurt. She leaves him and returns to her father's house for the second time. 'I have ended where I began – in my father's house . . . It is the will of our gods and my chi that such a misfortune should befall me.' (p.220)

Efuru fails partly because she tries to embody tradition and modernism is an extraordinary way. She might have succeeded if fate had not decidedly intervened against her. She has everything going in her favour initially. She is a good woman, loved and respected by all, a remarkable woman with very attractive qualities. She is noted for her industry and prosperity – 'It was not only that she came from a distinguished family. She was distinguished herself.' (p.7) She does good to all manner of people. For example, she provides medical care at her own expense for Nwosu and Nnona, and is broadminded enough to entertain the thought that Ogea may become Eneberi's third wife. Nnona proclaims her goodness and generosity to the world.

'I am back, our Nwashike, I am back. Your daughter has saved my life, I am well now. Your daughter is a good woman. A good husband will meet her. Good fortune will meet her. She will live long, nothing will happen to her. Her house will be filled with children.' (p.131)

It is therefore not for lack of goodwill that her two marriages fail. The explanation may lie in the fact that she eventually becomes a devotee of Uhamiri who cannot help solve her problem of childlessness – 'Can she give me children? . . . She cannot give me children, because she has not got children herself.' (p.165) Efuru may derive other benefits from her attachment to Uhamiri, but not the kind that can save her marriage from collapse or prevent Eneberi from bringing mighty disgrace to the family. Tragedy results in this case not from any display of personal ambition on the part of Efuru but from a cruel interplay of external forces which are clearly beyond her control.

The novelist has a better artistic reason for introducing the river goddess, Uhamiri. She has used the circumstances of the goddess to emphasise that the happiness of a virtuous woman like Efuru should not depend entirely on her ability to have a child. The goddess has other bounties to bestow. She can enrich a woman's life spiritually and help remove all the anxiety about having a child.

> She had lived for ages at the bottom of the lake. She was as old as the lake itself. She was happy, she was wealthy. She was beautiful. She gave women beauty and wealth but she had no child. She had never experienced the joy of motherhood. Why then did the women worship her? (p.221)

The novelist has used Uhamiri to symbolise the freedom of women generally and to indicate their ability to free themselves from the shackles imposed by society in favour of men. According to her, the goddess is real in the minds of Ogwuta people.[2] She occupies Ogwuta Lake. She is beautiful and independent, qualities which Efuru possesses. She is therefore a symbol of hope for all women so that her devotees such as Efuru can taste of her kind of freedom and happiness with or without children. Because Efuru has all the attributes of Uhamiri she can, as a devotee, become a visible representative of the river goddess and be happy without a child. This is an important statement of the novel and provides necessary justification for the emphasis placed on the importance of the river goddess.

The work is steeped deep in indigenous Igbo culture and way of life. The novelist creates a credible picture of Igbo village life before the turn of the century. The villagers are somewhat superstitious and allow their lives to be governed by the fear of the unknown. They revere their ancestral gods who play a dominant role in their lives, and are believed to guide and direct their every movement and action. They are largely ignorant of the world beyond the village and the ethnic group, but they are happy with themselves within the limits of their ambitions and achievements. It is an hierarchical and orderly society in which age and rank are accorded great honour, where the family as a functional unit is respected and age group organisations add to the pleasures of life. In such a rural situation gossiping becomes a pastime. The night is devoted, as appropriate, to story-telling and moonlight plays. The novelist shows a particular interest in stories because of their sociological and literary value, and often emphasises the immense pleasure the villagers derive in story-telling events.

However, there are strong indications in the work that this orderly and elementary mode of existence will not last for much longer. Some notable events are already taking place which are capable of disturbing the apparently smooth surface of village life. First, there is the war which gives prominence to the erratic behaviour of soldiers. The soldiers, according to reports, behave like savages.

> No soldier had ever returned to the little town since the war began, but they had heard fantastic stories about soldiers. Soldiers ate human flesh. If they were hungry and there was no food to eat and nobody to eat either, they cut their own flesh and ate it raw. If they were thirsty and there was no water to drink, they drank their urine. (p.186)

Secondly, there is the introduction of monetary economy which brings in its wake greed and an insatiable thirst for wealth. Life has become less secure, as people become more ruthless in their search for easy money, according to this conversation between Gilbert and Efuru.

> 'Onicha market is a terrible place. A market where you can see all sorts and conditions of men. There is nothing under the sun that is not sold there. I am sure that if one looks for a human head, one can easily find it in that market.' . . .
> Gilbert laughed. 'Most of the things you buy there are not genuine. One must be very careful before one buys anything from that market, especially medicines and cosmetics.'
> 'You are right,' said Efuru. 'You know I bought a tin of powder the other day and when I opened it I saw that it was starch.'
> 'Since buying M & B tablets from the market and discovering that they were white chalk, I don't buy medicines or powder from the market,' said Gilbert. (p.113)

It is against such a changing social and cultural background that the principal actors in the novel play their parts. The actors are mainly women. This is not surprising in a novel devoted mainly to home and family life. Apart from Efuru, there are other women who play crucial roles. Ajanupu, for example, symbolises the spirit of economic and social independence which traditional Igbo culture encourages in women. She is extremely knowledgeable about the affairs of the village and gets called upon to help out with social and medical problems. She is presented as a strong character throughout and is Efuru's constant support in times of distress. Efuru becomes attached to her because of the many different ways she has proved useful. Ajanupu appears to be the hidden voice of the author in this work both in her assertion of the rights of women and the way she lashes out at men on every conceivable occasion. 'Some men are not fit to be called men. They have no sense.

They are like dogs that do not know who feeds them. Leave Adizua with this woman. He will soon be tired of her...' (p.58) She accepts the woman's responsibility to her husband, but insists that the man should remain a respectable head of his family. Otherwise, he loses his self-respect and hardly deserves the respect of others. She severely rebukes her sister for bringing up Adizua wrongly, thereby directly encouraging his recklessness.

'Why don't you go in search of your son?' Ajanupu raised her voice. 'Why don't you, as you went in search of your husband many years ago. You are the cause of your child's bad ways. You never scolded him because he was an only child. You delightfully spoilt him and failed to make him responsible. You failed to make him stand on his own so that now he leans on these rich women not because he loves them, but because they are rich. (p.80)

The work bears testimony to other good qualities in women. For example, their industry is not in doubt. 'Women of our town are very industrious. They rise when the cock crows.' (p.194) They also in the main accept their traditional role as loyal and submissive housewives, as the lives of Ossai, Amede and Nwabata would tend to suggest. Ogea grows from the weak position of a domestic to play significant roles in family affairs. However, it is to their important role as mothers that the novel focuses attention. The work is almost a manual of mothercare. It contains details of what a woman should do at every stage of pregnancy, during childbirth and the upbringing of the child. The method of child-bearing and child-rearing reflects the beliefs, attitudes and customs of the people. For example, a pregnant woman should not 'go out alone at night. If she must go out, then somebody must go with her and she must carry a small knife. When she is sitting down, nobody must cross her leg'. (p.29) If at birth the child does not cry at once, you 'took hold of its two legs, lifted it in the air and shook it until it cried'. (p.31) The mother should put her legs together, or else she will not be able to walk properly in future. Breastfeeding should go on for a year or more. A mother should take personal responsibility for the upbringing of her children and not leave them to housemaids to look after. A girl's up-bringing needs special care and attention. Everything must be done to prepare her for her future role as housewife and mother. Ogea is a good example of a girl who is being so prepared. Even on a simple matter like sweeping the floor, she is told precisely what to do – 'Bend down properly, you are a girl and will one day marry. Bend down and sweep like a woman.' (pp.44-45) A child's proper unbringing is in the final analysis the responsibility of the whole village and the ethnic group. The ultimate aim is for him to become a responsible member of his community and to contribute his quota to the welfare of his people.

The author's knowledge of domestic matters, the relationship between Efuru and Ajanupu, the roles of Ogea and other female characters, Efuru's upbringing of children and disposition to her two husbands all help to make this essentially a woman's novel. The world of the novel is dominated by women and feminine practices.

> Efuru gave Ogonim a hot bath and put mentholatum in her anus. She then rubbed kernel oil all over her body putting it in every opening of the body. She tried to breastfeed her, but she refused it. Efuru put her on her back and in no time she was asleep. She brought her out again and put her on the bed. 'Now stay with her Ogea, while I go to Ajanupu.'
> Efuru walked as fast as she could, occasionally breaking into a run. Ajanupu was in. 'My daughter is ill,' she told Ajanupu before she sat down. 'She has a fever and she has lost her appetite. I have rubbed her with kernel oil.' (p.64)

Perhaps only a woman who is herself a mother can write such an intimate piece on mothercare. Such details impart realism to Flora Nwapa's characterisation.

However, the presentation of Efuru as an elegant, prosperous, infinitely patient, almost perfect village woman greatly respected by all, presents difficulties. As already indicated, the work abounds with examples of her goodness, and she is endowed with superhuman qualities. Gilbert spends the night out several times without notice and comes in the following morning without a word of rebuke (or complaint) from Efuru. Efuru takes care of the mother of Adizua who cruelly deserts her, decides on her own to get a new wife for Gilbert, her husband, and accepts her husband's boy by another woman even though Gilbert does not give him any previous warning about the boy.

Efuru is perhaps too good to be a convincing character. She reminds one of Ihuoma in *The Concubine* where Amadi attempts a beautiful, almost perfect character. Amadi's character achieves credibility because of the author's method of delineation. The reader, through the author's use of appropriate details, comes to regard Ihuoma as a rational human being and accept the nature of her connection with the Sea-King. 'The creation of perfect or near-perfect characters,' says Eustace Palmer, 'is a task of considerable difficulty, which Amadi has undertaken with great success. Ihuoma's goodness, politeness, courage, chastity, modesty, good sense, selflessness and beauty, are not only commented on but demonstrated.'[3] Flora Nwapa gives no reason for Efuru's goodness and does not offer enough detail to make her role in the novel completely acceptable.

Idu is the same kind of novel as *Efuru*.[4] Both novels thrive on assumed childlessness and there are cross references from one to the other. There is, for example, a reference to Efuru's house in *Idu*. Also the Woman of the Lake appears in both novels and in each case she is given the same kind of role, an omnipresent god who directs the affairs of man. She is endowed with enormous mysterious supernatural powers. Efuru dies because she is a devotee. Idu is victimised because of her over-emphasis on children.

In this work the novelist pursues her interest in home and family life. She portrays different kinds of marital connections in order to highlight what factors make for success or failure in married life. Adiewere and Idu provide the most enduring connection between man and woman in the novel. They are presented as a happy couple who are experiencing matrimonial bliss. Adiewere, we are told, 'is such a good man. There is no one like him'. Idu too 'is a good woman. She is like her mother. Her beauty, hair, even the way she laughs . . . God has a way of doing things at times. He has a way of bringing two people together'. (p.2) These two are extremely pleased with each other and may have been a shining example to others but for the fact that they have no child. Childlessness is again made a disruptive force. Without a child immediately after marriage, the woman is assumed to be barren, and barrenness is a curse is this society under focus. The man must immediately take another wife who will bear him children, restore confidence in the system and allay public anxiety. Happiness in marriage is desirable and welcome, but without a child, it avails little. It is a society which places a lot of premium on the ability of a couple to have children and, to that extent, undermines every other form of human achievement – 'What we are all praying for is children. What else do we want if we have children?' (p.150)

Societal expectations create hardship for Adiewere and Idu. For Adiewere they result in a nightmare. He is 'not at heart a polygamist'. (p.16) Yet he is compelled by force of circumstances to take another wife who proves irrational and ungovernable. Even with the arrival of his son, Ijoma, the problem is not solved because Idu has difficulty having a second child. The fact that the couple are happy with one child is unimportant to the villagers. No man is qualified to choose for himself a life-style different from what custom and tradition would allow. No couple, however popular or prosperous, can defy the expectations of society with impunity. It is in their attempt to satisfy others that Adiewere and Idu get into trouble. Idu convinces her husband to take a new wife. Adiewere finds a way out of present difficulties through drinking and late night parties. He contracts a mysterious disease which leads to his sudden death. Given the inestimable love which has existed between the two, it is not surprising that Idu becomes demented after the death of 'her husband. Life without Adiewere is worthless to her; she has lost the will to continue to live.

> 'I will not weep. That's not what we agreed. Adiewere and I planned things together. We did not plan this. We did not plan that he would leave me today and go to the land of the dead. Who will I live with? Who will be my husband, the father of my only son? Who will talk to me at night? What are you telling me? Asking me to weep? To weep for my husband? I was with him only yesterday. We did not sleep early. We talked making plans and today he is dead, he is a corpse lying there, a corpse, and you tell me to weep for him.' (p.210)

She dies only a few days later.

The marriage between Ishiodu and Ogbenyanu is presented as an example of a situation where, with children, a couple are not happy with themselves. In this sense, it provides a foil to the relationship between Adiewere and Idu. Ishiodu is a senseless husband of a more senseless wife. The two are lazy, quarrelsome and unsuccessful in business. The man is improvident, and relies solely on Adiewere, his brother, and Idu for his livelihood. Although there is some indication that his social circumstances may improve in future, the reader is not satisfied that he will be able to provide enough comfort and security for his wife and five children. The novelist may be suggesting that, although it is desirable to produce children, it is also frightfully important that parents have the means of bringing them up properly.

In the same way the relationship between Amarajeme and Ojiugo is used to demonstrate that childlessness in marriage is not always the fault of the woman, as is generally believed. Ojiugo marries Amarajeme despite his previous 'loose life'. She stays with him for a long time, but is not able to have a child. Then she moves to one of his friends and has a child by him. Amarajeme becomes dejected and inconsolable. As we are told, 'In spirit he was dead, but he lived on'. (p.127) He refuses to believe that Ojiugo has deserted him and very much hopes she will soon return.

> What Ojiugo, my wife, did is childish. She will come back to me. Mark my words. The devil tempted her. She will see reason. What did I do to her? I did not ill-treat her. She was my wife as well as my sister, for as you know my mother had only two of us. I have no sister. When I married Ojiugo, she became my sister and my wife. We lived

together, peacefully. She was so pleasing to my eyes that I liked the dust she trod on. Then you tell me now that she has gone to my friend to be his wife. That was not what we agreed on. It cannot happen. (p.107)

When it becomes clear that his wife will not return to him, he commits suicide. Amarajeme hangs himself not because of any mighty love for Ojiugo, but because she has all along kept to herself the secret of his impotence. Now that she has had a child by another man, the truth is out for all to recognise. He kills himself because he is too weak morally to face the truth about his circumstances in life.

Amarajeme's case is indicative of some of the changes which are gradually taking place in the village. In her presentation of facts the novelist reflects the time lag between the events described in *Efuru* and those of *Idu*. We still have something of the gaiety and simplicity of village life – story-telling, moonlight play, merriment, especially during the harvest season, age group organisations. The elders still try to inculcate a high standard of morality in the young, who are becoming lazy and careless. From time to time the erring ones are told, 'That is not how our people behave'. (p.105) Village training has been extended to include useful skills like fishing and swimming. This training is now systematically imparted.

'In our childhood days,' Nwasobi began, 'our mothers took us to the stream and threw us into the water. We struggled, and when we began to sink they got us out again. Then they threw us in again, and brought us out. They continued in this way until we knew how to swim. I did this to all my children, and now all of them know how to swim. I must tell Ogbonna. It's a shame that his son doesn't know how to swim.' (pp.64-65)

Western-type education has become popular, and more children attend school. However, the emphasis of the work is on the changes which are gradually disturbing the peace and stability of village life. Because of the increasing contact by women with the outside world, prostitution has become the order of the day. This is deprecated by all – 'Prostitution is bad for our women ... Our Woman of the Lake frowns at it' (p.39) – yet it flourishes. There are cases of fire disasters, dog bites and of people going mad. Armed robbery has brought about a feeling of insecurity to life and property, especially after Okeke is killed by thieves. The situation is aggravated by the fact that some of the robbers live in the village. 'It is not only the people from up-country who are thieves. We have thieves among our people here.' (p.176) These are disturbing changes which make village life less attractive than it ought to be. The

58

characters in the novel play their parts in these changing circumstances.

The novel, as is usual with this novelist, is packed full with women, many of whom play significant roles. Nwasobi is the counterpart of Ajanupu of *Efuru*. She is Idu's best friend and constant support in times of difficulty. She is always anxious to help others – she helps Ogbenyanu when she has a miscarriage and is in attendance when Idu delivers Ijoma. She is a village elder who, with Uzoechi, imparts goodness to other people, especially the young ones. Anamadi, Idu's sister, benefits from her interaction with others in the village who are older and wiser than herself. She starts by being a wayward and difficult girl, something of a problem child who acts only to please herself. Idu and Adiewere do their best to give her a good upbringing, but she takes some time to respond to treatment. Like Ogea in *Efuru*, she eventually becomes a useful member of the family and plays a positive role in family affairs. On the other hand, Onyemuru is an outstanding village gossip – she is often referred to as a witch – who makes life difficult for all who have anything to do with her. She is a cantankerous old woman who pries into other people's secrets and then reveals them to the whole village. She is an unpleasant person who is either disturbing the peace of the village, looking for a lost hen or upsetting traders in the market by underpricing their goods. She is disappointed with life, having lost all her important relations and any hope of a decent life. To a great extent she is the cause of her own misfortune, and therefore deserves little sympathy. Her role in the novel is an entirely negative one. She is introduced to show the variety of people who inhabit the village and the different kinds of activities they engage in. The novelist is trying to realise in full the background against which she writes.

The heroine, Idu, is naturally the most important character in the novel. On her a great deal of creative attention is focused. Like Efuru, she is presented as infinitely good and beautiful. Her goodness is demonstrated by acts of love and kindness to Adiewere and others. Her love for her husband knows no bounds. She stands by him in life and in death. She emphasises only the good sides of people and plays down their faults and weaknesses. She is concerned with the welfare of relations, neighbours and business associates – she brings Anamadi up to a socially respectable standard, she makes an attempt to help Uberife's son and undertakes to send Okeke's son to school. All the evidence points to the fact that she has been good all the time. 'Idu was never wayward as a young girl . . . She did not spoil herself at all. She was not like other girls. No man saw her nakedness before she married Adiewere.' (p.194)

Given Idu's goodness as a young girl and as an adult, why does her married life end in disaster? Why is she denied the joys of motherhood?

The novel provides no satisfactory answer to these disturbing questions. True enough, there is the anxiety caused by assumed childlessness, to which reference has already been made. But in this case, unlike that of 'Efuru, there is no mention of any active supernatural intervention nor any social or cultural inadequacies on the part of the heroine. What we have instead is a record of great devotion of Idu and Adiewere to each other and the sacredness of married life. 'God created the two of them together and said that they must be husband and wife. Do you know that if one is sick the other one becomes sick too. It is strange.' (p.150) Why then are the two not allowed to benefit from their nobility of mind and steadfastness of purpose? The problem of tragic responsibility in this novel is not particularly well handled. The heroine falls not because of any personal faults or the decisive imposition of external forces beyond her control. A situation in which husband and wife die suddenly one after the other without satisfactory explanation must be regarded as contrived and therefore artistically invalid. One cannot but agree with Yinka Shoga's opinion on this matter.

> The novels of Flora Nwapa have a diffused quality that prevents them having a very strong impact. The lot of woman is developed in a personal rather than a social term. The limitations imposed on the woman by the society is accepted by the character as well as the novelist. Consequently the novels lack that universal importance, that amplitude of reference which comes from the clash of human aspirations with destiny. So, the untimely death at the end may be pathetic, even shocking, but definitely not tragic.[5]

However, Flora Nwapa shows some signs of artistic maturity in *Idu*. Although there is still the use of material in a sociological way, dialogue is freer and the novelist displays an incisive knowledge of the content and tenor of village gossip. Signs of great improvement are clear right from the beginning of the book:

> 'You had a maid, what happened to her?'
> 'She has gone. Her people came for her one day, and she went with them; I did not even know. She took all the dresses I made for her, and left my youngest daughter crying.'
> 'This is bad. Who are her people?'
> 'She is from Esu,' Nwasobi replied.
> 'They are like that. You cannot rely on them. Look, there's Idu. Idu, our Idu, are you well?'
> 'I am very well,' replied Idu. 'I have come to fetch some water. My husband is not very well today.'
> 'What's wrong with him?' Nwasobi asked.
> 'He had a headache yesterday, so . . . (p.1)

Here dialogue is free and relevant. It is used not only to introduce some of the principal characters of the book; it also touches on a theme which is central to the action of the novel.

In this book the author seizes every opportunity to dramatise the fears, beliefs and doubts of the people. Often she attains heights of dramatic tension, usually achieved through the exploitation of the people's rural simplicity. The appearance of an eclipse is a case in point. The novelist uses this incident to expose the people's ignorance of a natural phenomenon. They are thrown into a panic and cease all normal activities. They are shown to be men and women of very limited mental horizon:

> It was the end of the world. Who among the people could claim that he had ever seen the night in the middle of the day? How could night occur twice in one day? It was unheard of. The world was full of evil men, and God was manifesting His works among men of the earth. The darkness had come so suddenly, without a warning. To the Christians it was the coming of Christ. He was to come like a thief in the night, unheralded, so they had to be prepared. (p.82)

Even greater confusion arises when Ijoma is presumed lost. The whole community is involved in the search and the novelist uses this occasion to bring about communal solidarity. Idu's pathetic cry: 'My Ijoma, where is my Ijoma, where is my only son? where is my only child? Has he drowned? Maybe he went to the lake and was drowned. In that case we shall see his body floating tomorrow morning,' (p.189) gives the signal for an intensive search in which practically every villager takes part. The genuineness of the people's distress and the thorough and energetic manner in which they show their concern attest to their love and respect for Idu. The author's achievement here is obvious in the way she successfully mobilises the people for a humanitarian purpose.

Never Again

Never Again is devoted to the ravages of war, especially its effect on human beings.[6] In particular Flora Nwapa concentrates on the capture of Ugwuta by the Federal troops during the Nigerian civil war and its recapture by the Biafran soldiers. The work owes its dramatic impact to the way the author uses incidents at Ugwuta to highlight the nature and extent of the conflict between the two sides. Ugwuta is important because of its nearness to the Uli airstrip through which Biafra gets its supply of ammunition and other materials. Uli is the only reliable line of communication with the outside world. Once Ugwuta is captured, it will require only a little more effort on the part of Federal troops to take Uli which is so essential for the resistance. Given this importance, it is not surprising that the author devotes so much attention to the people's resolve not to see Ugwuta fall. The strategic importance of Ugwuta is always stressed.

> At Ugwuta we did not sleep properly if we did not hear planes at night because that meant that arms and ammunition were not coming in. But when there were planes, we woke up greatly relieved, and dared the Nigerians to continue their war of aggression on a young progressive Biafra. (p.64)

The novel devotes a lot of space to the people's fear that the village may be taken by enemy troops. This is based on past experiences in Enugu, Onitsha, Calabar and Port Harcourt and the human suffering which accompanies the evacuation of captured places. The amount of destruction is enormous, and there is a total disruption of human activities. The greatest fear, however, comes from the possibility of being permanently uprooted from one's village, of being denied access to one's ancestral land. Many Ugwuta citizens articulate this fear in their reaction to the situation in which they find themselves. The deliberate lies told by people, the mutual suspicion with which they regard one another, the frequent designation of any disagreeable person as a saboteur are only some of the external manifestations of the great fear which has enveloped the whole community.

Even so, the villagers continue to hope that nothing serious will happen to Ugwuta. Part of this is based on false assumptions. There is the belief by many citizens that the Biafran army is invincible. At least, the troops are thought to have the ability ultimately to repel any invader, even where there is an initial setback. Therefore, if the Federal troops enter Ugwuta, they will immediately be sent back by the determined forces of Biafra. This is, in fact, far from the truth. The troops are not always disciplined. They are for the most part ill-equipped, ill-trained, and they often behave in a most despicable manner. They terrorise the inhabitants, tell them lies under the pretext of boosting their morale, loot their property and generally impose themselves on the people they have cowed to submission. They frequently take undue advantage of their position.

> At the beginning of the war when a soldier told you he was from a war front, you gave him drinks if you met him in a pub. Or you invited him to your home, and he ate with you and your family. If he was an officer, and you had daughters, you did not mind if he slept with one of them or even took her away the next morning. (p.18)

The citizens of Ugwuta base their hope of survival mainly on Uhamiri, the Woman of the Lake. They worship her as conscientious devotees and rely on her protection in all their endeavours. That is why they are able to say when Ugwuta is threatened: 'We can't leave Ugwuta for the Nigerians. Every place can fall, not Ugwuta. Only the night before, we sacrificed again to the Woman of the Lake.' (p.39) The absolute confidence of the people in their goddess is somewhat shaken when Ugwuta does fall. But this situation is soon reversed. The enemy attack is repulsed in circumstances which gives great credit to the goddess. The Nigerian gun-boat is sunk in the Lake 'as the people thought not by artillery fire but by the Woman of the Lake . . . She sank it for daring to carry war to her own beloved people'. (p.80) So in the end Uhamiri is rehabilitated in the lofty esteem of her people. Considering the use Flora Nwapa has made of the goddess in her previous novels, it is a great relief that she emerges triumphant here. It is one thing for a people to lose their material possessions and suffer the deprivations of war; it is quite another thing for them to be forced to abandon the spiritual anchor they have relied upon for so long. The author's intention is to emphasise that, even if as a result of these events the reputation of the goddess is dented, it is certainly not destroyed. In the end, we are told, 'the only thing that stood undisturbed, unmolested, dignified and solid was the Lake . . . It was calm, pure, peaceful and ageless.' (p.80) The author's emotional attachment to Uhamiri is clearly demonstrated in her attractive presentation of the goddess.

Flora Nwapa successfully dramatises the human dimensions of the war. The painful experiences of Kate, her husband, Chudi, and members of their family are typical of the hardship which the war brings upon the citizens. They have fled Enugu, Onitsha, Port Harcourt and Elele, and are thoroughly tired of moving from place to place. Now they are required without much notice to flee from Ugwuta. Kate and Chudi necessarily become sceptical about the ability of the secessionist army to contain the onslaught of the Federal troops. For this they are called saboteurs by their friend, Kal, who threatens to hand them over to the army. The situation is so confused that it is difficult to know when it is safe to talk or whom it is safe to talk to. Lepers mingle freely with other people and are occasionally recruited into the army.

The suffering of the people is exacerbated by other factors. The endless meetings called by the elders and the erratic behaviour of members of the war cabinet exasperate the villagers. The nocturnal searches by the army, and the threat of the deadly disease, Kwashiokor, combine to create an atmosphere of fear and insecurity. The gloom is heightened by a number of pathetic cases: Madam Agafa is temporarily separated from her children and suffers mental agony as a result; Ona refuses to leave Ugwuta in good time during the evacuation of the village and is shot dead by the invading forces; a pregnant woman, who is trying to escape, falls into labour by the wayside and dies in the presence of other helpless citizens. That is the end of the war for her but not for the others, as the novel philosophically points out.

> We stood. Others joined us. We watched. Then a rocket, another, and yet another. We took cover. We lay on our stomachs. The body was peaceful. It had no need to take cover. She was at peace with her God. God had ended her suffering. She would no longer suffer. (p.56)

Aniche is brutalised and killed by the Federal troops; so also is Ezekoro who, in a fit of madness, attempts to drive away well-armed soldiers with his fan. One gets the impression that some of these catastrophes might have been averted if the people had not been so consistently fed on a well articulated, false propaganda.

The author leaves no one in any doubt that she regards the war as a mad pursuit by both sides. She takes a balanced view of the whole affair. War brings untold hardship to people and ought to be avoided at all costs. The leaders on both sides should have adopted a rational approach to a peaceful settlement. In her view secession hardly solves a political problem because 'there was already oppression even before the young nation was able to stand on her feet'. (p.50) On the other hand, Nigerian soldiers should not have attacked Biafra with such brutal force. That only makes matters worse. Consideration ought to have been given to the close affinity between the two sides.

> Why, we were all brothers, we were all colleagues, all friends, all contemporaries, then, without warning, they began to shoot, without warning, they began to plunder and to loot and to rape and to desecrate and more, to lie, to lie against one another. What was secret was proclaimed on the house tops. What was holy was desecrated and abused. NEVER AGAIN. (p.70)

If such reasoning had prevailed in 1967 the Nigerian civil war would not have taken place and perhaps *Never Again* would not have been written.

One is Enough

In *One is Enough* the novelist continues to show interest in home and family life.[7] The emphasis here, as elsewhere, is on the disastrous effect on the woman of childlessness in marriage in a traditional society. Amaka gets into trouble not because she is a failure as a wife but because, after six years of marriage, she has not been able to produce a child. She obviously possesses the sterling qualities which should ordinarily endear a woman to a man. She is well domesticated and works hard to please Obiora and his people. She is successful in business and is willing to use her wealth to make her household comfortable. Furthermore, she is a good family woman and regards married life as honourable and sacred.

Amaka had always wanted to be married. She envied married people, and when at last Obiora decided to marry her, she was on top of the world. She was going to show everybody that a woman's ambition was marriage, a home that she could call her own, a man she would love and cherish, and children to crown the marriage. Although things had not worked out as she had hoped, she was desperately anxious to preserve her marriage. (pp.3-4)

Unfortunately these qualities are not enough in the circumstances. Without a child, Amaka cannot command the respect of the villagers. Nor does she have their sympathy or consideration. She is, in fact, rated lower in their esteem than the woman who has two children for Obiora but who 'did not know her right from her left' and who 'behaved atrociously and embarrassed Obiora'. (p.120) This other woman is clearly idiotic and a total misfit. Even so, she is brought to the house to displace Amaka. When Obiora eventually realises his folly and wants Amaka back, he is prevented by force of tradition from carrying out his legitimate wishes. So little importance is attached to the element of love in marriage. The marriage between Obiora and Amaka might have succeeded if the villagers had not held a childless woman to such merciless ridicule.

Fortunately the same cannot be said about the relationship between Amaka and Izu (Rev. Father Mclaid). The situation here is entirely different. It is such that it creates more problems for the man than the woman. In this case there is no genuine love between the two. The attempt to forge a union comes only with the arrival of twin boys. Izu expresses his desire to marry Amaka not because he loves her but because he is already a father. The marriage, if contracted, would not have had a chance of succeeding. For one thing, Amaka is not interested in a permanent union with Izu. He has been useful in helping her establish herself in Lagos. He has helped with the award of contracts and supplied the money with which to execute them. Above all, he has made it possible for her to become a mother. These are all the benefits Amaka wants to achieve from her connection with Izu. She looks at the relationship only from the selfish angle of personal gains and rewards. The matter is even more complicated from Izu's point of view, and he leaves no one in doubt about the dilemma in which he finds himself.

As a man of God, sworn to celibacy, what did he think he was doing? Cheating God and cheating his flock? He knew he was committing a mortal sin, but he did nothing about it. At one time, he had thought of going to the Bishop to confess all, but he did not have the courage. Yet he did his job well. He was respected by both his congregation and his colleagues. Sometimes he felt so guilty that he was afraid to associate with his colleagues lest they know his thoughts. Sometimes he imagined that they knew and would one day expose him and he would leave the priesthood in disgrace. (p.107)

Izu's position becomes intolerable. He makes a half-hearted attempt to leave the church. But at the earliest opportunity he confesses his sins to the Bishop who gives the necessary dispensation for him to continue his pastoral duties.

The novelist seizes every opportunity in this work to show how corrupt and unwholesome life in the city of Lagos has become. Lagos is experiencing the aftermath of the civil war when several girls rush from the war zone to the city in search of quick money. The situation is chaotic – corruption is rife and prostitution among girls is the order of the day. Detestable war habits acquired from the different battle fronts are introduced to the civilian life of Lagos. The result is a dramatic fall in moral standards which soon attains a level of social decadence such as Lagos has never witnessed before. The work is packed full of instances of appalling behaviour. There is, for example, the case of Madam Onyei who lets her eldest daughter loose among men in order to get contracts. Contractors often collect money for work not done. Government officials usually receive bribes from contractors who for the most part perform unsatisfactorily. Generally speaking, monetary advantage to the officials concerned is a priority consideration in any business arrangement. Promotion in the Civil Service is no longer awarded on merit, and in a particular case of mass retirement many innocent people suffer. Public and private life has become so corrupt that it is difficult for anyone to live an honest life in Lagos.

Amaka soon becomes an embodiment of this corruption. As soon as she arrives in Lagos she abandons her rural virtues for the corrupt methods of the city. She becomes so mercenary in her motives that any way of acquiring wealth, however mean or degrading, is acceptable to her. Her moral deterioration takes only a short time. In a year she has acquired a house, car and driver, and accumulated so much money that she qualifies for membership of the debased Cash Madam Club. This club brings her in contact with other women who have made money through dubious means, prostitute themselves to secure contracts, and live a flamboyant and false life. Amaka immediately establishes contact with an Alhaji who goes to bed with her freely in exchange for money and contracts. When she meets Izu for the first time she decides to go 'for the kill' and 'tempt' him. As soon as she succeeds in putting him in trouble she decides against marrying him. She is probably conscious of the fact that, given her recent history, she can no longer make a good housewife.

> 'I don't want to be a wife any more, a mistress yes, with a lover, yes of course, but not a wife. There is something in that word that does not suit me. As a wife, I am never free. I am a shadow of myself. As a wife I am almost impotent. I am in prison, unable to advance in body and soul. Something gets hold of me as a wife and destroys me. When I rid myself of Obiora, things started working for me. I don't want to go back to my "wifely" days. No, I am through with husbands. I said farewell to husbands the first day I came to Lagos.' (p.132)

The novelist devotes a lot of space of Amaka's psychological degeneration. She starts life as a decent, responsible and reliable housewife. Against the background of social rejection in the village and the craze for money in the city she deteriorates so fast that in the end she is only a little better than a common prostitute. So far has she departed from the path of honour that she rejects the offer of another opportunity of living a respectable married life.

The work is interesting in the way it differentiates between good and bad, between the old and new. Traditional life is sharply contrasted with modern experience in a way that reveals the inadequacies of both. Representatives of traditional authority – Obiora's mother and Amaka's mother, for example – are so callous and insensitive to the feelings of others that they do not make a favourable impression on the reader. So also is the woman dibia who by her performance might have redeemed the situation. She is made to behave in such a ridiculous manner that one suspects she is introduced only to be satirised. So, this group is disgraced. In the same manner, the elements of modernity – Ayo, with her expensive life-style, Amaka, the Cash Madam Club – are rejected. They have embraced the worst aspects of modern life and thrown moderation and social prudence to the winds. The way forward is indicated by the activities of Mike and Adaobi. Their marriage is based on genuine love which is shown in the way they share each other's burden in times of difficulty. It is a fact that Adaobi is gradually being contaminated with corrupt ideas from her friend, Amaka. But there is no indication as yet that she will ever become remiss in her duties as a wife and mother. Through the activities of this couple and other people like Nanny the novelists shows that it is still possible for honest people to survive in the city of Lagos. This is particularly reassuring, given the depressing picture of city life portrayed in this novel.

This is Lagos and Other Stories

This is the first of two collections of stories.[8] There are in all nine stories in which the author deals with a variety of topics. Her main concern, as usual, is the position of women in the social set-up. The woman is either insisting on her honour and integrity, as we have in 'The Traveller' or asserting her individualism, as in 'This is Lagos' and 'The Delinquent Adults'. In 'The Loss of Eze' the woman enjoys the pleasures of being loved and making a suitable choice. 'The Road to Benin' deals with the problem of juvenile delinquency while 'My Soldier Brother' underlines the adverse effect of war on human ambition. It has not been considered necessary to study all the stories in the collection. Six of them are treated in some detail.

'The Traveller'

In 'The Traveller' the author portrays Bisi as a girl of great integrity. She is ready to socialise with Mr Musa and attend various social functions with him. Her intentions are purely platonic and she will not engage in anything that is morally indefensible. Mr Musa has no such qualms of conscience. He is a traveller who moves rapidly from place to place, and in these places any girl is fair game. So he makes immoral demands of Bisi, adopting the very subtle method of a Lagos man.

> He locked his side of the car, came to her side and took her by the hand. She allowed her hand to be taken, but she remained doggedly on her seat.
>   'All right. If you don't want to go in, let's go for a walk.'
>   'For a walk, at this time of the night, not me.'
>   'What do you want me to do now?' Musa asked in despair.
>   'Go to bed and let me go home.'
>   'You have refused to come in?'
>   'Yes, I have refused to come in.'
>   'What is your reason?'
>   'Reason, you don't do things always with reason.' (p.5)

Mr Musa acts with a sinister motive and does everything possible to go to bed with Bisi just for the fun of it. There is no evidence of love between the two. To Mr Musa love is not an essential element in the relationship between man and woman. All he wants is a girl of easy virtue to serve his

68

pleasure. Bisi shows that she is not such a girl. She remains as courteous and helpful as ever, but does not disguise her contempt for Mr Musa – 'Musa, what kind of man is he? And what kind of woman does he think I am?' (p.8)

The author uses the story to call attention to some unattractive aspects of Enugu life. People in the upper middle income bracket live a life devoted to cocktails, dinners, parties and pub-crawling. The impression is given that these activities are not beneficial to the people and sap the energy which might have been diverted to more gainful pursuits. For example, cocktails are regarded as a means of killing time and not as any constructive contribution to the happiness of the people.

> It was not a bad cocktail. But it was the same pattern. One heard the usual questions asked at parties. 'How is the car behaving?' Conversations on promotions. Nothing on the international or national level whatever. (p.6)

Taxi drivers drive in a way that embarrasses other road users. 'They know what to do. It is just sheer irresponsibility and lack of patience'. (p.2) Doctors 'abuse' the privilege of engaging in private practice. The author points out the foibles of society, examines their causes and precribes remedies. Bisi shows by her actions how the city vices brought from Lagos by Mr Musa can be resisted or contained in a place like Enugu. The implication is clear. If other towns can show the same amount of resistance, the traveller will not be able to spread his vices around the country. In this lies the attraction of this short story and the significance of the author's approach.

'This is Lagos'

'This is Lagos' develops a theme in which the author has shown infinite interest in many of her works – the corrupting influence of city life. Soha comes from the rural area to Lagos as an innocent hard-working girl of twenty. She devotes all her attention to her work at home and at school. Then she meets Mr Ibikunle who pampers her with money, puts her in the family way, marries her in secret and virtually turns her against her parents and all they hold dear.

The emphasis of the story is on the changes which ultimately overwhelm Soha. These changes come gradually and in different forms. But they eventually have the effect of turning an obedient and respectful country lass into a wayward girl lost to the vices of city life. At the beginning of the work we are told,

> Everybody in the 'yard' thought how dutiful Soha was. Her aunt's

husband who was a quiet man praised Soha, and told his wife that she was a good girl. Her aunt was proud of her. Since she came to stay with them, her aunt had had time for relaxation, she did less housework, and paid more attention to her trade, which was selling bread. (p.9)

But once she meets Mr Ibikunle she becomes remiss in her duty to her aunt and other members of her family. She spends long periods out of the house without informing her aunt and entertains men privately without permission. She takes to drinking and late night parties. She tells lies freely and becomes completely mercenary in her outlook. Money is the deciding factor in all her actions. Mr Ibikunle often gets her to serve his pleasure by giving her money. Occasionally he has to give her money before she agrees to go out with him – 'Maybe you will buy dresses for me before I go out with you . . . He pressed a five pound note into her hand. She smiled and they went out.' (p.13) Soha has become a self-conscious city girl who works hard to entice a man of her choice.

> Soha was still in front of the mirror admiring herself. She was not in a hurry at all. Her mother had told her that she should never show a man that she was anxious about him. She should rather keep him waiting as long as she wished. She was wearing one of the dresses she sewed for herself when she was at home. (p.11)

Once a girl is addicted to the pleasures of the city, she loses her sense of propriety and often behaves irrationally.

Soha marries Mr Ibikunle without reference to the wishes of her people at home or in Lagos, thus defying tradition and setting in motion a conflict between the old and new, between the village and city. It is on' this conflict that the story thrives. Mama Eze, Papa Eze and Mama Bisi, as representatives of traditional authority, are flabbergasted by Soha's action and put this down to the wrong ideas imparted to the young ones at school. They insist that the requirements of custom should be fulfilled before the union can be regarded as valid. 'We don't marry like that in my home . . . Home people will not regard you as married.' (p.17) The young people stand their ground because they are convinced of the rightness of their cause. They refuse to go to the village and validate their marriage by performing the necessary traditional rites. They get away with their nonchalance. They have brought about a revolution in the method of marriage and asserted their individualism and freedom. They have indicated the need for change and the right of individuals to be guided in their actions only by a personal code of conduct. This result is edifying, even if the method of achieving it has not altogether been wholesome. The young couple have truly demonstrated by their action that 'This is Lagos. Anything can happen here.' (p.17)

The story is well executed. Within a short time the reader is brought face to face with the apparent moral decline of Soha. Once he comes to appreciate the purpose of the author, the various episodes assume their true importance – the conflicts in the Eze family between Mama Eze and Papa Eze, Eze's support for Soha and her husband, Mr Ibikunle's overconfident behaviour. In this context Mama Bisi's activities as Soha's unofficial mentor become meaningful. The author achieves character differentiation through the adoption of a level of speech appropriate to person, place and circumstance. Dialogue is employed not only to quicken the pace of narration and tempo of activities, but also to focus attention on the various aspects of the topic.

'Don't you work on Saturdays?'
'No.'
'Go well then,' Soha said.
'When am I seeing you again?'
'I don't know. I have no car.'
'Let's go to the cinema tonight.'
'No, my mother will kill me.'
'Your aunt.'
'Yes. She is my mother. You said you will buy something for me today.'
'Let's go to the Kingsway Stores then. I don't know how to buy things for women.'
'Don't you buy things for your wife?'
'I told you, I have no wife.' (p.12)

Here dialogue is used to introduce the important characters of the story and dwell on matters which form the central pre-occupation of the work.

'The Road to Benin'

In 'The Road to Benin' the author deals with the problem of juvenile delinquency which has proved intractable for many Nigerian families and communities. The story is based on a paradox sustained by the activities of Ezeka who brings sorrow and disgrace to his parents at a time when they are beginning to look at him as their source of joy. He raises their hopes and then immediately dashes those hopes because of his acts of irresponsibility. His admission to Government College, Umuahia, has been a matter of great jubilation to all. His parents do

71

everything possible to make him realise his ambition and establish himself in society after leaving school. Instead of paying close attention to his school work, as he has done in the past, he joins a group of youngsters to commit crime and he is sent to prison. The parents are bitterly disappointed and cannot understand why such a great tragedy should befall them.

> How could they be so lucky in the beginning and suddenly become unlucky. It was not often these days, colonial days, yes, but not these days, that the son of a labourer gained admission into such a school as Government College, Umuahia. Why was this sudden light, which had illuminated his poor family which had been in the dark all these years, suddenly turned into darkness? They thought that the light was going to burn forever. It was not the kind of light that was easily extinguished. It was difficult for it to enter in the first place into your household, but once it gained entrance it remained there forever. Who was extinguishing the light? An enemy? Fate? If it were fate, what brought it in, in the first place? It was not easy to comprehend. For simple folks like Nwanyimma and her husband it was mysterious. (pp.37-8)

The author provides the reasons which lead to tragedy. It is true that Nwanyimma and her husband are hardworking and frugal in their ways. They are anxious for Ezeka's progress and strain themselves to make sure he succeeds in life. The work bears testimony to the transparent honesty of the two, especially the wife in connection with her trade in fruits and vegetables.

> She did not only sell to white women, she also sold to cooks of white men. Thus she was in a very privileged position. Her customers were those who were able to pay any price. She did not cheat them, she had the best and sold them to her customers. When she had bad carrots or onions, she persuaded her customers to go elsewhere. Or she went and bought the things she did not have for her customers. (p.30)

Why do such diligent and loving parents come to grief with their most promising son? Ezeka and his parents are equally to blame for his moral ineptitude. The parents, especially the father, virtually abandon their parental responsibility as soon as the boy enters college. The father, for example, thinks the boy can now take beer – 'You should have given him the beer.' (p.33) The mother feels 'there was no sense in worrying about her son. The school would take care of him . . . she had handed over her son to the authorities of the school'. (p.32) They fail to assert their parental authority, leaving everything to the teachers in the college. They fail to realise that the home is a very important agency of education and that, even though their son is attending a reputable college, they ought not to have abandoned their crucial role as his spiritual mentors. Parents must be willing to contribute significantly to the effort to wipe out juvenile delinquency, and not leave this thorny problem to the school and state. It is through the combined effort of home, school, community and state that any success in this matter can be achieved.

But why does a brilliant boy like Ezeka turn a delinquent at a time that he should be highly motivated to read? Why does he prefer the 'loafers of Onitsha' to his school friends who probably would have kept him out of mischief? His moral degeneration seems to have come with his admission to college. It is during his first term holiday that his parents notice undesirable changes in him. Home-life is no longer as satisfying to him as it used to be. He despises his old friends – 'he had left them far behind, and he had nothing in common anymore with them.' (p.36) – and virtually becomes a problem child.

Ezeka became more aloof every day of the holiday. He was becoming quite a problem. He came in late and woke up when his parents had gone to work. He lorded it over his brother and the two sisters. He ordered them about, and they complained to their mother each time she returned from the market. When his mother talked to him, he did not listen. What was she going to do? What had gone wrong with Ezeka? (p.33)

It is understandable that his exposure to college life will liberate him from many previous prejudices. But it should not normally cut him off entirely from his roots. Ezeka's problems are therefore to some extent psychological. It is the failure of his parents to apply the correct remedy in good time and arrest the situation before it gets out of hand that leads to tragedy.

'The Delinquent Adults'

'The Delinquent Adults' shows active concern for a widow who is molested by close relations after the death of her husband. The harassment takes different forms, but has the cumulative effect of making Ozoemena miserable. She is so completely fed up with life at a stage that she blames fate for her plight – 'Oh God, why did you allow my husband to die? Chukwuma, why, why . . . ' (p.80)

The author dramatises the greed and avarice which close relations display on the death of a member of the family. Chukwuma dies in tragic circumstances, leaving behind a wife and many children. Instead of thinking of the comfort of his widow and children, his relations show interest only in the money he has in his bank account. Several people at different times ask the same question. 'Tell me, is it true that your husband has several bags of money in the bank?' (p.63) 'Have you found out how much your husband had in the bank?' (p.71) Ntianu thinks it is important for her daughter to retain any money and property left by her husband while Uzonwane wants the money for himself. The latter is so deeply interested in the matter that he threatens to bring in a dibia to adjudicate. The situation becomes explosive and ultimately leads to a direct confrontation between Uzonwane and Ntianu – 'I am prepared for anything. My daughter is in there. If anything happens to her, I shall hold your responsible.' (p.65) Ozoemena cannot understand this shameful display of immaturity by adults. She is shocked that her relations want to enrich themselves at the expense of her welfare and that of her children. 'What were these old people up to? . . . What was more important? The memory of her husband or the amount of money left in the bank?' (p.67)

The author introduces an element of mystery into the whole affair. Before Chukwuma dies, his wife dreams that her husband goes on a long journey and discusses his fate with another man.

'So you knew he was going?'
'Of course I knew. That was why I did not want you to go with him.'
'And you allowed him to go?'
'And you, could you stop him from going?'
'No.'
'Well then.'
'Won't he come back?'
'No.'
'Why?'
'The journey takes years.'
'What journey?'
'You are asking like a child.'
'I am not a child.' (pp.59-60)

Ozoemena is naturally worried, but she is not bold enough to relate her dream to her husband. When the man dies this action is held again her. She is said to have had a foreknowledge of the death of her husband and kept it to herself so that she can inherit his money and property. This provides apparent justification for those who are bent on disturbing the woman's peace of mind. Ozoemena becomes confused and to some extent mentally disturbed. There are some aspects of her present cir-cumstances she does not understand and others which seem to be beyond her comprehension. Whatever it is, she has clearly been unlucky not only in her husband's death but also in the behaviour of his people and her own mother after his death.

So this is life she said to herself several times. She too was being accused indirectly of killing her husband. And the dream? It was only a dream. She had had so many dreams which were just dreams. But why did she dream that her husband was going on a journey, and it turned out to be that he was really going on a long journey of no return? Was it predicted then that her husband would die? Who predicted it? God? What God? Impossible. It was an accident, true and simple. It could not be anything else. Accident. The lorry driver was careless. He had no brakes, so he crushed her husband while he was returning from work, her husband who was returning to her and his children. But why must it be her husband? Why couldn't it have been another man, another woman's husband. Why was it Chukwuma? (pp.68-69)

The title of the story is justified on another score. On the pretext of trying to help her daughter Ntianu arranges for Ozoemena to marry a rich elderly person who will send her to school and make her and her children comfortable. One cannot but condemn such an arrangement made without reference to Ozoemena and without regard for her convenience, education or orientation to life. The whole situation is intolerable – the method of approach is crude and the man's behaviour is nauseating. He is too conscious of the power bestowed by wealth and in his ability to acquire Ozoemena, or any other woman for that matter, with money. He is shocked when he is turned down and made to look small. 'So that's how girls are hooked? . . . Then she looked at the man, and the whole thing became unbearable. It was so revolting to her'. (p.79) Ozoemena asserts her personal rights in difficult circumstances, and gets away with it. She rebels against traditional authority, as represented by the 'delinquent adults', and comes to no harm. She shows by her resolute action that a widow can stand on her own in spite of difficulties put in her way by close relations. She need not suffer or become an object put up for sale.

'The Loss of Eze'

In 'The Loss of Eze' the author uses Amede's experiences to comment on the gaiety of life in Lagos. Lagos is a place of endless parties which go on up to the small hours of the morning. Many of the people who attend these parties over-enjoy themselves and often behave irrationally. The only exception is the case of Tunde and Amede who emerge from one of such parties with a serious purpose which they intend to exploit to mutual advantage. But generally speaking, the impression which is created is of local residents who eat, drink and womanise excessively, especially when these facilities are provided at other people's expense.

> This is a wretched country . . . Damnable country. Day in day out, parties. A friend who recently returned from Britain, after going to four parties in one night, asked me when Nigeria did her thinking. I told him that nobody thought in Nigeria. (p.86)

Lagos life has other limitations. The knowledge of the country of a typical Lagos man does not usually extend beyond Lagos. 'Many of them have not been to Ibadan, not to mention outlandish places like Ado-Ekiti.' (p.90) Nigerians study 'the geography of the British Isles, Canada, Australia and New Zealand' (p.87) instead of that of Nigeria. To qualify for a Lagos girl 'you must cast off all decency, scrape your eyebrows sort of'. (p.89) It is altogether an unattractive account of Lagos and Lagosians.

It is against this gloomy social background that Amede acts her part. A lover, Eze, has only recently been snatched away from her, and she is feeling disappointed and bitter.

> For six whole months, I did not know what to do with myself. You are lost when you suddenly find yourself left out, when you suddenly discover that you have lost someone who was life itself to you. You grope in darkness, you ask yourself so many questions which you can't answer, or questions whose answers frighten you. You are empty inside you, and you want to fill this emptiness depending of course on the kind of person you are. I was sensitive as a child, I think I still am. At first I was gripped with fear, fear of the world, fear of human beings, fear of all around me. (p.81)

Tunde comes in to wipe out this emptiness in her life in a pleasant way. She meets him at a party and immediately falls for him. 'It was indeed an enjoyable party. Tunde has made it so for me. I am sure that but for him, I would have gone home long ago'. (p.90) Tunde is rated very high in Amede's estimation because he displays greater maturity and urbanity than one finds in many Lagos men. He wins Amede's heart not through the use of money or display of wealth but through his pervasive good manners and kind consideration for a potential future partner. This discovery is particularly edifying, given the picture of Lagos social life which emerges from this work.

'My Soldier Brother'

'My Soldier Brother' is devoted to Adiewere whose life is inextricably

76

bound up in the Biafran war. The story concentrates on the human dimensions of the war, especially its disruptive effects on individuals, groups and communities. Adiewere's life ambition for which he has worked so hard and successfully has to be abandoned for him to join the army. He has had to forgo his studies at the University of Lagos to return home. There he encounters a nationalistic fervour and passion for war which become difficult to resist. People clamour for war without counting the cost or thinking of the dreadful consequences.

> It wasn't long after Adiewere had come home on long vacation, that our Military Governor declared the zero hour. Father was restless, everybody was restless. War at last. It was welcome news. The people were feverish with excitement. I heard sayings like this: 'Let them come by sea, land or air, we are ready for them.' I was excited myself, because the adults were excited. What did I know about war? Father did tell us about the last war in which a brother of his lost his life. He also said that things were scarce, and that many people died because they could not have salt. It was all so intriguing to me. (p. 113)

Adiewere's bright prospects as a young man either as a lawyer or a classroom teacher are ruined. He is sent to the battle front without much preparation. He is wounded and later dies. He is one of the very many casualties of a thoughtless war. He is used as an example of how warmongering first oppresses the human soul and later destroys it.

The author succeeds in making Adiewere's death a painful one because of the expectations of greatness he has aroused in early life. He has been particularly well behaved, dutiful and clever. He passed his School Certificate Examination in grade one and, as an encouragement, 'Father went to the "Esquire" and bought Adiewere a suit, a tie and pair of shoes.' (p.105) Soon he passes his Higher School Certificate Examination 'again with honours', and is admitted to the University. Apart from his academic brilliance he is a sober and thoughtful person.

> Adiewere was quiet, but very deep. He never argued with Father. But he did not do what he did not want to do. I admired him very much, but sometimes, I was afraid of him. There was something in him. Something impenetrable, even mysterious about him. I could not understand what he felt for Aunt Monica. We all did not like her and said so amongst ourselves. But Adiewere didn't easily tell us or other people his likes and dislikes. (p.107)

The fact that he can restrain himself from showing open dislike for Aunt Monica is a great personal tribute. For she is a rude and quarrelsome woman who is at loggerheads with practically every member of the family, and tells her brother off openly, even in the presence of his children. Adiewere is presented as a good, sensitive and ambitious young man who is killed at the prime of life. In this way the author underlines the tragedy of war.

Wives at War and Other Stories

This is the author's second collection of stories.[9] There are seven stories in all. They deal mainly with women at war against one kind of injustice or other. They largely concentrate on the restoration of women's rights, the need for women to be given a free hand to plan their lives and decide their own social priorities. Four of these stories are briefly discussed.

In 'Wives at War' women agitate for their inherent right to represent their country abroad. They claim they have contributed as much as the men to the war effort and deserve to be compensated with a trip abroad. They are annoyed by the way they imagine the government has chosen women representatives without reference to their leaders. They threaten drastic action against the Foreign Secretary and all others who undermine the role of women in society.

> 'You wait until the end of this war. There is going to be another war, the war of the women. You have fooled us enough. You have used us enough. You have exploited us enough. When this war has ended we will show you that we are a force to be reckoned with. You wait and see. What do you think we are? Instruments to be used and discarded?' (p.13)

The fight here is based on incorrect information and is conducted in a way that does not command respect. Militant leaders, such as the women here claim to be, ought to have checked their facts before coming to the Foreign Secretary to talk about the Biafran government sending 'an unknown group of women to Her Majesty the Queen'. (p.12) They direct their militancy to an unworthy end and only succeed in upsetting a dutiful public officer. Furthermore, they fail to present a united front. Instead of forming one strong central organisation which can present their case forcefully, they are organised in four ineffective splinter groups. The various groups occasionally contradict one another. This is a weakness that exposes the women to attack and ridicule, as the Foreign Secretary makes clear.

> Why could not the women organise themselves in one body and have just one leader? Why must every one of them want to lead? In this world there were leaders as well as followers. But here in Biafra every

one of them must form her own group and dominate the other. He had to personally intervene in Enugu when two groups of women almost clashed openly. It needed all his diplomatic manoeuvres to calm them down. (p.11)

The rivalry between these women is so intense that one is not surprised that they are unable to make any favourable impression on the Foreign Secretary.

Bisi is more successful in the way she attempts to extricate herself from the social problems posed by the civil war. She returns with her husband, Ebo, to Onitsha and finds the war situation intolerable. She claims her husband is insincere and unreliable. 'He brought me here to live and die like a rat.' (p.7) She becomes violent and uncompromising in her demands to leave the war area. She declares war on her husband and finally achieves her objective. Bisi's militancy is more purposeful and disinterested than that displayed by the unruly women's organisations. It is a well-co-ordinated effort that richly deserves to succeed.

'Daddy, Don't Strike the Match'

'Daddy, Don't Strike the Match' is the story of how the civil war affects members of the Okeke family. They have been forced to flee from Kano to Enugu to start life afresh, but are having different kinds of problems. Ifeoma cannot settle down to work. She dreams and sees visions about her previous life in Kano, and desperately wants to get back there. 'I want to go back to Kano. I want the war to end so that I can go back to school. I like school, daddy. I like our white Rev. Sister.' (p.19) Ndidi observes that the good training she has so dutifully imparted to her children cannot be sustained in their new situation. Social facilities are crude and inadequate, and they have to make the best use of meagre resources. For example, environmental sanitation is in a primitive state. Ndidi is concerned about the effect of this on the children in particular. 'Why should this happen to her? Her children who were used to using toilets now went to the bush to do the thing. There was no toilet paper.' (p.24) Okeke becomes a chain-smoker in order to escape from the strains of the war. The stresses on him are such that he looks for a way of making his mental burden light.

Okeke's problems are not unconnected with his occupation during the war. He works in a laboratory which makes bombs and has by nature of his work to perform a lot of experiments. 'He had been setting up the experiment for some time, and he was succeeding.' (p.29) On one occasion he is so pleased with himself that he decides to relax after his arduous task.

He deserved a cigarette. He struck the match. Before he realised what had happened, he was in the midst of a formidable fire. Everything was ablaze. It was terrible. Nobody heard him shouting. Nobody was in sight until a few minutes later when smoke was discovered coming from the room by passers-by. They shouted. (p.30)

Okeke dies in the fire, a victim of the war and his own stupidity. Why does anybody act so carelessly and selfishly in a situation that calls for sacrifice and great presence of mind. The danger of naked light in a highly inflammable surrounding ought to have been obvious to a man of Okeke's training. He dies because he has over-indulged himself in smoking.

'A Wife's Dilemma'

'A Wife's Dilemma' tells the story of Chika who falls in love with Amma when she is still in her husband's house. She falls so easily for Amma because of his politeness and good nature. Her admiration for him is sincere, and she openly confesses it. 'He was one of the nicest persons I had ever seen.' (p.57) 'I liked the way Amma did things.' (pp.60-61) 'I enjoyed Amma's audacity.' (p.54) She claims that her husband has become too rich and busy of late to care much for her feelings.

When you were married for twenty years to a man who was very busy, who never complimented you on your dress or appearance; who never kissed you and never took you to a good restaurant to have a good dinner, then you would understand my admiration for Amma. (p.52)

So she puts everything she has into the love affair with Amma. She meets him frequently and enjoys being left alone with him. She experiences the courtesies and romance which have for long eluded her in her matrimonial home. 'My husband kissed me only when we were courting. When we got married, he forgot all about kissing.' (p.53) She feels honoured by Amma's attention and considers the wisdom of establishing a permanent relationship with him.

Chika is not, in a sense, a typical Lagos woman. She is presented as a woman with a strong conscience and some sense of responsibility to her matrimonial home. She gets involved with Amma through force of circumstances. She soon finds herself in a great dilemma. To start with, she is much older than Amma. To make matters worse, he is a responsible married man who is not keen 'to have a "cash madam" mess his life'. (p.61) Above all, there is the voice of conscience which constantly persecutes her.

Then I heard a voice. It was the voice I had listened to all my life. I heard it clearly. The voice said, 'Chika hold it. Be careful. Be patient. Don't . . .' I smiled. (p.58)

If she has always 'listened to' her conscience, why does she choose to ignore it this time? She allows her emotion to override her sense of propriety. She establishes an extra-legal relationship with Amma in a manner that puts her social integrity in doubt. She suffers the fate of all women who betray their husbands. Her affair ends abruptly with the sudden death of her lover.

'The Chief's Daughter'

'The Chief's Daughter' highlights the crisis of confidence which develops between Chief Onyeka and his 'beloved' daughter, Adaeze. The chief cannot bear to see his daughter get married. Because of her academic brilliance and sober upbringing he wants her to take care of his household and manage his business on a permanent basis. He relies on an obsolete traditional practice which permits 'a favourite daughter to remain at her father's home married to no one, but to have children who answered her father's name'. (p.85) He does not seek his daughter's consent for these arrangements because he considers her opinion on the matter irrelevant. He fails to realise that Adaeze, with her background of British education, would like to take personal control of her life and make plans for her future happiness. He acts in the false assumption that 'just as her mother obeyed me in all things so will Adaeze obey me in all things'. (p.84)

As may well be expected, Adaeze rejects her father's plans and goes ahead to marry her chosen lover, Ezenta, in a Marriage Registry in London. Her father violently objects and decides to annul the marriage. The gulf between the two widens. Adaeze threatens drastic action.

'Father, I demand to know whether you married my mother or not. I am not your wife, I am not your son. I am only a girl, your daughter, and if I don't marry Ezenta, you have lost me for ever. You will not see my face again. I shall disappear from the face of the earth. I shall kill myself and kill you, I shall oh . . .' (p.90)

There can be no doubt where the sympathy of the author lies in the matter. The chief is portrayed as one who refuses to change with the times. He plans to deny his daughter an opportunity of a happy marital life in order to satisfy his own needs. Why should Adaeze set aside her personal plans and stay home because none of her brothers is successful in life? Why should she be victimised for the failure of others? Why should she be denied the opportunity the boys have enjoyed of planning their lives according to their individual wishes? The author's sympathy is definitely with Adaeze who is about to be denied her basic human right. Her father has always proved difficult. When she returns home from London unannounced he declared that 'Adaeze had spoilt everything, by coming home like a thief'. (p.88) When the vicar alludes in a sermon to the possibility of Adaeze ever getting married, Chief Onyeka castigates him openly for it. Knowing her father as well as she does, Adaeze decides to make use of her superior intellect and resolve the matter once and for all. 'She was not going to use confrontation to fight her father. She would use her commonsense, her education and her charm'. (p.93) The beauty of the work is revealed partly in the painless and attractive manner in which Adaeze overcomes all obstacles, asserts her rights and achieves her heart's desire.

Literary Development

Flora Nwapa's literary career can be easily divided into two parts. The first is the glorious age of *Efuru* and *Idu*. She is one of the first African female writers to make any significant contribution to the outburst of literary activities which came with political independence. Her early novels, in their strengths and weaknesses, compare favourably with those produced by other notable writers. In these novels her discussion of domestic issues is rooted in reality and has helped to produce a social awareness of the gaiety and harshness of traditional life. Her world is limited to indigenous Igbo culture, but this culture is so deeply and thoroughly exposed that the reader comes to appreciate its value and relevance to the people's way of life.

This kind of achievement is not easily in evidence in the author's later writings. Her topics have become diffused. She has moved from the discussion of weighty traditional matters to topics relating to the social complications of modern life. In her novels and short stories of recent years the Nigerian civil war has provided most of the material. Because of her personal involvement with the war she has not always been able to write with the kind of detachment that produces great literature. The same kind of impression emerges from her preoccupation with the moral laxity in the city. What the reader gets for the most part is a weak dramatisation of the situation as it exists at the moment. Rarely is one's knowledge of the condition of man in society successfully and logically extended. Her art is limited to the exposition of facts. Little encouragement is given for reflection on the ideas put forward. One can only hope that Flora Nwapa will yet produce substantial works of art worthy of the glorious days of her early novels, and thus reestablish herself in the vanguard of literary activities in Africa.

Notes

1 *Efuru*, London, Heinemann, African Writers Series (AWS), 1966. Page references are to the 1979 edition.

2 Speech made at Calabar on May 20, 1981 at the International Conference on African Literature organised by the Department of English and Literary Studies, University of Calabar, Nigeria.

3 Eustace Palmer, *An Introduction to the African Novel* (London, Heinemann, 1972), p.120.

4 *Idu*, London, Heinemann (AWS), 1970. Page references are to the 1974 edition.

5 Yinka Shoga, 'Women Writers and African Literature', *Afriscope*, Lagos, Vol.3, No.10, October, 1973, p.44

6 *Never Again*, Enugu, Nwamife Publishers Ltd., 1975. Page references are to this edition.

7 *One is Enough*, Enugu, Tana Press Ltd, 1981. Page references are to this edition.

8 *This is Lagos and Other Stories*, Enugu, Nwankwo-Ifejika & Co Publishers Ltd, 1971. All page references are to the 1979 edition.

9 *Wives at War and Other Stories*, Enugu, Flora Nwapa & Co, 1981. All page references are to this edition.

CHAPTER FOUR

Adaora Lily Ulasi

Miss Ulasi's major contribution to novel writing is in the area of detective or mystery novels. She has so far written four such novels. The first two are colonial novels in which colonial administrative officers play dominant roles and dictate the trend of events. Colonial officers also feature in her fourth novel, but they are no longer as powerful as they were in the previous works. In each of these novels, Miss Ulasi introduces an element of mystery into the living experiences of her characters. This mystery is often overwhelming and is allowed to influence the thinking and behaviour of people to a large extent. Usually every important character in the book is ill at ease until the end when the mystery is resolved and necessary explanations are given for some inscrutable actions or uncanny experiences. This almost invariably calls for the use of suspense as a literary device. The greater the suspense, the deeper the mystery, the better the novel as a work of art. In this regard Miss Ulasi's artistry seems to have gradually improved, achieving her greatest success with her third novel. The fact that she has been able to produce four detective novels in a row shows to what extent she is determined to popularise this kind of writing.

Many Thing You No Understand

Many Thing You No Understand is a colonial novel concerned with the functions and problems of the colonial service and how ready it is to cope with emergency situations outside the ambit of the General Orders.[1] The aim of the novelist is clearly to expose colonial officers to ridicule. How else can one explain the amount of official inefficiency and indecision documented here? Why are so many officers with such divergent views brought together to tackle the unusual problems connected with human sacrifice? Because of the demands of tradition a criminal offence is committed. Each expatriate officer attempts to solve the problem to the best of his ability. Given the lack of unity in official ranks, it is not surprising that no satisfactory solution is found. Furthermore, each officer is humiliated in turn. An acceptable solution might have been provided by MacIntosh, the Assistant District Officer. But he is an inexperienced officer, new from Scotland, a man with fixed ideas of right and wrong. Why, one is entitled to ask, is MacIntosh, with his doctrinaire attitude, given primary responsibility in these matters which might have been quickly disposed of by the District Officer, the liberal and more experienced Mason? It is the author's deliberate doing that any chance of reconciling the views and positions of the villagers and the Administration is irretrievably lost.

The novel thrives on this conflict of aims and aspirations. Not only is there internal dissension in the Civil Service, there is a clash between the Service and the traditional authority of Ukana. The Civil Service is in complete disarray. At a crucial period like this, the District Commissioner, Mr Hughes, is bossy, arrogant and intolerant, and is not inclined to respect the professional opinion of any of his subordinate officers. So, against the professional advice of Hayes, the doctor, MacIntosh is sent back to Britain on grounds of insanity. Again, throughout the novel Mason is drawn in contrast to MacIntosh both in his understanding of local customs and his anxiety to avoid direct confrontation with the villagers.

'I suggest that we shelve this matter, Mac. If the dead man's brother cares to come again and lodge a new complaint quite specifically – and doesn't change his story the next day when he's slept on it – then perhaps we'd be justified in having them in for questioning. But the way this matter stands now we just haven't a leg to stand on. Look, Mac, your man said one thing; then he changed his story; now with this letter he's gone back to his first one again. He's just not consistent, is he?' (pp.75-6).

This plea for caution and moderation by Mason is not heeded. MacIntosh pursues his perilous course and initiates a course of investigation which leads to disaster. He makes a puerile attempt to apprehend two village elders, Okafor and Chukwuka, for criminal offences and unwisely discloses his intention to Chief Obieze. The two leaders are advised to go into hiding while a paid servant keeps them informed about the ADO's intention. Meanwhile, the ADO is made insane and Mason is ambushed and humiliated. MacIntosh's exercise in futility only helps to achieve a complete alienation of the traditional authority from the Administration.

However, there is no attempt on the part of the author to absolve traditional authority from blame. Their apparent victory over the colonial authority is achieved at a great price. There has been a mean exploitation of group loyalty which often prevents offenders from being apprehended by the law. There is also an unconvincing use of magic, as in the case of MacIntosh, or the use of brute force, as when Mason is ambushed. Chief Obieze, the custodian of traditional authority, has had to tell a lie to save Okafor and Chukwuka from the consequences of their action. These two elders are shown to be cowardly men who are too afraid to face justice. They hide away in a fortress and suffer just as much as MacIntosh and Mason. Chukwuka complains about the social deprivations to which they have been subjected.

> 'Chief Obieze, I no like for stay for fortress. And if A.D.O. stay here for Ukana he go catch me one day. I no know about Okafor. But for my own self I know say I no fit hide for fortress like animal him hunter look for, for the rest of my life! Fortress tire me. I no have woman for three day. I be married man with plenty wife and I live inside there like man who no get wife!' (p.147)

These leaders have lost their self-respect and can no longer be trusted to uphold the dignity of traditional life. If therefore, from the events of this novel, colonial authority has been weakened, there has also been a systematic erosion of traditional authority. No side can claim complete victory over the other.

Ironies of situation abound in this work, and it is usually through them that the reader comes to realise how far apart the two sides have drifted:

> 'I be D.O. for the whole of the Delta!
> If you touch me –'
> 'Shut up!'
> 'Look, I make bargain with you. Let me go, and I stop look for Okafor and Chukwuka. Agree?' They shook their heads. 'We no agree!'
> 'All right. Make you take me. But let the court messengers and driver go,' he urged.
> 'Ah, what kind people you take us for? You think we be fool?' (p.189)

The irony here arises from Mason's new status as a virtual prisoner in the hands of the villagers. He speaks in an entirely different situation in which the reader realises for the first time how implacably hostile to the Administration the villagers have become. Mason who, as a junior Administrative officer, was feared throughout Ukana for his ruthless efficiency and sternness is reduced to submission and, as a captive, finds himself pleading for the type of leniency he has often denied others.

Mason's often-repeated remark about Ezekiel – 'You get good honest face, Ezekiel' – turns out to be the greatest irony in the novel. Ezekiel has earned his praise through hard work; he is mistaken for an 'honest' and dutiful steward, loyal to MacIntosh, but, in fact, his first loyalty is to his people. MacIntosh is yet to learn the hard way that 'the indigenous protected their own' and takes Ezekiel into his confidence. Far from being honest, he brings so much trouble on MacIntosh by his dishonesty that in the end the latter openly regrets: 'Ezekiel did this for me, after all I've done for him!' (p.177)

An irony of a different significance is derived from the relationship between MacIntosh and Mason. This relationship reveals how chaotic the colonial establishment has become at this time. Highly-placed officers, even at a period of crisis, often abandon their official duties to concentrate on trivial personal matters. Mason is MacIntosh's boss and is the older and more experienced officer. He is therefore expected not only to show MacIntosh how to perform his official duties successfully but also to ensure that the inexperienced officer comports himself in a dignified manner and keeps out of mischief. Ironically it is Mason who tries to interest MacIntosh in local women and obscene behaviour.

'Are you a virgin, Mac?'
'No, I sampled at eighteen. It was awful. But I have had some happier moments since.'
'Thank God! But not since you've been here?'
'MacIntosh shook his head. 'But it doesn't matter. Is this an inquisition?' he took his eyes off the road to inquire.
'No,' Mason replied, grinning. 'But it'll drive you round the bend, my boy,' he added.
'The lack of it?'
'Yes.'
'What one doesn't have, one doesn't miss.'
'There are some sweet young things here, you know. Ezekiel could fetch and dismiss on your say-so.' (p.97)

Mason stands in pathetic moral contrast to MacIntosh and must take part of the blame for the ADO's failure to establish a bridge of understanding between his Administration and the people of Ukana. With MacIntosh's repatriation the Administration is discredited in much the same way as traditional authority has been.

The language of satire in this novel is mostly pidgin English. Enough has been written elsewhere to show that the author uses pidgin where good artistic sense would counsel otherwise.[2] Often the quality of the pidgin is so poor that it virtually destroys the basis of true characterisation. Unfortunately this artistic fault is carried forward to her second novel, *Many Thing Begin for Change* and to the Fourth, *The Man from Sagamu*. In the latter novel Yoruba people, in intimate family situations, are made to communicate with one another in unorthodox pidgin. Miss Ulasi's use of a linguistic medium with which she is not thoroughly familiar prevents her from communicating as effectively as she might otherwise have done, and detracts unnecessarily from the value of her works.

Many Thing Begin for Change

The events of *Many Thing Begin for Change* are a follow-up from those of the first novel.[3] They continue the author's tragic story and shed more light on her literary intentions. The main characters are mostly the same people, at times now playing more important roles. To link the past with the present properly in the reader's mind the author provides in the early pages of this novel a recapitulation of the events of *Many Thing You No Understand*. With the brutal murder of Mason in the hands of the villagers the stage is set for a direct confrontation between Hughes, the District Commissioner, and Chief Obieze. The gulf between traditional authority and the colonial administration is now so wide that there is no hope of compromise and accommodation between the two. The result is a deadly conflict in which traditional authority is, in the final analysis, worsted.

The author hardly disguises her revulsion at the activities of those who claim to be custodians of traditional customs. Obieze and his men not only commit a senseless murder, they also attempt to cover up their misdeed in a despicable manner. In the earlier novel two elders in the society commit a crime with the connivance of Obieze. In this novel it is on the orders of the Chief that the crime is committed. The Chief's activities are reprehensible. He acts the role of a common criminal, terrorises junior civil servants, sets up a powerful intelligence network to embarrass the Administration, encourages members of the secret society in their nefarious acts and demonstrates in inherent distaste for order and good government. The picture of him one gets in a passage like this is utterly disgusting.

This was the man who still made his own laws, despite the ones made by headquarters. This was the man in whose hands lay the power of who shall live and who shall die, whose property shall be taken away to teach the person a lesson, or whose should be returned, after consenting, willingly of course, to part with half of it to the Chief. This was a man who had spies everywhere. (p.78)

One would have expected Obieze as a literate Chief to show some regard for human life and be more diplomatic in his dealings with colonial officials. Unfortunately in his ruthless search for power he misses every chance of reconciliation with the Administration and, as a matter of habit, treats the District Commissioner shabbily. When he finally over-reaches himself and commits suicide, only his fellow criminals are sorry for him.

There is little doubt where the sympathy of the author lies in this work. The clear impression is given that colonial officers do not deserve to experience all the headaches and inconveniences brought on them by Obieze's criminal tendencies. Once a serious situation is created, the officers do their very best to find an immediate solution. The novelist paints a picture of a purposeful Administration determined to rescue Mason from the clutches of death, if he is still alive. The onus of locating the missing District Officer rests squarely on Hughes as District Commissioner, and he accepts the responsibility with all seriousness. He approaches the task with ruthless efficiency and organises search parties. Other officials, senior and junior, show equal enthusiasm. But all efforts are in vain. It is only human that in such a situation Hughes shows occasional feelings of exasperation and wishes that the matter is quickly disposed of.

But where could Maurice have got to? How could he have vanished into thin air, and with four court messengers and a driver who knows the whole of the region like the back of his hand? ... Ever since his success, which I learned of from hearsay, at Ichara, the man has become difficult to handle. And not only by me; my predecessors, I gather had their belly full of him as well. A little success, like a little education, is a very dangerous thing. (pp.45-6)

The novelist takes the opportunity of Mason's disappearance to show how well and quickly the Administration can mobilise its resources at a period of crisis. She also brings out the strains and stresses which usually accompany such a mobilisation. So we note that officers occasionally get on each other's nerves or cross each other's paths. When husbands become touchy as a result of pressure of work, they do not always relate positively to their wives, as we find with Arthur and Evelyn Johnson or George and Millicent Hughes. In spite of these handicaps and Obieze's

89

evil machinations these officers press ahead singlemindedly with the mission to rescue Mason. Hughes devises several ingenious plans to elicit the truth from Obieze and settle the matter once and for all. The Chief plays a waiting game, but later comes to recognise the superior tact and diplomacy of Hughes. When he realises that he is trapped he kills himself, thus saving the Administration the embarrassment of a harsh and perhaps unpopular decision. Hughes himself, a principal actor in the whole drama, describes vividly the course of events which leads to Chief Obieze's end.

> In each of us there's a still small voice ... When I first asked him to come down it was a call for help, nothing more. Had he come then, we'd probably have written Maurice off and this wouldn't have happened. But no, he chose to be stubborn, and not only that, he sent his men to remove the stones and wipe the road clean. When he did that my suspicion deepened. The debt has now been paid in full. (p.191)

Little more need be said about the reward of Obieze's bestiality in this novel.

One of the major attractions of this work is the way the author presents in fictional terms the changes in political and social life which have taken place after the period she writes about in her first novel. Things have indeed started to change. These changes are affecting every aspect of life, including the domestic life of Chief Obieze. We note for the first time that his wife, Iru, is allowed some discretion in marital affairs and is occasionally consulted by her husband on matters of administration or his reaction to particular problems. Although the Chief is still the undisputed overlord of his household, we witness here the early beginnings of women's liberation and freedom of action. This liberal attitude is encouraged by the creeping materialism and increasing secularisation which education has brought in its wake. There is need to beat back the frontiers of knowledge and free the people from ritual bondage. The yearning for education is truly widespread. Even Chief Obieze wants members of his family to benefit from it.

> I want my children go school for learn book because many thing begin for change ... I want my first son, Anyagu, to go England for finish school because plenty change, plenty trouble, go come. (p.142)

Once the villagers are educated, they will be liberated from superstitious fear and other cultural inadequacies. They will then expunge from their midst social handicaps like the secret society which is a drawback on communal progress. The novelist presents the society as evil and reactionary. It shows partial affection for its members and eliminates any person who stands between it and its diabolical plans. The members of the society are well known for their ritual murders. For example, in order to secure all leading posts in the mine for themselves they arrange to kill Ephraim Obi. This leads to a general strike of all workers, which brings life at Amaku to a standstill. The novelist throws a penetrating searchlight on the nefarious activities of the secret society and, through the investigation conducted by the dedicated journalists of *The Daily Observer*, exposes its members to ridicule and shame. Surely, these men can benefit from the craze for knowledge and social enlightenment which is the order of the day. This almost certainly is the view shared by the novelist.

A major change to which the author devotes a good deal of creative attention is the emergence of the Press as a dynamic force and an instrument of social change. A trained journalist herself, Miss Ulasi appears particularly sensitive to the powers of the Press in the formulation and direction of public opinion. She uses her intimate knowledge of the internal working of a newspaper office, especially the amount of hard work required for the production of a daily newspaper, to advantage here. *The Daily Observer*, with its experienced editorial staff, is made the mouthpiece of the aspirations of the people. So, when a crime is committed at the mine, the paper presents the case of the people fearlessly to the reading public and quickly gets to the root of the matter. Not even the threats of possible reprisals from members of the secret society deters the paper from investigating the matter thoroughly. The paper helps to generate intellectual ferment among the people, thus raising their level of political consciousness and economic activity. Through its effort criminals of the secret society are rounded up and sent to jail. The society ceases to exist, and social justice is restored to all the villagers. One leaves the novel with the impression that Amaku will now settle down to a long period of political and social progress. Such is the extent of the contribution of *The Daily Observer* to the happiness and prosperity of the villagers.

The Night Harry Died

Miss Ulasi's third novel, *The Night Harry Died*, is different from the first two in many respects.[4] It is set against the background of southern USA unlike the first two whose setting is in eastern Nigeria. The medium of expression in the third novel is standard English even though the author shows a fascination for the habits of speech of the people she writes about.

In *The Night Harry Died*, Miss Ulasi has an important theme and a consistent imaginative scheme. She appears to have submitted both this time, much more than she has ever done, to the process of creative digestion. The result is a story which is not only interesting in itself but reveals the author's creative inventiveness and artistic intelligence. Harry Collier is presumed dead, but appears bemused at his own funeral. The novelist shows great powers of description in the way she records the consternation of the people and the chaos which follows.

> The funeral party turned and froze. For there, standing and watching his own funeral procession was Harry Collier! There was a stampede, as the mourners thought they were seeing a ghost. Helm's appeal for calm and common sense went unheeded.
>
> 'Man alive!' shouted Isaiah, the undertaker, and sank into the nearest pew, while Wade, his assistant, loosened Isaiah's collar to give him some air. The undertaker rubbed his eyes, raised his head and took another horrified look.
>
> But just as suddenly as he'd appeared, Harry vanished. 'After him!' shouted the sheriff. Edna clutched the undertaker by the coat and demanded: 'Who's in the coffin, then, Mr. Watson? What have you done with Harry?' (p.29)

A serious situation develops and the mystery of Harry's death is not unravelled until a court action is instituted and the principal characters are made to confess their various roles. Part of the novelist's success in this work derives from the fact that, in the midst of this confusion and uncertainty, all is not death, all is not gloom. Through the use of humorous situation and sayings she throws some light on the mystifying episode and, in a way, lightens the burden of the people. If the situation is too serious for anyone to laugh heartily, it is at least helpful to have occasional moments of relief.

> There was the firm of Adams and Adams near the church. Harry's father told him that the first Adams built the law firm near the church because it was handy to nip and cleanse one's soul each time one had finished a property deal. (p.24)

The court scene provides the climax to this work and it is important in the way it gives the clue to the mystery which engulfs the town for so long. Nothing shows more clearly the improvement in the author's artistic ability than the way she handles this court scene. Compared with the court scene at the beginning of *Many Thing You No Understand* we see here a relevant experience fully integrated into the structure of the novel. No more do we have the needless tomfoolery in court and the purposeless ridiculing of court proceedings which are characteristic features of the previous attempt. Proceedings are now conducted according to the rules and with great adroitness.

'Now, I don't want any noise around here,' shouted the judge, glaring at the packed court through blood-shot eyes. He gave Lacey the signal to continue.

'You say you stayed with Mrs Collier, Sam. For how long would that be?'

'Reckon about a couple of months, sir'.

'And what happened between you two all that time you stayed with her?'

'I object, your honour,' cried Adams. 'It is a pretty insinuating question that the sheriff's trying to ask there.'

'Objection sustained,' the judge said.

'When you lived with Mrs Collier, did you help around the shack?' asked the sheriff, and Sam replied in the affirmative.

'Reckon we all here know there's nothing much to do around a shack like that. In what way did you help Edna Collier?'

'Objection, your honour,' Adams interjected again.

Judge Albert looked at the Lawyer, a little annoyed. 'Well, Mr Adams. I don't see you've much to object about.' (p.99)

The court scene brings together all the principal actors in the novel and offers an opportunity for judicial officers to apply their knowledge and expertise to a new situation. The sheriff performs brilliantly under pressure and, through his searching questions, exposes every offender. Consequently, when the culprits are jailed, the reader considers the verdict appropriate and just.

The author succeeds in dramatising the complexity of human nature and the confusion which often results from a flagrant display of greed and selfishness. A lot of attention is devoted to Edna who falls from the lofty height of an obedient housewife to the level of a traitor and liar. In her attempt to escape from justice in New Orleans where a tangled love affair results in murder she comes to Alligator Creek and stays with Harry Collier against her better judgement. She remains with Harry for so long because she wrongly believes this is the only way she can avoid being apprehended by law officers from New Orleans. She forms a criminal partnership with Sam Goodwin who, for love of money, agrees to help her get rid of Harry. It is in this attempt to satisfy their base desire that they unwittingly throw the whole of Alligator Creek into panic and chaos. Every citizen suffers as a result and life in the community virtually comes to a standstill. Individuals suffer in varying degrees. Roscoe Virgil appears to be one of the most severely hit.

The doctor looked tired and very old and suddenly didn't know which way to turn. He saw the lucrative practice that his father before him had built up disappearing now before his eyes, and tears sprang to those eyes. He never thought he'd live to see this happen to him. His reputation at stake, his whole life and work sinking into a pit. He shook his head hard as if in doing so, he'd shake the whole nightmare away. (p.131)

The novelist's approach to this detective story is attractive and successful. Suspense as a literary device is effectively employed to keep the reader guessing what happens next. It is not until the end of the book that the reader discovers what actually happens. To create an atmosphere of mystery, necessary for success in this kind of work, the novelist introduces two relations who look alike, Harry Collier and Duke Lane. Harry is well known in Alligator Creek, Duke has never visited the town. Nobody knows that Harry has any such relation. Little wonder then that when Harry appears to have resurrected from the dead with a twin brother, the confusion in town knows no bounds. Several theories are put forward, but none seems to satisfy the facts of the case. The situation is made intolerable by Harry's occasional appearance at strategic locations. The creative energy of the whole community is diverted to the problem posed by the appearance of two Harrys and the need to unravel the mystery in the interest of the people's happiness and security.

Lacey nodded impatiently. 'Yes, I saw the risen Harry. We all saw the risen Harry. But that don't mean a murder wasn't planned, or even carried out – or maybe backfired. Harry knew something. That was the reason why he disappeared. How he got out of the coffin, we don't know. But he got out. And now we have two Harry's. A man dies, and comes back, not alone but with his twin. Maybe I'm going crazy. Maybe the whole town of Alligator Creek's crazy ... (p.38)

The sheriff suffers more than any other official since he is the chief law officer and he is principally responsible for the maintenance of law and order in the town. He therefore goes in search of the ghost – a new dimension added to his work. His mission is a hopeless one. When his left arm is paralysed by the appearance of the ghost, law and order almost completely breaks down. It is only after a long period of suspense that the truth of the matter is brought out in court – that Harry never died, that the elaborate trick was arranged to test Edna's fidelity to Harry and find out her level of criminal involvement with Sam Goodwin.

One wonders why a whole community in a civilised situation should become so confused and disorderly as a result of a single incident. True enough, the occurrence is unusual. But do the events of the book not reveal some general malaise in society, a certain tendency towards anarchy and disobedience? Undoubtedly there is greed coupled with corruption and a high degree of criminality. That the people are also superstitious is demonstrated by the indecent haste with which they embrace the idea of a resurrected Harry Collier and are frightened by his ghost. This makes Harry almost the hero of the book, the man who dictates the pace and tenure of events. He has never been respected by his community. He now seizes this opportunity to take it back on society, to force his people to pay attention to him by disturbing their way of life on a massive scale and portraying them as a credulous and foolish lot. Furthermore, he now sits in judgement over them and justifies some of his own past activities.

> Harry Collier grinned again. 'I told you sheriff,' he said 'the whole town's got rabbit brains. But you didn't listen. There ain't a man or woman here in Alligator Creek with a brain in their head! Judge Albert's as bad as the rest of the town. As for the doctor, I always said he was no good. And sheriff, as for the gold nuggets I took to the bank, my pa, he given me that when he was dying. He got it from the gold rush out west before crossing through to St. Augustine, and coming out here to settle . . .' (pp.139-140)

The reader leaves the novel with a much better opinion of Harry than he had at the beginning. A man who can successfully devise a plan to expose his wife's weakness, confuse law enforcement agencies, make mockery of the judicial process and keep the whole town awake for several days on end certainly deserves a lot of respect. This in itself is a reflection of the high degree of competence which the novelist displays in this work.

The Man from Sagamu

This is another detective novel.[5] As in *The Night Harry Died* the element of mystery plays a decisive role in the events of the novel. Here, Olu Agege's activities result in confusion at a time the people of Sagamu are preparing for an important festival. This, as in the previous novel, attracts the attention of the police and the civil administration. There is widespread panic among the inhabitants until the whole mystery is unravelled at the end of the book. So this novel too benefits from the use of suspense as a literary device.

Any dramatic impact the book makes on the reader derives from Olu

Agege's activities. It is he who keeps the whole town, including the police and the colonial officers, in a state of panic for a long time. He is a man born in mysterious circumstances. As we are told, 'a cock crew at noon on top of his mother's thatch-roofed home on the day he was born, which in itself, according to them, was an unusual omen'. (p.6) He behaves in a peculiar way and conducts himself in a manner contrary to the norms and beliefs of his people. He keeps to himself most of the time and comes out only occasionally to distribute coins to children. Like Harry Collier of the previous novel, he is a man largely neglected by society. He may therefore want to do something to call attention to himself. When he disappears in broad daylight from the midst of the people he achieves the kind of recognition he has been looking for. The novelist quite rightly devotes much attention to Agege's disappearance since upon it much else depends.

> Agege was an important fixture of the town and the circumstances under which he vanished were not only unusual, but might even be suspect. It wasn't just a question of him having left town as he was entitled, as indeed any citizen of the country was entitled, as much as the fact that the man in question stood at a particular spot one minute, vanished in the next, and there were eye witnesses to testify to it. It was something that had never happened before. (p.11)

The Sagamu community finds itself dealing with an unusual situation. It therefore has to adopt equally unusual measures to solve the problem without causing any spiritual damage to the society.

An attractive aspect of this presentation is the way the novelist succeeds in conveying in its totality the background against which the Agege drama is enacted. The reader is told the importance of Sagamu, its strategic location on the way to Lagos, the progressive outlook of its people. The whole drama is connected with the yearly celebration of the Oshun festival, a festival of great cultural importance. The preparation for this festival goes on for a long period and involves all indigenes of the town at home and abroad. The Oba and his chiefs have crucial roles to play, and these roles are described in detail. It is when considered against this elaborate background and the massive turn-out of Sagamu people at home for the festival that Agege's activities assume a new importance. The emphasis is for the most part placed on the number of people who see Agege display his supernatural powers or are affected by his strange behaviour.

> This seemingly unnatural quietness among the first batch to reach the spot brought out a second batch who out of curiosity went to find out what had happened to the others. On reaching Agege they, too,

> experienced the same paralysis as they beheld the man the whole
> town had been looking for. It was nearly 8.15 a.m. A third batch
> followed, and were also mesmerised by Agege. Five minutes later,
> Agege raised his hands above his head and the spell broke. (p.113)

Undoubtedly the author has chosen for dramatisation such an
important period in the life of the people so that she can achieve the
greatest impact. Agege's disappearance at another time of the year
would either have gone unnoticed or certainly been a matter of less
concern.

In a sense this is a colonial novel. The events are set at the turn of the
century well before Nigeria became politically independent. The
novelist therefore takes the opportunity, as she does in her first two
novels, to examine the colonial set-up and administration. The aim
here, as elsewhere, is to satirise the colonial officers and the institution
which they represent. Whitticar, the Resident at Sagamu, is portrayed
as very ineffective. At first he is cynical about the whole idea of Agege's
disappearance. He uses his official resources at this crucial time in an
incompetent manner. He displays an abysmal lack of knowledge of the
way of life and beliefs of the people. He spends more time at tea with his
wife than in restoring law and order to a town in a state of panic. When
he finally comes to believe, after Adewunmi's awful experience with a
ghost, that Agege may, in fact, have magical powers, he does nothing
positive to assure the Oba and his people of their safety. Instead he is
preoccupied with his own comfort and pleasures. He insists on those
things which separate him from the generality of the people and prefers
to live his life between the Residence and the Magistrates' Quarters, the
two exclusive areas of Sagamu.

The novelist succeeds in communicating to the reader the activities of
the two distinct groups which inhabit Sagamu. We have the world of the
colonial overlords like Whitticar and Jones, and their wives. In this
world must be included white blackmen like Adewunmi, the
magistrate, and Akinyemi, the doctor. They use their level of sophistication and borrowed ideas to play down matters of grave importance
to the community, and concentrate on their drinks and women. The
behaviour of these Nigerian senior civil servants reminds one of the fate
of Akpan in Aluko's *One Man, One Matchet*. Jones demonstrates his ineffectiveness by indulging in practical jokes at a period of crisis. The
white officials and their Nigerian friends live in a world apart, a world
separated by a wide gulf from the strains and the legitimate social concerns of the community in which they live. The other world is that of the
common people, the ordinary Sagamu citizens who form the bulk of the
population. They have been brought up in an environment which en-

courages superstitious beliefs. They are therefore credulous by nature, but hold on tenaciously to their cultural heritage. When Agege disappears many preposterous theories are advanced about his powers. There are a lot of rumours in the air, including the fanciful one that he is armed. However, it is this same people who give the Oba their unflinching support and exert themselves in every way to ensure that Agege's secrets are known. In this way they contribute tremendously to the happiness of their community. Unlike the pleasure-loving whites they are mindful of the common good.

This novel has a positive message which becomes clear to the perceptive reader at the end of the book during the final dramatic encounter between Agege and his people.

> When Agege ended, a loud cheer went up from the crowd. There was, again, sudden silence, for where a man had been – the reincarnation of the Oshun deity had suddenly gone. Agege had left as he mysteriously came. (p.124)

What is Olu Agege's positive mission in the light of the extraordinary powers given to him? To start with, by his disappearance and the general concern which follows it he is able to bring together the two worlds described above. Whitticar at a stage is forced to react with court messengers and cooks, police constables and domestic servants on a matter of mutual interest. He visits the Oba and joins the crowd at the celebration of the Oshun festival. Even his wife tries to elicit information about Agege from her steward. By bringing the two worlds of white and black, privileged and underprivileged, rich and poor together, even for a brief period, Agege has helped to obscure an obnoxious line of separation which has existed for too long.

His second achievement is more important. Hence the significance attached to it by Agege himself.

> Of one thing he was certain. There would never be another festival like the one that was about to take place.
>
> The sea is deep, he thought on, and who but the gods know all that it harbours? The plants in the forest are legion, and it is only to the gods that the knowledge of their many and varied forms are given. Once, in a dream, he found himself surrounded by many plants. But he was able to identify them. To him, Olu Agege, had been given something, and he looked forward to using it, to carry out what he had been fashioned to carry out. (p.96)

Olu Agege is conscious of his extraordinary power. He intends to use this power to deliver his people from their superstitious beliefs and ritual worship. A once-for-all sacrifice, such is about to take place, is enough. With his own final departure no other sacrifice will be necessary. One is confronted here with the messianic idea of a living sacrifice who with his life and blood redeems mankind from wickedness and sin. If, indeed, Agege has been a sacrificial lamb who washes Sagamu free of its impurities his final disappearance should be regarded as a mighty blessing. This is the symbolic statement that the novel makes. This is the clearest indication we have of the success of the novel as a work of art.

Notes

1   Adaora Lily Ulasi, *Many Thing You No Understand*, (Michael Joseph, London, 1970). All page references are to this edition.
2   See Oladele Taiwo, *Culture and the Nigerian Novel*, (Macmillan, London, 1976), pp.48-53.
3   Adaora Lily Ulasi, *Many Thing Begin for Change*, (Michael Joseph, London, 1971). All page references are to this edition.
4   Adaora Lily Ulasi, *The Night Harry Died*, Educational Research Institute Nigeria Ltd., Lagos, 1974). All page references are to this edition.
5   Adaora Lily Ulasi, *The Man from Sagamu*, (Fontana Books, Second Impression, March 1979). All page references are to this edition.

CHAPTER FIVE

Buchi Emecheta

Buchi Emecheta is a comparatively new-comer to the literary scene. But she has achieved so much in recent years that she is now generally accepted as a major African novelist. She is extremely prolific, and in ten years of writing she has produced twelve novels which are widely used in various parts of the world. Some of her works have been translated into several European languages and are adopted for use in undergraduate and postgraduate courses. Several dissertations have been written on her novels, and many of her books are used as O level and A level texts in several parts of Britain. This is no mean achievement for a writer whose first novel was published only in 1972.

In an interview Buchi Emecheta talks of the circumstances of her. writing, her craftsmanship, the role of the African novelists and her achievement as a writer.[1] She had an inspiration to write very early in life, and this came from a number of sources. First, there were the stories told by the women in moonlight sessions in the villages when she was young. Her grandmother, whom she much admired, was a keen storyteller and succeeded in getting her to recognise storytelling as an important cultural event. She was fortunate in her early years to attend schools which paid a lot of attention to oral and written composition – Ladilak School and Reagan Memorial Baptist School, both in Yaba, Nigeria, for the primary and Methodist Girls High School (M.G.H.S.), Yaba for the secondary. Oral composition involved storytelling and narrating events one had witnessed or heard of. The standard of written composition at M.G.H.S. was high. To achieve the desired result the school insisted on careful oral preparation for every piece of written work. Although the English classes were not exactly designed to prepare pupils for a career in writing, they provided enormous encouragement for anyone who had a bent for writing. Buchi's English teacher at the upper forms was Mrs Mabel Jolaoso (now Mabel Segun), one of the earliest Nigerian female graduates and herself a keen writer. By her activities she fired young Buchi's imagination and became one of her early sources of inspiration.

But Buchi Emecheta's writing career did not start until she arrived in Britain and acquired enough experiences to write about. The experiences of her early years in Britain, as documented in her first two novels, were so devastating that she did not want to 'push' them right inside her. She had to get them out and set them down to avoid an emotional breakdown. After this stage she has been very happy with herself as a writer. Her craftsmanship is flexible, and is mainly dictated by the requirements of each novel. Generally speaking, she conceives of an idea and devises the episodes needed to put the idea forward, making sure always that these episodes hold together properly. Occasionally, she concentrates on the beginning and the end, the cause and the effect. As she writes she keeps the intended outcome in mind all the time. The greater the work, the more complex the style and approach. That is why, for example, the style of the *The Slave Girl* is vastly different from that of *Destination Biafra*. Whereas it has been appropriate to adopt the 'ballad style' in the former, such an approach would have been unsuitable for the complex situation of the latter which is a war book. Her general approach is to adapt the style to the content and circumstance of a particular novel.

Buchi Emecheta is satisfied with the amount of recognition her writings have brought her so far. She has won several awards: 1978, Best Black Writer in Britain; 1979, Jock Campbell award; Daughter of Mark Twain – an American Literature Award. She is a member of the Arts Council of Great Britain and of the Advisory Committee to the Home Secretary on Race and Equality. She gets invited to conferences and seminars in various parts of the world and frequently enjoys the advantage of addressing teachers and students in schools where her novels are adopted as texts. On the religious side, she is a member of the choir of Christ Church, Highgate, in North London.

She is greatly concerned about the future of the Nigerian novelist and the fate of the literary artist generally in Nigeria. She believes a conscious effort should be made to establish writing as one of the career options open to young graduates who have a flair for writing. This would involve the teaching of courses in creative writing in colleges and universities, through which potential writers will improve their skill. These courses should be taught by specialists, preferably renowned authors. Each university should have at least one writer in residence who should act mainly as a resource person. He should be available for regular consultation by staff and students, and should have only a light teaching load, if he has to do any teaching at all. For writing to become a worthwhile occupation, the government should come to the aid of the universities in their attempt to mount the necessary courses and give every encouragement to the writer before he is fully established. Unless the government helps, the writer can hardly hope to succeed on his own in a very competitive society.

Miss Emecheta supports the feminist movement because of her belief in the individuality of everybody, man or woman. All citizens must be able to act in freedom and dignity. No sex should attempt to dominate the other. Women should be free to discuss every available topic under the sun – exploitation and oppression, sex, class and race. There should be no attempt to gag them just as they too should not attempt to dominate their menfolk. She does not consider marriage compulsory for women; it should be only one of the options open to them. Women writers should help to establish a female literary tradition, but should always avoid a narrow and short-sighted feminism. They should speak out clear and loud, in a way that can compel the attention of all citizens.

Buchi Emecheta writes to fulfil the urge for women to speak for themselves. Although other African women are writing novels, her attempt must be considered a significant literary intervention whose content and approach deserve attention. The beauty and harsh realities of inherited culture, and the love and respect for the past provide the motivating force for her early works. Undoubtedly tradition stands at the centre of this literature. But at the same time the novelist is concerned with the historical processes of fragmentation and decay. The reader is therefore from time to time reminded of the need for change, especially the catastrophe which usually accompanies the inability or unwillingness to make the necessary social adjustment at the appropriate time. The statement is clear and unambiguous: a legitimate concern for indigenous culture invigorates society, but the belief in culture and tradition should not be allowed to stand in the way of progress.

The aim of this chapter is to consider to what extent Buchi Emecheta succeeds in establishing a link between tradition and modern experience in her novels. The aspects of traditional and modern life which are highlighted in these works are examined, and an attempt is made to show how successfully she dramatises the perplexities and social problems of the present. The approach here involves occasional references to text in order to point out the type of material the novelist has used to reflect her awareness of a given situation. To start with, it is necessary to pose a few questions.

What culture provides the background for these novels and what are the traditions of this culture? What changes are considered desirable and how can they be·effected without offending the sensibility of the people or causing any social and political upheaval? These questions touch on some of the central concerns of the early novels which consistently exploit and dramatise Ibuza customs and traditions in all their rigidity, sternness and heavy-handedness. No exceptions are made; no citizen, in traditional setting, is allowed to violate with impunity any of the laws of the land. Social conduct and group behaviour are regulated by certain traditional beliefs and practices which may appear unacceptable to the modern mind: a girl is inferior to a boy; a wife is valuable only as a source of producing children; a woman without a male child is despised by the society; a father is allowed to marry off his daughter to any man of his choice – the girl and her mother have no say in the matter. We have a picture of a traditional society where the word of a man is law and where the woman exists only to serve his pleasure and obey his every command.

But the Ibuza citizen sometimes travels abroad, reacts with people in other countries and finds himself subjected to foreign laws. He develops modern ambitions and adopts new attitudes, some of which are at variance with traditional practice. How does the Ibuza man survive in these circumstances? To what extent can he, in a different social and political system, successfully observe the rules of traditional society? How do the changes in his new situation affect his sensibility and cultural awareness? Is indigenous culture resilient enough to withstand foreign influence? How generally does a man behave in a foreign land among unfamiliar people? These are some of the questions the novelist seeks to answer in her first two novels.

In the Ditch

In the Ditch, which is autobiographical, describes the social deprivations experienced by Adah and her five children in London.[2] There is a picture of cruel hardship only partly relieved by the state welfare system. Adah's immediate neighbours try to be friendly. But she never forgets the colour of her skin and the fact that her cultural orientation to life is different. She often misses the warmth of interpersonal relationships which Ibuza culture engenders. She vacillates between hope and despair and never attains true happiness. The link established between tradition and modern experience is unattractive.

Adah desires a life of peaceful co-existence with the inhabitants of the Mansions. But she soon discovers that any solidarity between her and her neighbours is based on a common desire to break the laws of the society and derive more benefit from the social welfare system than they deserve. She becomes disenchanted by a system that is open to so much abuse and by a group of friends who have no intention of helping themselves to stand on their own feet. She is disillusioned by the fact that she is not wholly accepted by the group not because of anything she has done wrong, but because of some in-built prejudice against her race. She says in disgust,

> Blast these illustrators. Who told them that the Devil was black? Who told them that angels are always white? Had it never occurred to them that there might be black angels and a white devil? (pp.10-11)

We are in this novel in a world of women who are assigned roles appropriate to the design and content of the work. There is a realistic portrayal of events and an opportunity to reach the inner psychology of the section of humanity the novelist knows best.

> 'That's why I like Jako,' Whoopey was saying. 'He lives in a one-room flat all by himself; you know, one of those new types of flats with a separate kitchen. And you know some'ink, if he asked me to come to his country, I'd certainly go with him.' Whoopey rambled on with her usual feckless optimism, and Adah not wanting to deflate her, found herself agreeing, while under her breath she cursed all African men for treating women the way they do. (p.127)

Here the author brings her personal experience to bear on the business of fiction writing. Adah survives in her given circumstance partly because she is willing to apply her traditional education to a new situation.

Second-Class Citizen

Second-Class Citizen provides a classic example of a mode of interplay between tradition and modern life.[3] Adah represents the modern Ibuza woman. In Lagos and London she is exposed to a great deal of social interaction with American and British middle-class workers. She benefits from such contacts to enrich her life socially and academically. She therefore lives the life of an enlightened housewife ready to experiment with strange ideas like the use of contraceptives, and play the role of breadwinner for the family. She readily throws overboard some traditional customs and beliefs when they clash with her new orientation to life. Not even her awful experiences with Trudy and the Nobles prove strong enough to disturb her confidence in the British way of life.

However, she is conscious of her responsibility to her husband and indigenous society and agrees to have more children under very difficult circumstances.

Francis, on the other hand, is a typical Ibuza man who cares little for Adah's new-fangled ideas. He believes men everywhere are the same and expects them to behave in the same way whether they are at Ibuza, Lagos or London. He therefore refuses Adah any freedom of action and frowns on her social interaction with Europeans. His attitude to women has not changed in any way.

> To him, a woman was a second-class human, to be slept with at any time, even during the day, and, if she refused, to have sense beaten into her until she gave in; to be ordered out of bed after he had done with her; to make sure she washed his clothes and got his meals ready at the right time. There was no need to have an intelligent conversation with his wife because, you see, she might start getting ideas. (p.181)

The dramatic conflict in the novel arises from the fact that Adah does not allow herself to be subjected to this kind of treatment. She would do as she pleased and arrange her life the way that suits her. The fact that her husband depends on her for his livelihood gives her unusual confidence and leads her to think that Francis will change with time. She is proved wrong. We are told 'Francis was an African through and through'. (p.30) He asserts his manliness and dominance over his wife and children without the means of fulfilling his obligations to them. He continues to falter and misbehave, and remains essentially an unhappy man. His refusal to change, when change is necessary, brings in its wake untold hardship.

This couple continues to drift apart. While Adah works strenuously for complete assimilation into British society, Francis looks for fellowship with the black community in London. In *In the Ditch* Adah's problems arise from her dealings with government officials and white people, in *Second-Class Citizen* it is the blacks who put the greatest obstacle in her way. She is disliked by her Nigerian co-tenants because of her assumed sophistication and ready acceptance of the British way of life. On the other hand, Francis works with the blacks for reasons of self-preservation. He is anxious to cultivate a sense of belonging and therefore stays close to the black community whose members share with him the common burden of being black. According to him, 'the day you land in England, you are a second-class citizen. So you can't discriminate against your own people, because we are all second-class'. (p.43) Adah rejects the status of a second-class citizen and feels the blacks have for the most part been responsible for their own misfortune.

The novel contra-distinguishes between life in Lagos and London, and this is closely linked with the past and present of Francis and Adah. In Lagos the couple live a comparatively peaceful and purposeful life. There is a measure of parental control and unsolicited advice. The demands of life are not overwhelming, and people are generally happy, as symbolised by this group of women dancers.

> It was a joy to hear and see these women, happy in their innocence, just like children. Their wants were simple and easily met. Not like those of their children who later got caught up in the entangled web of industrialization. Adah's Ma had no experience of having to keep up mortgage payments: she never knew what it was to have a family car ... she had no worries about pollution, the population explosion or race. (p.15)

In the complex situation in which they find themselves in London Francis and Adah have to worry about too many things. Housing conditions make family life difficult. The children have no amusement of any kind. Parents and children virtually live on top of one another in a small enclosed space. The situation is so bad that the author is able to say that 'the Obis lived not as human beings at all, but like animals'. (p.52) One is not surprised that in these circumstances it becomes impossible to continue to hold the family together. Francis loses his head, falls to pieces emotionally and eventually allows the custody of the children to be given to Adah who has painfully but steadily adjusted to her new environment.

The statement of the novel is clear. The social demands of London, representing the present for the Obis, are greater than those of their past in Lagos. Only strong-minded people, like Adah, can hope to survive in the new situation. Francis suffers mainly because he is unable to relate the past to the present. For, as Adah says, and she must know, 'Francis was not a bad man, just a man who could no longer cope with the over-demanding society he found himself in'. (p.110)

The Bride Price

The Bride Price is the first novel with a wholly Nigerian background.[4] In it the novelist highlights some important features of Nigerian social life in the fifties – education and culture, the relationship between men and women, town and country, and the consequences of any breakdown in these relationships. What is of particular interest to the novelist are the traditions which regulate the conduct of people of slave ancestry, especially as they relate to the payment of bride price. Several taboos have been built around these traditions: no free-born should mix freely with slaves, a girl's bride price must be promptly paid. If not 'she would never survive the birth of her first child'. (p.168) Despite such restrictions Ibuza is notable for its rural simplicity and candour, its citizens are reasonably happy and appear organised as one large family.

> Nearly everyone in Ibuza was related. They all knew each other, the tales of one another's ancestors, their histories and heroic deeds. Nothing was hidden in Ibuza. It was the duty of every member of the town to find out and know his neighbour's business. (p.68)

This is sharply contrasted with the complications which arise when an Ibuza man comes in contact with new ideas and develops a new attitude of life. This results in the duality of life when, for example, he worships the European God during the day and consults his ancestral gods in the night. Home and school invariably impose different standards for children, as they do for Aku-nna and Nna-nndo. These children, on their return from Lagos, find life in Ibuza too confined and restrictive. Yet they have no choice in the matter. They are, in the picturesque language of the novel, like 'helpless fishes caught in a net'. (p.82) The difference between town and country is dramatised in the relationship which exists between Ogugua and Aku-nna. Ogugua is a gentle but vivacious country lass who understands her cultural environment very well. She enjoys the unique advantage of a life not yet complicated by foreign ideals. She is not, like Aku-nna, one of the Nigerians standing bewildered at a cultural cross-roads.

The main preoccupation of this novel is the relationship between Chike and Aku-nna. Chike is of slave extraction and Aku-nna is a free-born. For these two to become man and wife is to do extreme violence to Ibuza tradition and to rock society to its very foundations. Aku-nna, with her modern ideas, calls it a 'savage custom . . . that could be so heartless and make so many people unhappy?' (p.122). Chike in his own interest prefers to think that such a tradition does not exist. But this does not help matters. The elders in society stick to their guns and lead the resistance to change. Okonkwo, for example, warns in an authoritative voice:

> Aku-nna, Chike Ofulue is only a friend. You must remember that. Now that you have grown, that friendship must gradually die. But die it must. (p.116)

To the vast majority of people such a relationship is unthinkable. No citizen has the right to assert his individualism in such a way as to destroy the foundations of society. No one considers it important that the two young people are greatly in love with each other, that they may

107

be allowed to try something new and set out on their own without undue interference from society or the imposition of a burdensome bride price.

The novelist comes down on the side of modernity. The events of the novel are presented in such a way that Chike and Aku-nna are the only two convincing characters. They show inestimable love for each other, and the necessary background is provided for such a genuine love to flourish. There is a consuming desire by the two to keep together under all circumstances. Aku-nna's cry of anguish: 'I want to marry you for many, many reasons which I feel in my heart, although I can't name them all' (p.149) is only one of the ways she demonstrates her love. Another is the method she adopts to disentangle herself from the clutches of Okoboshi when she is kidnapped. She puts her life and reputation at great risk in order to be re-united with Chike. When they escape to Ughelli, their preparations for a new life are such as might have succeeded if fate had not stood in the way. The novelist undoubtedly displays great artistic skill in the way she handles the love affair between these two. The intensive continuity of the narrative during the last anxious moments Chike spends with Aku-nna shows to what extent the author intends to portray these lovers as victims of circumstances.

One leaves the novel satisfied that, although tradition has been upheld, there has been an undeniable emphasis on the need for change. At every point the impression is given that nothing can stop the march of progress. The slave will eventually mix with the free-born. Rural people will become urbanised and literate. More Ibuza people will go to the universities to study and to the towns to work, and thus come in contact with progressive ideas. The elders may dominate the present, but the future certainly belongs to people like Chike and Aku-nna, and their friends, Adegor, Rose and Chima.

The Slave Girl

The same kind of conclusion is tenable for *The Slave Girl*.[5] But the circumstances are different. Any success recorded in this novel is achieved through sweat and blood. Ojebeta experiences so much physical hardship and mental torture that, although she returns home a wiser person, she never forgets her days in slavery. For, as Ama Ata Aidoo has said,

> whatever is sweet has some bitterness in it, then we have to determine the amount of bitterness we take from the sweetness of the present. Otherwise, they'll be so much bitterness, we shall never know there was anything else around.[6]

Ojebeta encounters so much bitterness in her inter-personal relationships with other people from within and outside her family that she doubts whether there is any sweetness left anywhere around the world. Through the judicious use of internal monologues her thoughts are laid bare to the reader, especially during the periods of her greatest anxiety and dissatisfaction.

The work derives its strength from a conflict of aims and interests. Okolie, for purely selfish motives, sells his sister into slavery which is, traditionally, a source of cheap labour and occasionally a way of settling a debt. What is unusual in this case is that a brother condemns his sister to servitude for a paltry amount required for an age-group dance. Okolie has a successful outing and plays a prominent role on the occasion. It is ironical that he has had to sell his sister to be able to achieve some status in society. To underline this ridiculous situation he is given in public praise names which contrast sharply with his private misdeeds.

> Look at him, a young man as strong as the strongest tiger, as fast as the arrows of the gods . . . Who makes the earth shake when he walks? . . . Who has a body like those of the polished images made by wood carvers? (p.86)

The sarcastic intent of the novelist is obvious in the way she allows such encomiums to be showered on a man of little moral stamina.

The slave empire of Ma Palagada for which Okolie has acted as a recruiting agent falls to pieces after her death. The seeds of destruction are there all the time. With increasing Westernisation, citizens are getting exposed to external influences and becoming conscious of their rights. The British Administration is opposed to slavery and does everything possible to stamp it out. Under Ma's benevolent dictatorship the slaves are allowed to attend literacy classes and go to church on Sundays. These are, in a sense, special slaves who are allowed to benefit from the changing circumstances of their time. The novelist often points out the fleeting advantages of a condition of slavery. With her usual eye for detail she compares a slave girl with the girls at Ibuza.

> She was an attractive grown girl of about fourteen with large breasts. She looked well fed and so fresh and plump that her skin reminded him of smooth, ripe mangoes, ready to burst open oozing out rich, creamy, sugary juice. He wondered why Ibuza girls were not like that; they were usually thin, with long legs and narrow faces. (p.47)

One has the impression that so long as Ma is there, she may be able to hold the slave kingdom together. Once she is gone, there will be nobody left with enough force of personality, drive and organisational skill to manage the great household efficiently. The death of Ma symbolically brings to an end the dark days of slavery. No force will be strong enough to prevent the slaves from dispersing. They will now return to their homebase and use for their own benefit whatever lessons they have learnt from the iniquitous system.

As with slavery, so it is with marriage. By Ibuza tradition, marriages between young people are arranged by their families. Jacob and Ojebeta change all that – they introduce the element of love and arrange to be man and wife by direct negotiation. Jacob asks for Ojebeta's hand in marriage and brings about a revolution in traditional custom.

> 'Ojebeta, do you like me? Do you love me? I would like to marry you if your people will accept me.' (p.173)

This union, based on modern beliefs and practices, deserves to succeed. But traditionally disaster awaits any unredeemed slave like Ojebeta. Even after Clifford has been given the ransom money of £8, she still considers Jacob her 'master' and 'new owner'. The sort of mutual confidence and respect which should exist between equal partners is yet to be fully established. Although she talks of feeling 'free in belonging to a new master from my very own town Ibuza' (p.189) the slave mentality has not been completely eradicated. She has experienced change, but not enough of it to make her absolutely free.

The Joys of Motherhood

The Joys of Motherhood is one of Bucki Emecheta's very complex novels.[7] Themes barely mentioned in the other novels are treated here in some detail. Not only is there a fuller discussion of the private and public life of the Ibuza citizen, he is put in circumstances where he needs more than native intelligence to survive. He now lives, as steward or cook, in the same compound with a European master. He works in big corporations and learns the ways of the white man. He is recruited into the army and renders service outside his country. As a student he attends some of the best schools in Lagos and travels abroad for his university education. The Ibuza man is certainly making greater contacts with the outside world. Therefore many of the conservative ideas on which traditional society thrives are, as a result of these contacts, yielding place to a new progressive way of thinking and living. However, indigenous culture shows remarkable resilience in the way it accommodates some of these new situations.

The story is told against the background of the second world war which, like any other war, brings great hardship to many people and homes. In this case, it makes life unbearable for Nnu Ego and Nnaife who are in any case finding life in Lagos extremely difficult. The novelist's description brings vividly to the reader a picture of excruciating poverty. She exhibits great literary powers in the way she visualises a scene and brings it in a cinematographic manner before the reader's eyes. Take, for example, the scene where Nnu Ego tries to commit suicide on the death of her son, or this chilling record of the rewards of poverty.

> Their poverty was becoming very apparent and Oshia was constantly hungry. He was lucky if he had a good meal a day. His mother had not been able to go out to evening market since the birth of his brother, so she would make a display stand outside the house, with cans of cigarettes, boxes of matches and bottles of kerosine, and ask Oshia to sit beside them. (p.103)

Poverty in this novel partly results from the practice of polygamy which is an accepted way of life. Nnaife inherits his dead brother's wives and children, and further worsens his precarious financial condition. Adaku, a newly acquired wife, is a constant source of embarrassment to Nnu Ego who now finds her position as senior wife untenable. Because she has no male child, Adaku does not command respect and is finally driven to prostitution. Nnaife soon takes another wife. The novelist's treatment of polygamy is uninspiring. By making Nnaife so completely ineffective as the head of an extended family, she may be suggesting that polygamy is one of the traditional practices which need to be changed.

A substantial portion of this work is devoted to Nnu Ego's conception of the joys and responsibilities of motherhood. She does not like the role allotted to the woman in the scheme of things. Traditionally the woman bears the burden of bringing up her children against the background of standards set by men for male children. She is blamed for producing girls as if this is her fault. She does all the worrying and is left alone to care for the children 'when they are small; but in the actual help on the farm, the upholding of the family name, all belong to the father'. (p.122) She advocates a change of attitude towards female children and believes the change should be initiated by women themselves. A woman can contribute just as meaningfully to the growth of a society as a man.

These are some of the principles which have guided Nnu Ego in the upbringing of her children. She is reasonably successful in her attempt.

> Her joy was to know that she had brought up her children when they had started out with nothing, and that those same children might rub shoulders one day with the great men of Nigeria. That was the reward she expected. (p.202)

The children are doing well, and she is satisfied with the results. But there is a sudden change of fortune when she appears deserted by many people, including her sons in America and Canada. She dies a lonely and forsaken person. How she deserves this shabby treatment in her last days is not easy to discover. But we are told she is given

> the noisiest and most costly second burial Ibuza has ever seen, and a shrine was made in her name, so that her grandchildren could appeal to her should they be barren. (p.224)

She is undoubtedly one of the most complex characters in the whole of the Buchi Emecheta canon. She readily reminds one of the conception of tragedy in Igbo traditional society.

> Tragedy in the Igbo situation is not in the feeling that nothing goes right for the individual, but that any success he attains is followed sooner or later by a bigger and more terrible misfortune. This is a constant reality in Igbo life, which among some Igbo groups is described as the phenomenon of Ume.[8]

The overall emphasis of the novel is on change. Much has changed at the end of the work. Nnaife is sent to jail for attempting to use brute force in a situation which calls for discussion and reason. Ibuza of Nnaife's childhood has changed a lot, as he discovers when he returns there for good. Nnu Ego's tragic end results partly from the fact that she is not mentally prepared for the series of changes which finally overwhelm her.

It becomes obvious from a consideration of these five novels that the attempt to forge a link between tradition and modern experience poses many problems which Buchi Emecheta has tried to solve in several ways. Some solutions have proved more attractive than others. Her approach in the main has been to dramatise an important aspect of culture or a well-known tradition in a way that its significance becomes obvious to all. However, this is done usually against the background of change. The important issues of bride price, polygamy, childlessness and domestic slavery are highlighted in this manner. In novels based on experiences in Britain, Africa provides the metaphysical landscape. The impression is given that the African in Britain, even when he lives in depressing circumstances, has something to gain from British culture.

The novelist has done what she knows best how to do. She has created a world of women where, for the most part, men play subordinate, often uncomplimentary, roles. This inordinate attempt to portray male characters in unfavourable light may be an intentional device to take it back on the men because of the image of women in the novels written by men. For example, most male characters in *In the Ditch* are social misfits. Pa Palagada in *The Slave Girl* is a terror to the slaves. Nnaife in *The Joys of Motherhood* and Francis in *Second-Class Citizen* are irresponsible heads of families who are mostly insensitive to the needs of their wives and children. Chike in *The Bride Price* is probably the only acceptable important male character in these novels. But he is tainted with slave ancestry, which places some doubt on the validity of his actions. It must, however, be acknowledged that the novelist makes her presentation convincing through the application of great imaginative powers and an impressive display of technical skill. For, as Kofi Awoonor has rightly pointed out,

> The traditional artist is both a technician and a visionary. There is no division between the two roles for him. His technical competence enables him to select and utilise material . . . which in themselves carry a spirituality or an innate essence. It is from here that the transformation into the visionary realm is primarily fed. Forms and motifs already exist in an assimilated time and world construct, and so he serves only as an instrument of transforming these into an artistic whole based on his own imaginative and cognitive world.[9]

Buchi Emecheta not only utilises material of great worth but also makes her novels infinitely attractive by her dramatic presentation of events.

These novels emphasise the need for change, and this is attributed to many factors: differences between town and country, between Lagos and London, increasing westernisation and secularisation. The man in Ibuza, in his traditional setting, will cling to his home-made gods, respect the customs and lore of his people, obey his elders in society and accept their word as the law. He will be satisfied with the little he earns from his farm, enjoy whatever pastimes and pleasures his locality provides and generally live a contented polygamous existence. But when he leaves Ibuza and finds himself in the monetary economy of Lagos and London, he behaves differently. He joins in the rat race and develops ambitions for himself, his friends and relations. He embraces other beliefs and religions and, in the process, makes light of traditional customs. The novelist presents these changes as inevitable. They are indications of man's attempt to overcome a difficult environment and make material and spiritual progress. The novelist is so much interested in the need for change that she pursues this theme in some of her other novels.

The Moonlight Bride

In *The Moonlight Bride* Buchi Emecheta demonstrates her concern for

113

the preservation of traditional customs while at the same time indicating the need for change.[10] Women are in the forefront; they are assigned important roles and made an instrument of change.

Two village girls, Ogoli and Ngbeke, are excited at the fact that a moonlight bride will soon come to the family. They go to the deep banana grove in search of clay to make lamps and pots for the bride. This innocent intention of two industrious girls triggers off a chain of events which keep the village busy for many months and provides an insight into the role of individuals and groups, and especially the hierarchical nature of traditional society. Women are expected to make the general preparation to receive the new bride and, in the process, display any artistic talent they may have. Work requiring masculine prowess is naturally reserved for the men. So, when Ogoli and Ngbeke discover a python in the banana grove, it is the men who go and kill the python and flay its skin for presentation to the bride.

The author rightly makes great capital of the role of the elders. They have the grave responsibility of presiding over the affairs of the community and making sure that societal norms and customs are preserved intact. Any deviant behaviour is chastised and any performance which falls below expectation is publicly deprecated. However, this responsibility is not without its share of honours. As we are told,

> the older an Obi was, the more share he would get. So in Ogoli's family, there was always a large supply of eating-meat, because not only was her father an Obi, he was very old as well – one of the oldest in the whole of Ibuza. My father was an Obi too, but much younger, and he had not been an Obi for long, so he was not so illustrious. (p.45)

The emphasis is on the elder's public responsibility to the younger ones and to the community at large. Hence the elders of Odanta do not spare Chiyei, the village lazy man, whose preoccupation appears to be eating and drinking. In several ways they exhort him to imbibe the community spirit of hard work. They devise their own method of teaching him the benefit of self-reliance and the need for him to contribute his quota, however small, to the total output of the community. They drive their message home by constantly reminding him that 'God needs human, working hands to make his world go round'. (p.29)

Happily it is partly through her use of Chiyei that the novelist indicates the need for change. Chiyei has been a burden on society, a man who goes from hut to hut drinking and devouring other people's food. His unusual behaviour is a source of embarrassment to all, and his people do not hide their feelings.

The pity of it was that Chiyei was well aware that he was unwanted. Whenever he stood up to talk, people would shout him down and say 'sit down, Chiyei, this conversation concerns full men, not half men.' In this way they referred to his wifelessness and childlessness. How could he contribute anything sensible to the pool of ideas when he's never had children of his own? (p.72)

Little wonder that when it is announced that Chiyei is the prospective husband of the moonlight bride everyone is surprised. The villagers doubt his ability to make a good husband and father. The bride herself, an albino, would ordinarily have been unacceptable. But she has been so gentle and kind to Chiyei that his people no longer mind her complexion and origin. The whole community warms up to her and gives her a rousing welcome to the village, such as very few moonlight brides have received before. She is offered many gifts, including the special python mat. She settles down happily with Chiyei to experience a successful marital life. The indication of change is worth quoting at some length.

Alatiriki, our fair wife, stayed with us and, less than a year later, used the very python mat for delivering her first baby boy. And even though he was fair, he was not an albino like the mother. Our Alatiriki put up with our Chiyei, and persuaded him to be a little more responsible. He still ate a lot and drank too much, but he knew that now he had a wife and a child to care for. They had many more children, none of them albino . . .

Well, we did not mind. Our Alatiriki of a wife had the best sense of humour in all our umunna, and she taught us it matters little the colour or superficial beauty of any person, the most important thing is the beauty of the heart. And our wife Echi, or Alatiriki, had that. (p.77)

In this way the author indicates the change that is gradually taking place. The community may impose its norms and expect conformity. But there is always the possibility that a man will assert his individuality in order to make progress. So it is with Chiyei who on his wedding day 'walked so tall and proud that the limp which had been his handicap now became a mark of distinction'. (p.72) He has risen from the level of a village lazy man to a notable personality who from his sale of yams is able to buy a very big goat to feed the community at large. With Echi the change is even more spectacular. By her demeanour and show of affection to relations and friends she brings about a revolution in people's way of thinking and of evaluating others. This is an important change of attitude which underlines the novelist's achievement in this work.

In *Naira Power* the novelist provides a sarcastic commentary on the social life of Lagos.[11] She is concerned with the lack of social facilities. There is no constant supply of water and electricity, no good programme on the TV, the telephone system hardly works and the traffic congestion is unbearable. The government attempt to solve the traffic problem by introducing the odd and even number system for cars on the road has only helped to aggravate the situation. Because of the oil boom Lagos inhabitants have rendered the law ineffective by buying more cars. What with the open drainage system, mini-lakes on the roads, especially during the rainy season, filth and uncollected refuse all over the place, the people's suffering continues unabated. Because suitable accommodation is in short supply, people have to live in crowded houses. At times twenty-four people live in one room! Government is doing precious little to alleviate the suffering of the people and establish a reliable social welfare system. The oil boom has brought in its wake many social problems which have proved intractable for the government. Nigeria appears 'condemned to choke' in her oil wealth.

One of these problems is the need to eradicate corruption which has thoroughly permeated public and private life. The author uses Amina as a narrator to highlight the many manifestations of bribery and corruption in Lagos society. People are so anxious to get rich quick that they hardly wait to consider the moral implication of their behaviour. Citizens go to any length to amass wealth. If necessary, they commit murder in the process. Smuggling and drug peddling are the order of the day. Even the country's law-makers openly engaged in smuggling.

> Auntie, you remember the day we came for you at the airport. You remember that many of the senators returned in the same plane. You saw all the goods they brought in. You saw that all the airport officials were saying 'yessir, yessir,' and nobody searched them. You saw one of them carrying a bale of lace openly, flouting the law they made for ordinary people like us. (p.30)

The whole country is enveloped in corruption. It is a place where 'big thieves who can swindle the government of millions of naira are respected and honoured, pickpockets are not'. (p.34) What a scathing remark! The author sees very little hope for a country where practically everybody is corrupt.

Polygamy is seen as one of the social evils which must be uprooted if corruption is to be wiped out, and individual liberty and freedom of action for women restored. Lemonu's household of three wives and several children is used as a case study of the social inadequacies of a polygamous family. Lemonu is an honest man who has earned for himself the title of 'the fearless, the blameless' for his incorruptibility as a sanitary inspector. But he has complicated life for himself by taking on more wives than he can maintain. Because he has many children he cannot afford to send them to school. Some of them, like Ramonu, live a dishonest life. His wives turn out to be unreliable and wicked. Idayatu allows Ramonu to go to bed with her while Simbi, through the use of a love potion, makes it impossible for Lemonu to have sexual intercourse with his other wives. We have here an example of a family disunited in purpose, scanty in resources, and weakened to its very foundation by jealousy and greed.

Such a family is not uncommon in the Nigerian society. But why does the novelist link this situation with the fact that the family is a Muslim and polygamous one? Similar situations abound in monogamous and Christian families. The situation is even worse when a rich man, Christian or Muslim, maintains women and children in different homes in separate locations in the city. The novelist appears to be more concerned here with some vague feminist ideals than the reality of Lagos life. Lagos provides a good example of a society in a state of flux, where social values are undergoing a process of change. Therefore, the author's attempt to contra-distinguish between polygamy and monogamy, and present one as superior to the other is not particularly helpful. Lemonu is in trouble not because he is a polygamous man and a Muslim, but because he piles upon himself a greater social burden than he can easily carry.

Ramonu is a by-product of the social strain noticeable in Lemonu's family. He is presented as a personification of all that can go wrong with life in the city. He has no formal education, but he is extremely anxious to acquire wealth. He leaves home early to fend for himself. When he surfaces again, it is as a rich man, willing to dazzle people with his wealth. He has been involved in large-scale smuggling, drug peddling and trade in human heads. As we are told, 'in this age of the naira, anything is possible, if it brings in naira power'. (p.87) He is lionised by his people and regarded by many as a symbol of success. In fact, he is an ex-convict who has served long jail sentences during his several 'disappearances' from home. He has committed many murderous acts and has often put his own life at risk in his search for money. He is finally apprehended and burnt alive in public. The novelist quite rightly disapproves of his activities and orientation to life. She uses him to make the most important statement of the novel.

The tragedy that was Ramonu was the fault of nobody, but that of a society that respects any fool who has naira. However intelligent or

creative one is, if one has no naira, there is no place to rest. The
language of naira is universal here. (p.102)

The message is clear and unambiguous. Naira may be powerful. It
may be a source of prestige or illusion of grandeur for many. But it has
to be acquired in an honest manner for it to bring permanent joy and
peace of mind. Ramonu has made his money in a dishonest manner and
bribed his way through all kinds of situations. But on the appointed day
his naira cannot save him because he is now dealing with one 'who
cannot be bought or bribed with naira. The Owner who sees and judges
all things. Allah!' (p.108). It is on such a philosophical note that the
author rests her urgent warning to all those in Lagos and elsewhere who
have come to accept corruption as a way of life.

Destination Biafra

Destination Biafra is a fictional presentation of recent national history
in an unfavourable light.[12] It is a vivid fictional record of the unwholesome events which started with the pre-independence elections in
Nigeria in 1959 and the proclamation of the Republic of Nigeria to the
secession of Biafra and the civil war which ended with the triumph of
the idea of an indivisible Nigeria. The novelist dramatises twelve years
of political mismanagement, civil commotion, personal and communal
greed, unabated selfishness and corrupt leadership which lead
ultimately to social chaos, deprivation and death. The high
functionaries of the state, civil and military, act with such reckless
abandon that nothing but calamity and widespread suffering can result.

The operators of the state machine are vividly described and
categorised. Each group is satirised in turn and castigated for acting
below national expectation, thus contributing to an impending doom.
Those who set the stage for disaster are the politicians. They openly rig
elections and behave in the most riotous manner during campaigns.
Election results are flagrantly falsified. Politicians indulge in con-
spicuous living and a shameless display of wealth. Samuel Ogedemgbe,
for instance, believes fervently in the power of money even when this is
acquired by corrupt means. In his adoration of tribe, wealth and
political position, he is made the personification of the corrupt Nigerian
politician. He is in politics for what he can get out of it. For, as the
novelist asserts,

As a responsible person in Nigeria, one did not just go into politics to
introduce reforms but to get what one could of the national cake and
to use part of it to help one's vast extended family, the village of one's

118

origin and if possible the whole tribe; at least in this way much of the ill-gotten money returned to the society. (p.16)

The politicians who start the country down the slope are Odumosu and Durosaro. These leaders act without regard for the welfare of their people and throw Western Nigeria into confusion in their struggle for personal aggrandisement and political supremacy. It is as a result of this trouble and the subsequent emergency which is declared that the army boys cultivate the idea of military intervention in Nigerian politics. Nor are the politicians from the East, Dr Ozimba and Dr Eze, any better. They are shown to be just as politically unreliable and corrupt as their Western Nigerian counterparts. For instance, they encourage Abosi to secede and establish the Republic of Biafra. But they do little in concrete terms to help sustain the young Republic. Instead, they concentrate on their own personal interests and try to benefit from the ravages of war. While the children of poor people are conscripted into the army to die, they send their own children to school abroad. Their wives make huge profits from the 'attack' trade and accumulate wealth inside and outside Biafra. Certainly, these leaders do not have enough moral stamina to give the new nation the political guidance it badly needs. No wonder not many Igbos take them seriously. When finally Dr Ozimba defects to Nigeria, only a few people are surprised.

Nor are the army boys shown in a better light. The coup which they organise flops, thus putting to question their credibility as a disciplined group. The apparent partiality with which the coup is carried out and the fact that corrupt politicians are killed selectively help to put Nigeria on the brink of disaster. Mutual suspicion creeps into the rank and file of the army, and the officers exploit this to their personal advantage. Saka Momoh and Chijioke Abosi are portrayed as characters ready to wreck the nation in order to achieve their personal ambition. They both behave in a most reprehensible manner. At Aburi they show bad faith. At home they falsify truth and promote the ideals of war. When Biafra appears to be gaining ground with the capture of Benin and Ore, Abosi becomes over-confident and impervious to reason. When the federal troops regain Ore and Benin they treat captured Biafran soldiers and civilians brutally. What the novelist presents is an atrocious war fought in the most primitive manner without regard to the recognised rules of the game. That it went on for so long is partly the fault of Abosi who resorts to deceiving his people when he knows that he is not only losing the war but also alienating, by his executions, the Igbos on the west bank of the Niger. The concept of Biafra has become odious to these people, as one western Igbo woman makes clear.

Biafra, Biafra, what is Biafra? You killed our man from this part,

Nwokolo; the Nigerian soldiers came and killed what your soldiers left. We are Ibuza people, but we now live in the bush, thanks to your Abosi and your Biafra. Our town is now a ghost town. Go there and see Hausa soldiers killing and roasting cows. They shoot anything on sight, and kill anyone who gave shelter to your people. And when we needed you, where were you? Where was your Abosi when our girls were being raped in the market places and our grandmothers shot? Please go back to your Biafra (p.230)

Once the unity of the tribe across the Niger is disrupted, it is only a matter of time before the war is lost. When Abosi finally realises the game is up, he abandons his people to their fate and escapes from the country with members of his family.

The novelist highlights the fact that in this war Nigerians have allowed themselves to be used by foreigners as tools of self-destruction. The divide-and-rule policy of the British colonialist is brought tactically into full play and made to succeed. Foreigners fan the embers of war for their own selfish ends and manipulate one side in the conflict adroitly against the other. In fact, the colonial power plays a significant role in sowing the seed of distrust among Nigerians in the first place. For example, colonial officials make it quite clear before the pre-independence elections are held that it is in the interest of Britain that the party from Northern Nigeria wins. To achieve this, even before all the results are announced, Nguru Kano is proclaimed Prime Minister and invited to form the government. This government, as one may well expect given the strengths of the various political parties, is weak, ineffective and corrupt. It is this situation that leads to the coup on which foreigners capitalise for their own gains. The British naturally regard Nigeria as their sphere of influence and intend to do everything possible to keep out the Russians. They see Nigeria only as an opportunity for achieving cold-war supremacy over the Eastern Bloc. Grey makes this clear in his official actions and dealings.

But the Englishman, despite his avowed love for Nigeria, still felt that the country's wealth should be shared with the powers of the West, preferably Britain; with the ambitious Ibos at the helm, trade agreements with the Russians might be signed. So even though he congratulated his old friend upon being head of state, Grey's congratulations were too brittle to hide his mistrust. (p.73)

Foreign intervention intensifies as the war progresses, with each side relying on foreign military advisers and weapons. When mercenaries arrive, the war escalates. Peace is not achieved until a secret deal is concluded on how to share Nigeria's oil wealth. The novelist underlines the fact that foreigners are not interested in peace in Nigeria for its own sake, but have come to fish in troubled waters for the economic advantage of their home countries.

As in her other novels, Buchi Emecheta gives prominence to women in this work. The heroine, Debbie Ogedemgbe, is given decisive roles to play at crucial stages in the events of the novel. She is made to grow in our estimation from the spoilt, well-educated child of a corrupt politician to a responsible, loyal citizen of Nigeria who possesses an idealistic vision of her country's greatness, and is ready to make a lot of personal sacrifice to achieve the ideal. She joins the army to prove that a woman can be just as useful to the country as a man in times of distress and national reconstruction. She believes fervently in the liberation of women from the submissive role which custom and tradition thrust upon them in the home and society. She is anxious to maintain her personal independence and be in complete control of her life. She finds the marital life of her parents a negative example in this regard and decides to continue to assert her individuality in domestic and public affairs.

> She loved both her parents very much. It was just that she did not wish to live a version of their life – to marry a wealthy Nigerian, ride the most expensive cars in the world, be attended by servants . . . No, she did not want that; her own ideas of independence in marriage had no place in that set-up. She wanted to do something more than child breeding and rearing and being a good passive wife to a man whose ego she must boost all her days, while making sure to submerge every impulse that made her a full human. Before long she would have no image at all, she would be as colourless as her poor mother. Surely every person should have the right to live as he or she wished, however different that life might seem to another? (p.45)

She needs this independent spirit and more if she is to contribute maximally to the search for a solution to the problems raised by the war. She is sent on a peace mission to Abosi and, in the process, suffers a great deal of hardship. This does not deter her from pursuing her mission or even developing some idealistic concept of what Biafra stands for. To her Biafra represents an ideal which every true Nigerian should work for, the first real fight for independence.

> It is not a war between Abosi and Momoh. This is our war. It is the people's war. Our very first war of freedom. Momoh and Abosi started the purge, to wash the country of corruption and exploitation. Now there is a danger of the two men putting their self-interest foremost. If that is the case, the war will be taken out of their control

and put into the hands of responsible leaders who will see the purge through and restore to us a new clean Nigeria. (p.160)

The two leaders prove unreasonable and prolong unduly the suffering of the people. Debbie's costly mission fails to achieve its objective. She, however, displays great resourcefulness abroad as the propaganda officer for Abosi and Biafra. She achieves a measure of success here, but she is still disappointed that Abosi will not see reason and stop the war. She is sad that the high hopes for Biafra are fading, and disillusioned that so much corruption, greed, selfishness and inefficiency have crept into Biafran life. When in the end she discovers that Abosi has been in touch with South Africa all the time, she becomes dejected and puts the blame for the war on Grey and his group of foreign interlopers.

Look, we even have a South African plane here offering the same help you are offering. But how did they know about tonight? And how did you know, white man? Oh, Abosi, I wish I had succeeded in killing you. To make us sink this low! If future generations should ask what became of Biafra, what do you want us to tell them? (p.259)

However, it is in her relationship with her white lover, Alan Grey, that Debbie asserts her independence and individuality in the most sensational manner. Here she may be acting as spokesman for the novelist and all others who believe in women's liberation and freedom. The fact that she is openly in love with a white man in a tribal society shows to what extent she has become detribalised. She sleeps with him quite frequently without any thought of marrying him. Her ideas of marriage are unconventional and demonstrate little regard for traditional beliefs and practices. She decides to join the army to show that if a woman can have complete freedom of action, she can contribute positively to the development of the country and help resolve thorny problems. She and her friend Barbara are so completely liberated from restrictive traditional social norms that some of their actions constitute an embarrassment to elders like Mrs Ogedemgbe.

I don't know what has come over you girls. We all want freedom for women, but I doubt if we are ready for this type of freedom where young women smoke and carry guns instead of looking after husbands and nursing babies. (p.108)

It is this independence of action that Grey often exploits to his advantage in his dealings with Debbie. But he underrates her nationalistic feelings and patriotic intentions. He is disappointed in the end when Debbie rejects him and takes a stand in favour of Africa and African womanhood.

I see now that Abosi and his like are still colonized. They need to be decolonized. I am not like him, a black white man; I am a woman and a woman of Africa. I am a daughter of Nigeria and if she is in shame, I shall stay and mourn with her in shame. No, I am not ready yet to become the wife of an exploiter of my nation . . . Goodbye, Alan. I didn't mind your being my male concubine, but Africa will never again stoop to being your wife; to meet you on an equal basis, like companions, yes, but never again to be your slave. (pp.258-9)

In devoting so much space to the psychological development of her heroine and endowing her with so much education and ability to perform so well at crucial times, the novelist directly raises the status of African womanhood. She achieves this at some price – a large-scale departure from historical facts. Debbie is an imaginative invention devised not merely to demonstrate the equality of women with men but particularly to highlight areas in state and politics where women can excel men. So we see that on many occasions Debbie constitutes an important factor in the execution of the war. She is acceptable to both sides of the conflict and, through Grey, has connections with the British imperialists. Even so, she shows no political ambition. Her motives are always genuine – to identify herself with the suffering of her people and help her country out of present difficulties. These are indeed noble aims which Debbie prosecutes single-mindedly. The novelist thus succeeds in endearing her heroine to her readers. After this, no longer can the woman be expected to play the role of a second-class citizen, as we have in the novel of that title; no longer will people be too interested in academic feminist writing, but in situations, such as we have here, where women show their mettle and class. This is an important area of achievement in this work.

Other areas of achievement concern the novelist's approach to the work and her attractive narrative prose. She appropriately captures the atmosphere of war and, as one may well expect, makes it almost a women's war. The common man suffers most. As an enlisted soldier he dies fighting; as a civilian he suffers all the deprivations that war brings on a people. The men are usually quickly eliminated. The women are kept alive somehow to experience the greater hardship. This is the case during Operation Mosquito when women are trapped in the bush between Benin and Asaba in their attempt to escape from the brutal might of the invading federal troops. The women are made to experience the bestialities of war, and the novelist records these horrible events without mincing words or wincing.

The pregnant woman now began to wail as she was dragged from the main road to the side bush, pushed mercilessly with the butt of a gun;

the woman was falling and getting up again, and calling to her husband Dede to help her. Debbie wondered what had happened to the child. She heard the tired, strangled voice of the woman calling out in Ibo, begging for mercy as they took her to a different part of the bush. (p.133)

When Debbie is raped we are told,

she could make out the figure of the leader referred to as Bale on top of her, then she knew it was somebody else, then another person . . . She felt herself bleeding, though her head was still clear. Pain shot all over her body like arrows. She felt her legs being pulled this way and that, and at times she could hear her mother's protesting cries. But eventually, amid all the degradation that was being inflicted on her, Debbie lost consciousness. (p.134)

To such horrors the environment, as it were in sympathy, is made to respond.

But the night insects still buzzed. Crickets from the undergrowth cried, 'Shame on you humans', frogs from nearby ponds went on croaking and owls drawled their mournful complaints. This was a place for animals, this was their time of day; humans should be in their own habitat, in their built-up homes, not in this belly of the thick African forest where it was impossible to tell people from trees. (p.170)

These are direct forceful narrations which cannot fail to make a lasting impression on the reader.

The novelist is particularly successful in the description of events, persons and attires. She has a good eye for detail, and this helps to impart realism to her work. She often uses to advantage her intimate knowledge of local styles of dress and modes of behaviour.

'I am sorry to have kept you waiting,' breathed Debbie as she sailed in wearing a brightly coloured Itsekiri outfit, with two pieces of vivid cotton George material tied round her. Her flaming red silk headtie was intricately and artistically knotted, so that for a moment Alan thought that the beautiful woman standing in front of him was Mrs Stella Ogedemgbe transformed. She looked very like her mother but with some touches of her own: her bold smile, the confident thrust of her head, the way she looked him straight in the eye when talking, were gestures which Mrs Ogedemgbe had never acquired. When Debbie walked in her native attire she seemed to move with measured grace; it gave her an air of still formality, almost bordering on artificiality, but all told it added grace and femininity, qualities which were lost when she put on shapeless green army trousers she had insisted on wearing of late. (pp.111-112)

The novelist has no doubt matured and now uses language as a dynamic force in the work of artistic creation. This high linguistic competence manifests itself also in the narrative sections of the work. Because the subject-matter is war the narrative intensity of the prose helps to heighten emotional tension, as we have here in the report of the emergency action taken in Ibadan.

> The Nigerian army heads did not sleep. They were in all parts of Ibadan, commanding the still untrained local recruits, keeping an eye on the residences of ministers and important businessmen, patrolling the streets. The few shots they fired were only to scare; a stray bullet did hit one man in the leg but the injury was not too bad. Those who died did so as a result of beatings by their opponents. Some of the ringleaders were captured and taken to the army barracks, since it seemed the police had played a disappearing game. As soon as they saw the spirit of the thugs and guessed that some of them were on a suicide mission, the police ran for cover. But meanwhile the soldiers were everywhere like locusts. (p.52)

In conception and execution, therefore, this is a successful work, the most ample that the novelist has written so far and perhaps the most memorable. The author has written well, but has she also written with bitterness? The work starts with a dedication to her close relations who died during the war and goes on in an Author's Foreword to say: 'Yet it is time to forgive, though only a fool will forget.' It might be argued that unless forgiving includes a measure of forgetting, it becomes only a partial act of grace. The proper role of historical fiction is not to leave scars in the heart of readers but to put them in a frame of mind to benefit from the achievements and failures of the past. Without its emotional dedication and an unusual author's foreword *Destination Biafra* will easily pass for a work devoted to the ideals of national unity and stability.

Literary Development

During her short career as a writer Buchi Emecheta has successfully written on different kinds of topics. She started with the ones which touch on her early life and attempts at personal survival. This is why *In the Ditch* and *Second-Class Citizen* have autobiographical overtones. Then she moved on to topics of social and cultural significance in *The*

Bride Price and *The Slave Girl*. But her most complex works were to come later – *The Joys of Motherhood* and *Destination Biafra*. In all these, the novelist has shown how competently she can handle a variety of topics ranging from love affairs, slavery, home and family life, culture and tradition, politics and war. She has also demonstrated her ability to portray human beings of different classes and situations in life. So one finds in the novelist's works all manners and conditions of men in public and private life – in the armed forces or political arena, as businessmen or civil servants, village elders or factory workers.

She completes the picture with a work which will soon be published. One year as a member of staff at the University of Calabar, Nigeria, has yielded her first novel based on university life. *Double Yoke* is the story of Nko, an undergraduate, who tries to cope with the double yoke of tradition and that of modernity. Should Nko lose her identity in marriage to her boyfriend and be a good woman in the traditional sense? Or should she try and get a good degree by encouraging the love affair with the Dean of her faculty and, in the process, be labelled feminist, rebellious – in short, a bad woman? How is she expected to carry the two burdens on her shoulders at the same time? These are the difficult questions posed by this work. The story is as usual well told, and helps to confirm the novelist's established position as 'one of the true story-tellers to emerge from Africa in the past decades'.[13]

The characteristics of Buchi Emecheta's writings should be fairly obvious from the foregoing analysis of her works. In each novel she takes an important aspect of life, examines it critically, asks appropriate questions and leaves an unresolved dilemma. Women are usually in the forefront in her portrayal of life. As mother, housewife, bride, girl-friend or slave, they are given a significant part to play. Their roles are sometimes so crucial that without them men cannot function effectively. This assumes greater importance as the works become more complex. So we find that in all her novels the most complex role given to a woman is that of Debbie in *Destination Biafra*. The picture of a woman performing so efficiently in a theatre of war must be considered one of the novelist's greatest contributions to the feminist ideals of justice and equality. It is a far cry from the humble and humiliating roles women have had to play in her early works and shows to what extent the novelist has developed intellectually. She has opened up new horizons for women as an unmistakable sign of her own maturity. The growth in artistic imagination has resulted in vastly improved works of art.

Notes

1   Interview between Buchi Emecheta and Oladele Taiwo at Briston Grove, North London, on 3 April, 1982.

2   *In the Ditch*, Allison and Busby Ltd., London, 1972. All page references are to the 1979 edition.

3   *Second-Class Citizen*, Allison and Busby Ltd., London, 1974. Page references are to the Fontana Books 1980 edition.

4   *The Bride Price*, Allison and Busby Ltd., London, 1976. Page references are to the Fontana Books 1979 edition.

5   *The Slave Girl*, Allison and Busby Ltd., London, 1977. Page references are to the Fontana Books 1979 edition.

6   Ama Ata Aidoo, *Our Sister Killjoy* (London, Longman, 1977), p.115.

7   *The Joys of Motherhood*, Allison and Busby Ltd., London 1979. Page references are to the African Writers Series edition, Heinemann, London, 1980.

8   Ernest N. Emenyonu, 'Who does Flora Nwapa Write for?' *African Literature Today*, No.7, Heinemann, London, 1975, p.31.

9   Kofi Awoonor, 'Tradition and Continuity in African Literature' in Rowland Smith ed., *Exile and Tradition*, Longman, London, 1976, p.166.

10 *The Moonlight Bride* (O.U.P., London, 1980). Page references are to this edition.

11 *Naira Power* (London, Macmillan, Pacesetters Series, 1982) Page references are to this edition.

12 *Destination Biafra*, Allison and Busby Ltd., London, 1982) Page references are to this edition.

13 Matchet's Diary, *West Africa*, London, 6 February, 1978, p.238.

CHAPTER SIX

Grace Ogot

Grace Ogot is one of Africa's outstanding storytellers. She went into the lead early and has worked hard ever since to remain there. She has written several collections of short stories and full-length novels in English and Luo. *The Promised land, Land without Thunder, The Other Woman, Island of Tears* and *The Graduate* are established and well received. The writings in Luo – *Ber Wat, Miaha, Aloo Kod Apul Apul, Simbi Nyaima* may be new to many outside Kenya, but they have proved extremely popular at home. For example, a recent dramatisation of *Miaha* in Luo-speaking areas of Kenya excited the people and showed to what extent drama could be used as a medium of transmitting indigenous culture. The drama version of two stories from *Land Without Thunder* – 'The Rain Came' and 'The White Veil' – staged by the Albert Wandago Production at the Cultural Centre, Nairobi was also well received and had almost twenty runs. So, not only has Grace Ogot been writing stories and novels, she has also been promoting creativity in other directions. A few of her books have been translated into several international languages and some have been adopted for use as school texts for the O level in Kenya.

In an interview she talked about her new books in the press, her motivation for writing, her craftmanship and the recognition that writing has brought her so far.[1] She has three completed novels in the pipeline, two of them she has worked on for ten years. These two are historical novels. *In The Beginning* deals with the history of the Luo people from about 97 AD to about 1300 AD when the people make a Wi-nam settlement, and what compels then to leave this settlement. For greater effectiveness the story, usually referred to as the story of the

128

spear and the bead, concentrates on three generations of one family. It hinges on a family spear, an inheritance of great cultural worth, which has to pass from one generation to another. At one stage a member of the family makes a mistake and an elephant walks away with the spear. The owner of the spear refuses compensation. So the man at fault goes in search of the spear. This action eventually leads to the separation of two brothers who later found two nations. The second novel, *Princess Nyilaak*, virtually continues the historical fiction where the first has left off. Nyilaak was born around 1517 AD, and her story takes us up to about 1750 AD. She is the daughter of the ruler of the Luo people. In the absence of a male child she is designated to succeed her father. For this reason the oracles decree that she should not marry. Her mother does not like this decision and does everything in her power to oppose it. Nyilaak has an encounter with Ochak, a prince from another part of the land, marries him secretly and becomes pregnant for him. Ochak is hunted down by Nyilaak's father, and is killed and cremated. Nyilaak is banished from the land and her twin sons are to be killed. However, through the intervention of the elders, she is reprieved with her two sons and she later becomes a ruler. Nyilaak later founds the Alur society in Uganda, and one of her sons succeeds her as ruler.

The third novel, *A Call at Midnight* is different in texture and orientation from the first two. It will be published by Anyange Press at Kisumu and is being prepared for dramatisation by Alika Mboya. It is a social comment on family life, expecially the responsibility of the father to his wife and children. A father deserts his family, and ten years after he has left home there is a telephone call to his wife that her husband is critically ill in hospital. The wife says she has no husband. The ward sister replies that dying men don't just call on any women in the city. All the time the man has been away from home he has maintained an illegal contact with another woman in a smuggling business. This woman dupes him of a large sum of money, dopes him and leaves him unconscious by the road side. This is why he goes to hospital in the first place. He recovers from his illness, paralysed, and returns to his matrimonial home. The wife is rather unhappy about his return, but the children feel it is much better to have a crippled father than not have any at all. When these three novels are published they will confirm Grace Ogot's position as an outstanding female novelist in modern Africa.

Grace Ogot is a highly motivated writer. She comes from a family of storytellers. Some of the early influences on her came from her maternal grandmother who was an accomplished storyteller. Her stories made great impact on the mind of the young Grace. For example, Grace heard the story of Oganda – 'The Rain Came' – very early from her grandmother, and the details haunted her for a long time. She developed great personal feelings for Oganda and was often afraid as a young girl that she too might be asked to be sacrificed. Other stories like *Ber Wat, Miaha* and *Simbi Nyaima* came originally from her grandmother, although in some cases she has had to modernise the content and change a few minor details. Her father was another salutary influence. He was a school teacher and would often read Bible stories and translate them to her for her enjoyment. She so enjoyed these stories and the folktales her grandmother told her that she resolved: 'If one day I can write, I shall write the story of Oganda so that other people can know she was sacrificed for the welfare of her people.'

The urge to write was already in her when she met her husband, Allan Ogot, who made her aware that she could write. After she had written two love letters to him, he urged her to write poetry because the content of the letters was poetic. She was not confident she could write good poetry. Then Allan urged her to start writing short stories. So she started with the stories she had heard before and has never looked back since then. The fact that her husband is himself a writer and in academic work has certainly been a great help. All members of the family appreciate her contribution, and the family tradition has been carried forward by the children. The first son, David, is fast establishing himself as a prose writer and has written a number of books in the Okelo series, a series devoted to school adventures. The third child, Michael, is a poet and has produced a good number of highly rated poems.

Her approach to story-telling, Grace Ogot says, is simple and unadorned, although she finds that her penmanship has improved over the years. She tries to get a good framework for her stories before she starts. She conceives of the beginning, the middle and the end, and then tries to put the parts together with appropriate details. However, she has had the startling experience where the characters tend to rule the story and virtually dictate all else that happens. Again, in a few cases she starts by focussing her imagination on the end of the story, and then works backwards. She has not found short stories easier to write than full-length novels. The short story leaves the writer little room to manoeuvre. It therefore compels directness of narration and economy of words, and characters may not be as fully developed as one would have in a novel. These apparent restrictions have their own advantages. Her practice is to hit direct on the subject-matter without allowing the beginning of the story to drag, and leave something for the imagination of the reader at the end. She finds the story form more African than the novel – the novel, in any case, is a literary imposition on African traditional practice. However, it has its own advantages. It gives the writer a wider scope to tell his story and develop his characters. More details can be incorporated by way of background and analysis of events, as she has done in *In The Beginning* where three generations of the same family are fully developed.

Grace Ogot is satisfied with the recognition her writing has brought her so far and is particularly gratified that she has been able to bring so much pleasure to her people who speak and read only Luo. She is pleased that the dramatisation of some of her works have made them more popular and feels happy that drama is rapidly establishing itself as a medium of communication in Kenya. She is satisfied with the activities of the Writers' Association of Kenya of which she was founder chairman from 1975-80. The Association has helped to stimulate creativity, discover hidden literary talent, improve the freedom of artists and settle royalty problems in specific cases. It has sponsored a few seminars on creativity, notably the seminar on children's literature in November, 1981, and taken active interest in the collection, synthesising and publication of oral Literature.

After that extensive discussion of Grace Ogot's motivation and attempt at literary creativity, her works must now be considered in detail so that her contribution may be fully assessed. She made a name as a writer with the publication of *The Promised Land*. So it has been considered appropriate to start with this novel and the shorter piece, *The Graduate*, before going on to consider her various collections of short stories.

The Promised Land

The Promised Land presents in the form of a fantasy the tragic consequences of the restlessness of man and his eternal quest for power, wealth and social prominence.[2] The story is put in the context of Luo pioneers who in search of happiness and prosperity cross over from Nyanza to Tanganyika. The emphasis is on the dangers attendant on such journeys, the inconvenience of leaving one's family and immediate environment and the uncertainty of living in a foreign land. While upholding the spirit of adventure, the novel stresses at every important stage, either by way of social comment or through the experiences of the main characters, the possibility of ultimate failure and personal dissatisfaction.

The novelist clearly indicates that, as with the other Luo pioneers, a little bit of contentment on the part of Ochola might have saved him much embarrassment. There is abundant evidence that he will make good at home. He is successfully married to a hard-working woman who is liked by practically every member of his family. He is the first son of his father in a patrilineal society, which means he will eventually inherit his father's farms and other possessions. Although he has had difficult times as a youngster, he will almost certainly succeed now as a farmer with the help of his father and a sympathetic stepmother. Why does he abandon these prospects for the illusion of grandeur in Tanganyika. The novel provides the background against which Ochola takes his irrevocable decision.

> He was getting tired of living in Nyanza, with its unscrupulous tax collectors, its petty tyrants and its land feuds. Whatever money anyone could make went for school fees, hospital fees and so forth. Sub-chiefs regularly recruited forced labour to work on public projects. Why were people made to pay taxes as well, then? He pondered the beauty of Tanganyika in his mind. Perhaps people did not even pay taxes there. (p.14)

Furthermore, there is an unhealthy emphasis on wealth which Ochola unfortunately thinks will solve all his problems. When his father points out the adverse effect his decision will have on members of his family, especially himself, Ochola has a ready answer.

> 'I must go, father. I'll be more useful to you if I go . . . I'll be rich and all the money troubles we've had for so many years will vanish. Whatever I earn I'll share with the whole family.' (p.35)

All entreaties fail to move Ochola. Not even the taunting of his wife, Nyapoh, whose warning turns out to be prophetic makes any difference to him.

> 'Rich, rich, every man wants to be rich . . . It's all greed. Greed killed Okal Tako. This is the fate of men who want to get rich too quickly.' (p.27)

Ochola's illusion about Tanganyika is so great and overwhelming that nothing can now stop him from trying out his ideas of getting rich quickly. When a man of Ochola's vivid imagination is totally consumed by a fantasy, he does everything to remove all obstacles in the way.

The novelist devotes a lot of attention to this attempt at greatness. There is undoubtedly no intention to kill initiative and the use of discretion. So, Ochola and Nyapoh are put right in the centre of the story and are made to record initial successes in Tanganyika through dint of hard work and the help given by Okech and his wife, Atiga. The novelist shows particular interest in the psychological development of

Nyapoh who comes to be regarded by the villagers as a paragon of virtue.

> Nyapoh was a good wife! Many people in this new land had remarked how strong she was in the fields and how well she cultivated the land. Her hands were light during weeding time, she had also proven herself fertile in giving birth to a son. If she was able to brew beer, then her qualities as an ideal wife would be complete. (p.101)

A few months after their arrival at Musoma they are already rich and well-known in the neighbourhood for their prosperity. This is amply demonstrated by the large attendance at the house-warming party which they hold in their new house for their friends. Both hosts and guests are satisfied with the lavish hospitality and conviviality shown on the occasion.

> At sunset, the party came to an end. Several speeches were made, praising the hand that had brewed the strong sweet beer. They praised Ochola for his hard work, his friendliness and for the generosity which he had shown to his countrymen. They were convinced that in a few years' time Ochola would be one of the richest men in the land. As each guest left for his home, he blessed the generous host. (p.111)

Ochola and Nyapoh are now fully integrated members of the community and have the blessing and goodwill of their neighbours.

Given this auspicious start and Ochola's reputation for hard work, why does his stay in Tanganyika end in disaster? The novel only partially answers this question. The answer does not lie in what Ochola is able to do for himself and members of his family, but in what the gods have ordained for them. To start with, it is difficult to know how acceptable to the gods of his ancestors is Ochola's desertion of his ancestral land. This may have played a crucial part in his fate. What we know for certain is that he is a victim of a sordid aspect of the history of his people. The enterprising Luos had driven away by force of arms the original owners of Musoma and established themselves there. They now act as overlords of the place to the annoyance of the few aborigines left. One such is an unnamed old man who shows implacable hostility to Ochola. 'You Luo people . . . I hate all of you,' (p.128) he confesses. It is suggested that this old man, through the use of his extraordinary magical powers, is responsible for Ochola's troubles. This introduces a mysterious element into the work. Why, for example, does the old man single out Ochola for punishment for an offence committed by the ethnic group many generations ago? Many Luos have settled down in the land before him and prospered. Why is the old man endowed with such magical powers that cannot be countered by any other medicine man in the land? Magungu fails woefully in his initial attempt; so also is the white man's hospital. One must look for an answer to this mystery in the activities of the gods rather than those of men. At the beginning of his adventure Ochola has committed his fate to his ancestors and family god.

So hear my plea, mother! Ask God, on my behalf, to bless me and my wife, and guide our feet to the unknown land. (p.39)

It is only these gods who can save him in times of trouble. If, as in this case, they leave him to his fate and refuse to lift a finger to help him, it is probably an indication that they are not sufficiently appeased or that his plans do not enjoy their support. Even if one feels that Ochola does not deserve this kind of treatment, one still has to concede that the disposition of the gods is often beyond the understanding of man.

The work highlights the confrontation which exists between the old and new ways of life, between ancestral worship and Christianity, between traditional and modern medicine. Ochola is taken to Dr Thomson for treatment after he has been subjected to traditional medicine for several months. Dr Thomson, who is a mission doctor, fails and agrees that Ochola should be returned to the traditional healer. Why does Dr Thomson's sincere attempt to help Ochola fail? Is it because his faith in Christ is not strong enough or his practice of medicine is deficient? It is not easy to decide which is the more potent factor. The doctor launches into a somewhat unnecessary gospel teaching which offers for emulation by Ochola the example of Job. One finds that despite the pretensions of the Christian group Christianity is not firmly rooted among the people nor is it presented in a sufficiently glorious light. Consider, for example, the frequent quarrels between Dr Thomson and his wife, and the unruly behaviour of the Christian convert, Abiero, who in the name of Christianity breaks his father's precious pipe and objects to the singing of traditional songs. Surely such activities cannot help to make the Christian religion acceptable to the people. Little surprise then that in its encounter with traditional religion, Christianity is worsted, and this adversely affects Dr Thomson. Traditional medicine prevails but it is not triumphant. Its constructive aspect is used to save Ochola from dying. But it is because of a potent destructive magical force masterminded by the old man that Ochola leaves Tanganyika suddenly in the interest of himself and members of his family.

The climax of events in this novel comes at the end. The author displays a lot of narrative energy to make the end of the book convincing. Ochola has suffered so much that there is a need to provide justification for such a devastating experience. Part of the explanation may be the unfavourable attitude of his gods. Once a man puts the acquisition of wealth before everything else, he should be ready for any eventuality. It may well be that Ochola's experiences are devised to teach him the simple lesson that 'Wealth you can buy, but you cannot buy life'. (p.197) Or can it be that the author is against change, the type that Ochola's activities indicate? Is she, for example, against a sudden change in social status, such as Ochola seeks to achieve, or a movement from the known to unknown which Ochola attempts in going to Tanganyika? These questions are not directly answered, and the author leaves each reader to come to his own conclusions. However, the fact that Ochola loses everything at the end and returns to Seme practically as he left tends to lend credence to some implicit disapproval of his action by the author. Be that as it may, the narrative intensity of the prose and the realistic actions of Ochola at the end of the book do great credit to the novelist. The facts of the case are laid bare in the last pathetic scene when Ochola becomes demented and finds himself unable to face the truth. At this juncture there is need to put the records straight. Here Abiero comes useful as he consoles Nyapol.

> 'My sister, it's the will of God,' he said. 'We plan to go east, he turns our faces west. That my brother's wealth has to be left to the enemy tears my heart, but we have no choice, my sister. We must follow Magungu's advice.' (p.198)

Ochola returns reluctantly to Seme, but we are told that 'his soul would stay forever in his home in Tanganyika'. (p.205)

In this novel the author introduces certain literary devices which she uses to advantage in her other works as well. Her approach in each case is determined by the complexity of the work and the level of sophistication of the characters. It is mainly through their behaviour and speech that she contra-distinguishes between urban and rural characters. So, we find that because most of the events of this novel take place in a rural setting among people close to the roots of indigenous culture, a high sense of morality is everywhere in evidence. Town life is portrayed as inferior, and there we discover occasional lapses, like the misbehaviour of Father Ellis when he squeezes Apinyo's breasts. Town life is also characterised by a lack of regard for the other man's feelings and comfort, as Nyapol is compelled to point out.

> Nyapol was shaken and puzzled. Things were so different in the town. Politeness was considered a weakness that these town people exploited. Everyone looked after themselves. (p.56)

Through the application of appropriate linguistic skills the novelist gives a true picture of rural life, dignified in its setting and decorous in its speech and behaviour. She ensures that the level of speech is always appropriate to person, place and circumstance. Descriptions are apt and either add local colour or make an event more meaningful. Proverbs are used to bring out the deeper significance of an utterance. So when, for example, Ochola is offended by the treatment he has recently received from members of his wife's family he put his grievance, through the use of a proverb, in a way that the psychological damage done to him is clear for all to see.

> How can you put a calabash of water to my lips and suddenly remove it, leaving me to die of thirst? Night after night, I thirst for you, like the cracked sun-baked clay soil thirsts for rain. (p.10)

Again, when Ochola seeks Okech's permission to move out of the latter's house and build his own hut, it is through the use of a descriptive proverb full of images that Okech gives his reply.

> 'Our home is open to you and your wife, my brother, and you can stay as long as you like. But I can read your mind. You don't cook two cocks in one pot, and I can't blame you for feeling that the pot is too small for both of us.' (p.76)

More important than the application of proverbs is the use of speech and description is an edifying sort of way. The speech of rural people is always allowed to benefit from the characteristics of their first language. The closer the personal relationship between two people, the more intimate the language is allowed to be, as we have here when Nyapol addresses her husband.

> 'Son of my mother-in-law, don't let your sufferings ruin all the happy moments we used to share when you were well. Ochola, you're so ill, and you've gone through so much pain, but we're still man and wife. If God is kind and you get well, we may yet have a long life together. Now tell me, Ochola, what's the matter? Whatever I say is wrong. I know you don't want to go home to Seme, sick as you are. I have given in on that . . .' (p.191)

This is a moving request from a wife to her husband on his sick bed. The language is intimate and the tone mournful. We note in this address the predominance of the habits of speech, the style of one speaking direct to another. We are impressed by the rural simplicity and candour of the speaker. It is through such an open demonstration of her sincerity in words and deeds that Nyapol wins her husband's confidence and the respect of her neighbours. The novel also abounds in apt descriptions which indicate the tenure of events or reveal the potential of an individual, as we are given in this portrait of Magungu.

> Magungu was unkempt, his matted hair was so shaggy that he looked like some madman. His long twisted beard joined with the hair from his head, and his shabby moustache looked like a cat's whiskers. But that was not all. His eyes were as red as those of a cattle egret and one of his front teeth hung so loosely that it moved up and down while he spoke, as if it would fall out at any moment. A strip of goatskin was tied round his wrists, and a large cow's bone hung down his chest. (p.150)

Here the author shows a large degree of imaginative inventiveness and an eye for detail. What we have is a picture of a fierce-looking and experienced medicine man who is capable of performing efficiently. This is, in fact, what Magungu turns out to be. In the end he not only saves Ochola, but also makes sure he is out of further danger. It is in the use of such descriptions that the novel displays some of its attractive linguistic qualities. The author uses these qualities efficiently to raise the value of her work.

The Graduate

The Graduate highlights a complicated social problem which results from the political independence of many African states.[3] In Kenya, as in other parts, the Civil Service is dominated by Europeans, and there is the problem of putting Africans in strategic posts in order to Africanise the service. The government takes a bold step by sending Mrs Juanina Karungaru, Minister of Public Affairs, on a recruitment drive to the USA. She offers appointment to Jakoyo Seda who has initial difficulties in reaching her when he returns to Nairobi.

Using the plight of Jakoyo as background, the author raises many issues of fundamental importance. For example, how much control can the Kenyan government have over its own affairs in the face of the vested interests of Europeans? Europeans use their formidable positions in government to protect their group interests. Their first loyalty is not to the government which employs them, but to their ethnic group. They see themselves involved in a struggle for survival and will do anything, however mean, to remove any obstacles in their way. So they use their influence to block Jakoyo's appointment so that Ted may remain in his post for a little longer. The fact that Jakoyo is exceptionally well qualified is not important to them. They act to undermine government policy, conveniently set aside their oath of allegiance to their employers and generally provoke Jakoyo to the extent that he begins to regret his decision to come home in the first instance.

> He had been such a fool . . . He had been educated to use his brain. And on the first major decision he had to take in his life regarding his first job, he had made a tragic mistake. His colleagues had cautioned him to get a letter of appointment first before turning down a lecturership that covered his wife and children. He had turned his back against a legal contract, to take a verbal one which was turning out to be fake. (p.55)

The novel dramatises this conflict between Europeans and Africans. While the Africans are trying to consolidate the gains of independence, the Europeans hold tight to whatever is left of their former supremacy. This conflict is exemplified in the constant clash between Anne Brown and her assistant, Anabell Chepkwony. Mrs Brown, the confidential secretary to the minister, sees it as an essential part of her duty to protect European interests. So, she leaks all the secret information her kinsmen require to help Ted. She also makes it impossible for Jakoyo to meet the minister to discuss his appointment. Anabell quickly sees through this conspiracy, shows solidarity with her countryman and takes steps to ensure that he gets the post. In the process she improves her standing with the minister and earns for herself promotion to the rank of Personal and Confidential Secretary.

> Hon. Juanina Karungaru stood a while, looking at the girl . . . she looked mature, sensible and full of confidence. It needed a lot of courage and wisdom to hatch out that plan and execute it. She had used her talent so wisely that, even if it would take her time to match Mrs Brown's swiftness, at least she had her heart in the right place. It is her type that any minister would want as a secretary, the type that is loyal to Kenya. (p.70)

Anabell's promotion is well deserved. By her action she has shown an unflinching loyalty to her people and demonstrated the spirit of African brotherhood.

The novelist describes in some detail the psychological damage which is at times done to students abroad by the carelessness or irresponsibility of their home government. Students encounter much hardship abroad in their quest for higher education in the hope of becoming more useful citizens of their country. When they need help this is more often than not refused by the government. Ambassador Simiyu talks of the 'disillusionment, bitterness and mistrust' which such a callous attitude engenders in students. Little wonder they are reluctant to return home after their studies. This attitude may be pardonable with a colonial government, but becomes utterly indefensible with an African government which proclaims itself anxious for rapid development and increased supply of manpower. Given these circumstances, only a genuine spirit of nationalism and patriotism can move a student to leave the comfort and security of life abroad for the uncertainty of an appointment at home. This is the type of risk Jakoyo takes in what turns out to be a successful adventure.

The picture of Mrs Karungaru which emerges from the novel is that of a loyal, dedicated and patriotic minister. She works hard in the USA to win the confidence of students and gets them to agree to return home. She asserts her authority and acts promptly to defeat the attempt to block Jakoyo's appointment. She achieves positive results in parliament and uses her position to help the masses in every conceivable way. These are positive achievements which are meant to raise the status of Kenyan womanhood. The place of women in society is extensively discussed as part of the general background given to Kenyan social and political life. Mrs Karungaru's appointment is made in recognition of the noble role played by women during the Mau Mau emergency and their laudable political activities during the struggle for independence. She is a political activist, the only woman minister, who has proved particularly effective in the discharge of her duties. In placing a woman right in the centre of events in this novel and endowing her with such unlimited ability, the author may have been inspired by the feminist ideals of freedom and equality for women. The minister is offered a cabinet post by the President on equal basis with men and she uses the opportunity to the glory of her sex.

However, the author points out another aspect of Mrs Karungaru's life in which she has not been too successful. She has become remiss in her domestic duties to members of her family. One of her children, Nyokabi, recalls the adverse effect which her public duties are beginning to have on her domestic life.

> It seemed there were just too many people claiming her love and her attention that even Daddy was getting fretful, and was somehow always pushed out of the way. However hard she tried, she could not get near enough to her mother as she had always been. (p.6)

The attitude of the author, herself a mother and housewife, is clear. She strongly supports the idea of a woman holding a high public office and performing well. But she believes this should not be done at the expense of her husband and children. This is why perhaps the minister is endowed with enough energy to be able to cope with both aspects of life equally successfully.

Grace Ogot has so far published three collections of stories – *Land*

Without Thunder[4], *The Other Woman*[5] and *The Island of Tears*[6]. There are twenty-six stories altogether in these collections. Between them they cover a variety of topics which range from comments on several aspects of social and political life to a consideration of matters which have great cultural, supernatural or metaphysical significance. It has not been considered necessary to discuss each of the stories in detail. But a good many of them in each collection are critically analysed and evaluated either from the point of view of the author's approach to creativity or the ease with which she handles the various kinds of topics. The aim is to assess the value of these stories as a contribution to African Literature.

Land Without Thunder

(a) 'The Rain Came'

'The Rain Came' is one of Grace Ogot's earliest stories. She is sentimentally attached to it as it was passed down to her by her grandmother. The value of the story lies partly in the way it brings out most of the characteristics of the author's style of writing. In this story she deals with an important theme, adopts an imaginative scheme and utilises her great powers of concentration and description to put her ideas across. She also uses the techniques of conflict and comparison, humour and pathos to advantage. A song and an element of mystery are introduced at appropriate points to carry forward her artistic intentions.

The author is conscious of the limitation of space in the short story. So in this, as in the other stories, she goes direct to the subject-matter. In the first paragraph the two important characters, the chief and Oganda, the heroine, have already been presented. The problem of the villagers – the absence of rain – which the author intends to highlight has also been mentioned. Soon the reader is confronted with the enormity of the problem. The village has been without rain for a long time, and this is naturally causing great hardship to everybody. To have rain again, Oganda, the only daughter of chief Labong'o, will have to be sacrificed. So the gods have decreed. The chief is anxious that the rains come, but he is puzzled that the sacrifical lamb has to be his daughter. It is this dilemma that the author successfully dramatises.

> Never in his life had he been faced with such an impossible decision. Refusing to yield to the rainmaker's request would mean sacrificing the whole tribe, putting the interests of the individual above those of the society. More than that. It would mean disobeying the ancestors,

and most probably wiping the Luo people from the surface of the earth. On the other hand, to let Oganda die as a ransom for the people would permanently cripple Labong'o spiritually. He knew he would never be the same chief again. (p.161)

To achieve a resolution of this difficult problem the author adopts several literary devices. There is the irony of situation when the elders of the family are discussing Oganda's fate and the repercussion of her being offered as a sacrifice, but she thinks they are discussing her future marriage. There is the tense atmosphere which the author carefully builds up when Oganda's father and mother meet her to talk about her impending death. The author makes the situation extremely meaningful to the reader by the use of a sustained and descriptive proverb.

For a long time the three souls who loved one another dearly sat in darkness. It was no good speaking. And even if they tried, the words could not have come out. In the past they had been like three cooking-stones, sharing their burdens. Taking Oganda away from them would leave two useless stones which would not hold a cooking-pot. (pp.164-5)

The conflict in the story is revealed in the attitude of the people which Oganda finds basically selfish. The villagers shout:

'If it is to save the people, if it is to give us rain, let Oganda go. Let Oganda die for her people and for her ancestors.' (p.164)

They seem to be completely oblivious of the great personal agony and danger to which the girl is being exposed. She is mindful of this all the time, and it causes her mental pain and anger. She thinks her people do not love her; otherwise, they should have tried to save her. She becomes thoroughly disgusted with the whole affair during the farewell gathering the villagers arrange for her when girls of her age group get up to dance. Her mind dwells on the advantages which these girls now have over her.

They were young and beautiful, and very soon they would marry and have their own children. They would have husbands to love, and little huts for themselves. They would have reached maturity. (p.166)

So when she sings on the lonely path in the wilderness on her way to the river monster, it is a song of sorrow and contempt for her people's action. There is, again, humour arising from the action of a child who sends a small earring through Oganda to a dead relation. She, in her innocence, exposes herself to ridicule and laughter: 'when you reach the world of the dead, give this earring to my sister. She died last week. She forgot this ring.' (p.168)

141

Oganda is saved through the use of magic and fantasy. Osinda provides her with a leafy attire which, he says, has the power of protecting her 'from the eyes of the ancestors and the wrath of the monster'. (p.171) With this magic power they both escape from the forest to safety. Then, we are told, the rain came 'in torrents'. Here the reader has to suspend disbelief to go along with the author. If the gods have been so powerful as to cause the amount of anxiety and hardship we read about at the beginning of the story, how then can they be so easily defeated by a medicinal apparatus prepared by inconsequential Osinda? To make it credible, the use of magic needs to be put in a more convincing context than we have here. The author applies the power of magic and fantasy more successfully in *The Promised Land* and some of her other stories.

(b) 'Land Without Thunder'

'Land Without Thunder' is the tragic story of Owila. Misfortune followed his footstep at every stage. His boat capsizes on the lake, he knows no peace in his hometown, Agok, and even when he moves to Mombasa, the land without thunder, it makes no difference to his life.

The story derives its impact from the intervention of the gods in human affairs and the inherent contradictions in human behaviour, especially at a period of crisis. At times these two causes are so closely intertwined that they become inseparable. How does one, for example, explain the awful experiences of Owila and his cousins at the lake? They are capable fishermen and have had to contend with bad weather in the past. But this time, we are told that with a tremendous storm the canoe just breaks loose.

> The canoe became wild. The cousins let it drift where it wanted, while they battle to shovel away the hailstones that rapidly filled it. Ochuonyo, who had so far kept quiet cried out; 'What have we done to the ancestors that they should deny us the warmth of our huts?' (p.144)

The reference to the 'ancestors' is quite meaningful in the context and brings us close to the central preoccupation of the story. For there is the unmistakable impression that the gods have a hand in these matters. They may be teaching Owila a lesson for disobeying the warning not to go fishing on that particular occasion. This also explains the hallucination he continues to have in the form of the ghosts of his cousins and the fact that he remains tortured and restless.

But that can hardly fully explain the jealousy shown by relations because Owila survives the disaster while his cousins die. Nor does it throw much light on the contradiction in the behaviour of clansmen in Mombasa who start by embracing Owila – 'we cannot doubt the voice of the clan. Owila is our blood. His trouble is ours' (p.155) and later drastically change their attitude and insist that Owila should return home.

> 'Owila's cousins are angry with you,' one old man told Oyugi bluntly. 'They were bound to revenge sooner or later. Let Owila return to his hut and appease the spirits of his cousins.' (p.157)

In this story the author appears extremely anxious to emphasise the supremacy of the gods and the power they exercise over human affairs. Once Owiti has disobeyed the gods, he cannot expect help or favour from them or, indeed, from the other villagers who worship these gods. Hence his mental agony and harassment from place to place. Even when the medicine woman from Kajulu appears to be succeeding in saving him, the gods in the form of thunder destroys any hope of a positive result.

Owila's best chance of survival is in Mombasa. But here, again, fate and human intolerance are in the way. Owila's protective medicine which he carries with him from Agok is assumed to be causing horror and death in Oyugi's household. His children fall seriously sick. So his wife, Ambajo, becomes hysterical and grumbles – 'Take the medicine away from my house. I cannot bury two sons in one day.' (p.156) Oyugi becomes worried, informs the elders and they agree that Owila should leave Mombasa. So, for Owila there is no hiding place. The only indication in the story that he may ultimately regain his peace of mind is what he does at the Kisumu railway station when he returns home from Mombasa.

> Owila handed out the luggage to his cousin on the platform. He looked suspiciously at the *kikapu* containing the paraphernalia of his treatment and pushed it right into the corner of the train. If the spirits wanted it, they would find it there. (p.158)

This may well be a symbolic burden that he is throwing away and perhaps, with it, the pain and torture of his recent past. However, one cannot insist on this interpretation. The gods are so hard on Owila in this story that they may never relent.

(c) 'The Old White Witch'

'The Old White Witch' is a moving story of a rebellion by nurses in a mission hospital. Here the author utilises her knowledge as a trained nurse to include details of how a hospital should be successfully run and what things can possibly go wrong.

The conflict in the story arises from an apparent incompatibility between a group of nurses and the hospital authority as personified by Matron Jack – the old white witch. The nurses rebel against the ruling that they should carry bedpans, which the matron regards as part of the ordinary duties of any nurse. Her attitude is understandably overbearing since she regards the people as 'primitive, ignorant and irreligious'. Unfortunately the carrying of bedpans for girls has a cultural implication which Monica, their leader, puts forcibly to the matron.

'Long before you came, we agreed to nurse in this hospital on the understanding that we were not to carry bedpans. We want to be married and become mothers like any other women in the land. We are surprised that senior members of the staff have sneaked behind us to support you, when they know perfectly well that no sane man will agree to marry a woman who carries a bedpan. A special class of people do this job in our society.' (p.10)

The matron thinks that Christianity should have delivered the girls from such beliefs and refers to the situation in Britain where 'giving a bedpan to a patient was part of a nurse's job, and it was as important as feeding or bathing a patient'. (p.9) What the matron forgets is that nursing as a profession should recognise local differences.

The impression is given that nursing is linked with the Christian religion and that all beliefs and attitudes which form part of the Christian faith should automatically be reflected in nursing practice. Here the European management of the hospital appears to have gone astray. They do not seem to recognise the importance which Africans attach to cultural matters. If girls have to forgo essential elements of their culture to become nurses, then the sacrifice required of them is too great. Why, in fact, should they first have to be Christians to become good nurses? Why are the two so inexorably linked? Why should girls become cultural rejects and remain spinsters all their lives because they want to be nurses? The whole affair is badly managed by the authorities, and there is little doubt that the author's sympathy lies with the striking nurses. These girls act from a position of strength, especially as their action has brought to the surface the rift between the African and European senior members of staff.

The African members of staff did not say much. In a way they were happy that the women had gone on strike. Matron Jack had been treating them like children. They were never consulted on anything, and she was always supported, at least publicly, by her fellow Europeans. (p.20)

The weight of evidence is clearly against the European missionaries of the hospital. Even so, given the useful service they render, it will be unfortunate to disgrace them. This point must have weighed heavily in the mind of the author when writing the end of the story. She achieves an acceptable resolution of the events of the story. Monica falls ill and is brought back for treatment at the hospital which is then virtually closed to patients. With her presence, life returns to the hospital and all the various groups resume work, united in a common purpose to continue to serve humanity. Monica is reconciled to Matron Jack, and the hospital is reconciled to the community. The protest of the striking nurses has been upheld and, through it, revolutionary changes have occurred. In a dramatic action at the very end of the story Monica upholds the doctrine of peaceful co-existence and the reconciliation of all parties, which, in fact, may be the message of the author in this work.

Then, as the rain subsided, Monica gradually opened her eyes. Matron beckoned the dying girl's mother. The two looked at each other without uttering a word. Only tears on their eyes betrayed their thoughts. When Monica saw Matron Jack and Dr Joseph, she wept bitterly . . . When she stopped weeping she opened her eyes wide, and then whispered to her mother, 'Return to Father – I am staying with the Old White Witch.' (p.25)

The reader leaves the story satisfied that the foundation for peace and progress has been firmly laid and that every effort will be made by staff and management to maintain the high reputation of the hospital.

(d) 'Tekayo'

'Tekayo' is the bizarre story of Tekayo who gets so used to eating sweet livers as meat that he ends up disrupting the routine of life in his family in an attempt to procure sweet livers. From risking his life in the forest in several encounters with wild beasts to telling lies to his relations about his sudden disappearances, he ends up killing his grandchildren in order to take their livers and satisfy his savage appetite. A great crisis is created when the fact becomes known. This is how Aganda, Tekayo's first son, reports his father's misdeeds to members of the clan.

The children in this clan get sick and die. But ours disappear unburied. It was our idea to keep watch over our children that we may catch whoever steals them. For months we have been watching secretly. We were almost giving up because we thought it was probably the wratch of our ancestors that was upon us. But today I caught him . . . The man is no one else but my father. (p.59)

This speech in a way provides the climax to the events. The atmosphere is understandably charged. There is cry of 'Stone him now! Stone him now! Let his blood be upon his own head!' (p.59) As they go about preparing for the stoning ceremony, Tekayo hangs himself in his hut. Then we are told

> The men came out shaking their heads. The crowd peered into the hut in turn until all of them had seen the dangling body of Tekayo – the man they were preparing to stone. No one spoke. Such a man, they knew, would have to be buried outside the village. (pp.60-61)

The story is well told. The author sufficiently prepares the reader's mind for the tragic end of Tekayo. Once he becomes addicted to eating sweet livers, he will stop at nothing to procure them. He spends many days and nights in the Ghost Jungle, and has dreadful encounters with dangerous animals. Yet he is not persuaded to give up his preference for livers. 'The vehement desire within him blindly drove him on.' (p.50) After the death of his beloved wife, Lakech, it looks as if he will give up his blind desire. But the craving soon returns powerfully to him. After this stage nothing can now save Tekayo. His tragic role must be fully acted out. As with many tragic figures, his death is not only a personal tragedy; it also has repercussions for the whole community.

Consider, for example, the amount of gloom and uncertainty he leaves behind in the village. For Tekayo's offence he ought to be stoned to death as part of a ritual performance to cleanse the village and drive his evil spirit away. The author emphasises how important this is.

> Everyone in the clan must throw a stone at the murderer. It was bad not to throw a stone, for it was claimed that the murderer's wicked spirit would rest upon the man who did not help to drive him away. (p.60)

Tekayo forestalls this ceremony by committing suicide. How can the village be purified now without the ceremony of stoning? How can villagers be reassured that the evil spirit of Tekayo has left the village? Suicide itself calls for its own kind of purification. Nothing is said about the steps needed to accomplish this. True, we are told, 'that no new-born child would ever be named after him'. (p.61) Is that also a guarantee that no child will take after him?

One cannot help feeling that Tekayo represents a powerful scourge on the village. His original sin is unpardonable – he snatches a liver from a flying eagle, thereby depriving the poor bird of its meal and existence. From this incident he develops his mighty appetite for livers, which finally leads to disaster. The intention may be to emphasise the dreadful consequences that usually follow any act of cruelty to lower animals. Tekayo has paid his full penalty. But the innocent villagers should not suffer as a result. There is therefore a need for comprehensive purification both for the unusual nature of Tekayo's crimes and for the fact that he commits suicide. Only then can the villagers feel free to go about their daily work and play without the fear of molestation by the gods of their ancestors.

(e) 'Karantina'

'Karantina' is a social comment on the awful experiences travellers occasionally have. Dora and her friends are fascinated by the beauty and attractions of Cairo – 'the gate to the Orient, half African half Arab'. (p.65) So they decide to make a brief stop there on their way to Europe. What difficulties they encounter in Cairo and how they try to overcome them provide the material for the story.

The author uses Dora, the main character, to show how many obstacles unsympathetic officials can put in the way of travellers. Cairo airport officials are described as rude and abrupt in their treatment of passengers. Therefore they cannot be moved to show any consideration for Dora. Furthermore, they appear ignorant and unable to grasp the international dimensions of their work. For example, they insist on Egyptian money to the exclusion of any other valid international currency.

> Angelina pulled out a five pound note from her handbag and gave it to the man.
> 'Let him take what he wants, and you can refund it to me later.'
> 'What is this?' the man asked aggressively.
> 'Money,' Angelina said with sullen defiance.
> 'Not this,' the man threw the note back to her. 'I want Egyptian money – your money no value.'
> 'But what do we do? We have no Egyptian money.' Tears started in Angelina's eyes. (p.67)

The author's description of the situation in Karantina (quarantine) shows the amount of oppression of innocent individuals which goes on with official sanction. The inmates are treated like criminals and denied any kind of basic freedom. They are subjected to appalling living conditions. The whole place is filthy, and the inhabitants are ordered

147

around like school children. Even the porter issues commands which any inmate can only ignore at his own peril.

'If you want supper at night – pay now. Supper comes at ten o'clock. Only 99 piastres – pay now. I give you receipt – or else no supper.' (p.84)

The height of callousness is reached in the case of an old man, an Angolan refugee, who is being famished to death in the quarantine. They refuse to accept his money. So he cannot buy food and has had to depend on the generosity of others. His fate leads one to wonder whether the quarantine is conceived of as a health institution or a place of torture. If an old man, a refugee who is already undergoing a lot of physical and mental pain, a fellow African, can be treated in this way, then nobody is safe. Such a treatment of an African by another African establishment undermines the concept of the OAU and all that it has been trying to achieve. It certainly shakes Dora's faith in humanity and civilised behaviour.

The whole world is paying lip service to brotherhood of mankind – that is what it is. These people are no brothers to anyone. (p.83)

But all is not tragedy, all is not horror. The author uses some of the characters to show that, even in a difficult situation, people still show kindness to one another. So we note that Angelina and other friends do all they can to get Dora out of the quarantine, and when they fail, they take measures to reduce the harshness of her stay. Banale helps to solve some of Dora's immediate financial problems and acts as a faithful companion inside the quarantine. To kill time the two launch into a lengthy discussion of marriage during which Banale gives an ingenious explanation of honeymoon.

'When the European girls took to eating the forbidden fruit in a big way, they could not stay home to face their inquisitive relatives. So the idea of honeymoon was born. Today it is regarded as one of the hallmarks of a civilised wedding.' (p.79)

So we find that the story makes comments on several aspects of life – the erring officials at the airport, the sadists working at the quarantine, friends who help one another out in times of difficulty and youngsters who adopt the wrong attitude to marriage.

(f) 'The White Veil'

'The White Veil' is a love story between Owila and Achola which almost goes sour because of the rigidity of Achola and the intervention of

148

Felomena. Achola loves Owila dearly. Even so, she will not allow him to go to bed with her before marriage because of the demands of custom. Owila becomes restless and insists on what he considers his right. But Achola's faithfulness to tradition is such that she finds her hands tied by the tribal commandment which says

> A girl must be a virgin on the day of her marriage. This is the greatest honour she can bestow upon the man she is marrying and upon her parents. (p.120)

Owila deserts Achola for Felomena, but this affair comes to nothing in the end.

The author, as usual, uses the story to raise issues of social and cultural significance. There is the comparison between African and European social demands as regards the relationship between a boy and a girl before marriage. There is also an inherent conflict between indigenous culture and modern life, between Bible commandments and tribal commandments. The relationship between Achola and Owila is compared frequently with that between John and Jenny who are British. Owila is John's friend, and John encourages him to demand sex from Achola, as he sleeps regularly with his girlfriend, Jenny. This is why Owila feels cheated and leaves Achola for a girl who is free with sex. What he forgets is that the cultural demands of Europe and Africa are different, and that in a tribal society there is a limit to which one can assert one's individuality and independence. Achola's stand on this matter is culturally sound and praiseworthy. Furthermore she has a clear vision of the role she is playing to uphold the dignity of African womanhood. She will not allow herself to be diverted from a right course by the unacceptable behaviour of Jenny.

> She had made up her mind. It was all very well for Miss Hannington to give. But she was lucky because she was a European. Perhaps her people did not demand the bedsheet to be returned to the grandmother the day after the wedding. (p.120)

Achola is justified in the end. Not only is she commended for her behaviour by a priestess: 'You are a noble woman. Unlike other educated women, you have not taken to the white man's way. The god of our ancestors will reward you', (p.130) she ends up marrying Owila.

But Achola's achievement is not without its contradictions. Given the strength of her love for Owila, it ought to have been possible for them to get married without the complications that are introduced into this story. Achola's love seems to control her every word and deed. When Owila changes his attitude to her, the difference it makes to her life becomes obvious for all to see. The author elaborates in detail the physical and psychological deterioration of the girl.

> Achola had long miserable days and touchy sleepless nights that robbed her of the health and gaiety of youth. She had never known sorrow to this extent . . . This was a kind of sickness that was eating all her heart away, burying the past and blotting out the future she had so carefully planned. People who saw her walking thought she was alive, yet in her heart Achola knew she was a sick woman, moving in a big town among thousands of people without really seeing them. (p.122)

Why does a girl who is sincerely in love have to pass through all this mental agony to win her man? Why should it be necessary for her to seek the help of a priestess? The author leaves these questions unanswered. Instead she creates a long period of suspense when the reader is kept guessing how the problem of two possible bribes for one wedding will be resolved. The resolution comes in a sustained irony which makes it possible for priest, Owila and congregation to mistake Achola for Felomena. By the time Felomena arrives, Owila and Achola are already man and wife. What we have can hardly be called a happy wedding, but it is sufficiently valid to enable Achola to be married in her heart to the man she has always loved. This is a tangible reward for her stout defence of an important aspect of traditional culture.

The Other Woman

The Other Woman is Grace Ogot's second collection of short stories. There are nine stories in the collection, a few of them very long. They are not substantially different in content and orientation from the stories in the first collection. But, as will become obvious, the author's techniques are becoming more sophisticated and her topics more broadly-based and varied. Because of space it is not considered necessary to discuss all the stories in detail. Only five of them are briefly considered below, with the limited aim of bringing out the distinctive features of each story.

In 'The Middle Door' the author employs her well-known devices of direct narration, conflict, tension and humour. The story starts with Mrs Muga in a state of tension hurrying to catch a train for Kisumu and not knowing where her husband is. Such a mental strain at the beginning of a journey hardly portends good. Little wonder she is in conflict with practically everybody she reacts with throughout the journey.

150

The story is built on conflict, which reaches its dramatic height with Mrs Muga's encounters with two policemen who are travelling on the train with her. These constables are supposed to provide security for travellers, but paradoxically they harass Mrs Muga and insist on having sex with her.

'You give it to other men – who give you money. We must have it too, with or without money. Look at your painted nails. Look at your hair and polished face. You are not married to one man, we know it. The type married to one man are the ones like the woman you chased away from your compartment. The simple housewife. Not you.' (p.31)

Undoubtedly the intention of the author is to satirise the police force. These constables are ignorant, uncouth and given to the use of vulgar language. They show disrespect to a decent married woman and deliberately cause her great annoyance. In the violent confrontation which ensues they show how cowardly they are by piping down at the sight of a gun pointed at them by the woman. They make themselves an object of ridicule at the police station when it is discovered that what terrified life out of them is a toy gun, not live ammunition. Certainly these two men are a disgrace to the police force. They cannot be relied upon to provide protection for the citizens or impartially enforce law and order.

The clash between Mrs Muga and the woman who shares her compartment with her for some time is on a somewhat smaller scale. But it is used by the author to highlight a few important issues. These touch on the existence of class differences in society and how independence has brought a feeling of freedom and equality to the common man. The woman comes into the compartment with a bunch of bananas and a cock. The situation is inconvenient for Mrs Muga who wants to get on with her writing, undisturbed. The woman ignores Mrs Muga and, in fact, shows some irriation at her supercilious attitude. She insists on her rights and feels justified in her stand because of her contribution to Kenya's struggle for independence.

Where were you at the time when I and my kind nursed the wounded men during the struggle for Independence? Where were you when we went without food and water? You rich woman, when we carried the little food we could steal to feed our men, where were you? And what do you know about dying or sacrificing for a nation? Now you are proud because you are educated. You can write books. You have good clothes, Yes. You are proud, But it is not my choice that I am a village woman, it is fate. (pp.21-22)

This clash shows all the signs of a class struggle between the proletariat and the bourgeoisie. The woman considers Mrs Muga as a parasite on society, reaping plentifully where she has not sown. To Mrs Muga the woman is no more than a piece of nuisance which should be disposed of quickly. Given the way the matter is amicably resolved, the author may be wishing to stress the need always for compromise and accommodation, the paramount necessity for peaceful co-existence in a society where everybody, high or low, plays his part for the benefit of all. This is what makes the title of the story particularly meaningful.

'The Other Woman' emphasises the need for mutual love between husband and wife if a stable married life is to be maintained. A distinctive feature of this story is the way the author achieves a delicate balance between the conflicting claims of husband and wife. She appears more impartial here than in 'The Wayward Father'. No attempt is made to heap all the blame on the man. Nor is the woman prevented from asserting her individuality. The situation augurs well for the display of equality between the two partners, Jerry and Jedidah. Both are well educated and occupy important public positions. They earn reasonably good salaries and live comfortably. Their only problem is that the wife gets so busy with her public duties that she usually has little time for her domestic life. Then the husband has to fend for himself. What he does at such times is not always edifying or morally defensible. The story dramatises this conflict of interest which results in Jerry's sinister love for house girls. When matters finally get out of hand the author leaves no one in doubt that Jedidah has unwittingly put herself in the wrong.

> The image of Anna Jura seemed to stand temporarily between Jedidah and her Jerry. Jedidah remembered Anna's words, 'When you have no time for him, he will go to another woman.' (p.58)

The author provides in this story conditions which lead to the success or failure of marriages. She stresses the need for both parties to invest emotionally in the home and cherish each other. In this connection Anna is the voice of wisdom, the medium through which some stability is brought into the Oda family. She advises her friend, Jedidah, frankly on the important part sex plays in sustaining a happy marriage and that her role in this respect needs to be more positive. When Jedidah tries the new approach Jerry becomes a changed man, settles down to a quiet domestic life and concentrates more on his hobby, painting. There are frequent confessions of love and adoration on both sides. Husband and wife enjoy matrimonial bliss for as long as it lasts.

> 'I am lucky to possess the whole of you – you who are nothing but

152

loveliness. Your skin in smoother than the surface of a pearl; your sleepy eyes have the beauty of water lilies; and your features, or to use technical terms, your contours, are as delicate as those of a wild antelope. Continue to love me as you do now, Jedy.' (p.50)

Such a panegyric is possible only when both lovers have the highest regard for each other.

As is at times the case with this author, the climax of the story comes at the end. Jerry gets round again to his old game of putting house girls in the family way. First, it is Achola. Now it is the new girl, Taplalai. There is a dreadful encounter between the girl and Jerry who tries to rape her. Into this serious situation the author introduces some humorous episodes through which the girl succeeds in making her master look ridiculus. She stands for the sanctity of married life and the highest dictates of traditional morality. However, because her life is in danger she allows Jerry to have his way. The author reserves a lot of creative energy for the last scene where Jerry is found in bed with Taplalai. The successful detective technique she employs is directly conveyed to the reader by her detailed description.

She glanced at her watch. It was about 11.00 a.m. She tiptoed bare-footed towards the bedrooms. Her bedroom door stood open. Voices from the guest room greeted her ears. She drew closer. She heard a woman moan. A man grunted as though engaged in some laborious job. Enraged by what she heard, Jedidah drew the knife from her bag and flung open the door. Her eye rested on what very few human beings ever witness in their life-time. (p.57)

Confusion and uncertainty follow this scene. Fortunately out of this chaos later develops an atmosphere of calm from which Jedidah and Jerry can piece together the remains of their married life.

In 'The Honourable Minister' the author pursues her interest in city life and shows what makes it inferior in quality to village life. The heroine, June, has recently moved from the village to the town and initially intends to retain her village virtues. She finds she can only achieve this if she is willing to remain poor in the midst of plenty. This she is not willing to do. It is this conflict in June and the way she tries to resolve it that the author highlights in the story.

So long as June upholds rural virtues and norms, she seems happy and safe. However, she soon becomes discontented with a simple successful married life with Jared. She is consumed by the desire to own a house like her sister Alice and live a glorious life. The Coffee Group is used as the instrument of her moral degradation. The secretary of the group, Amelia Waswa, makes sure the voice of conscience in June is silenced and acts as the devil incarnate. She puts before June an easy, but dishonourable, way of achieving a comfortable life. June soon becomes dissatisfied with herself and decides to start a new life.

> In my present natural look, no man was going to look at me and be tempted. For very few men in Nairobi cared for women in their natural beauty. Nairobi was a city of over-worked men who needed artificiality to stimulate them. Nature was a thing of the past: beauty of the olden days was only left in the rural areas where life was relaxed and men enjoyed the original charm of women. (p.91)

June is now cut off from her roots and has broken faith with nature and traditional virtues which alone nourish the soul and keep man away from the temptations of the city. It is not surprising therefore that as from this point she begins to deteriorate morally until she becomes a social disgrace at the end of the story.

The relationship between June and Kim Mawanga, Minister of Housing, is central to the author's preoccupation of showing how city life destroys. When June meets Kim at a party, she is a relatively honest, humble and respectable housewife. But once the Minister promises a new house, she debases herself to please him. The author shows incisive knowledge of city life and rightly devotes a lot of space to June's moral degeneration. Her subsequent meetings with Kim are intended to show the stages she passes through in her capitulation to evil. However, the author is also careful not to portray her as a reckless city adulteress or a woman without a conscience. After all, she is a new member of the Coffee Club and will need at least a few years of practice to achieve the expertise of older members like Amelia. So she is allowed to exercise a keen conscience and an awareness of the moral issues involved in her illegal connection with Kim. Therefore, even at the end, when she goes to meet him for a weekend rendenzvous, the voice of conscience in her is still alive.

> I clenched my suitcase and walked confidently to the reception desk. 'Oh June!' the voice within me cried. 'Don't have any dealings with this Minister, turn back to the road and take a bus to your home. Your body is the temple of God.' But I shook the voice away from me. 'A woman whose body is the temple of God has no place in the city and there cannot be many of that type of women anywhere nowadays.' (p.110)

June's conscience is now mortgaged to the evils of the city. She will buy a house of her own and establish herself in luxurious comfort as a member of the Coffee Club. But she will achieve this status at a high price. She will lose not only her peace of mind but also the security and respect which only a happy domestic life can give. This, almost certainly, is the message of the story.

'The Family Doctor' shows the author's continuing interest in the welfare of city dwellers. The story concentrates on the problem of medical care, especially the difficulty of obtaining quick and adequate medical help when one needs it. Minya is sick, and the mother, Asuna, tries in vain to secure the services of a doctor at home or in hospital. The author intentionally magnifies her problems by putting every imaginable obstacle in the way. Her husband is away and none of the four doctors she contacts is immediately available. The hospital is not in position to give even a temporary relief. The child is at the point of death. As we are told,

> Minya had developed acute pneumonia. The middle lobe of the right lung was almost collapsed. He knew it would be a great struggle to isolate the infection to stop it from spreading to the other lung. (p.138)

It is against this gloomy background that one must consider Asuna's restless effort to save her son. The mental strain is enormous.

> Her eyes had not known any sleep, and fatigue was beginning to numb her limbs. Numerous bad thoughts came and went and she felt like a person under persecution. Why were her children never well? Was the house cursed or was she being punished for her past sins? And what were these sins? Many children from poor homes went about naked, scavenging from dustbin to dustbin. They never seemed to fall ill. But hers who were well-fed and well-clad were permanently sick! (p.134)

Asuna introduces a metaphysical element into the whole affair. Why is there no doctor readily available to help Minya? Is it because of the poor state of health care delivery or sheer hard luck? Why is his 'acute pneumonia' proving difficult to cure when several of such cases have been cured in the recent past? Is some evil spirit visiting the household to make life difficult for everybody? Is there an ancestral sin to atone for? The story pays a lot of attention to the mysterious aspect of the situation. Dr Jasinda gives every kind of medical help to Minya, but he does not improve. Finally he considers the boy a hopeless case and gives up. The parents are confused and sorrowfully wait for the inevitable end. Then the mother suddenly decides to go down on her knees and pray to God.

> Asuna closed her eyes tightly till the skin around her eyelids ached. 'God,' she whispered. 'Please listen to me: Please look down now — and let your eyes shine on my son. Extend your hands now, and touch my

son. You took away the son of the widow in the Old Testament, but you gave it back to her alive . . .' (p.141)

After this the boy gradually recovers from his illness.

This process of recovery leaves many questions unanswered. Does the boy get better because of his mother's prayer or as a result of the cumulative effect of Dr Jasinda's close attention or a combination of both forces? The metaphysical argument is tenable because Asuna has spoken of the possibility of a curse on the family. If this is the case, Western medicine is not the answer. An alternative may lie in traditional medicine, the use of supernatural powers or a ritual appeasement of the ancestral gods. Instead of all these, Asuna decides to turn to God, itself an act which requires a good deal of faith and spiritual energy. It may be the intention of the author to emphasise the part played by faith and the supernatural in African life. However, the way the story ends it is clear there is no intention to disgrace western medicine. Dr Jasinda returns to re-establish himself as the family doctor, regain the confidence of the sick boy who acknowledges his help and writes with great delight 'a case history of this child who had miraculously come back to life'. (p.144) Furthermore, he decides not to charge any amount for his services. This certainly is an excellent example of where faith has been used successfully to complement the work of medical science.

'Fishing Village' is a short complex story of Ojuka who overreaches himself in the village and escapes to Kisumu. In the Fishing Village he causes hardship to various people and is generally given to mischief. The author utilises his lack of seriousness to demonstrate how human talent can be wasted. He devotes his energy to cheating his people, and enjoys making them look ridiculous. He robs Ombara of two oxen and sets the whole village ablaze with suspicion and worry. From this event several ironical situations develop. The people after a brief initial period of sympathy come to the conclusion that 'Ombara is very rich. He is the man to offer a sacrifice for the well-being of the village'. (p.182) The author derives humour from this situation which is essentially tragic, thus appearing to make light of the matter.

So that is how it was. While Ombara and his family mourned, and while the tribal police put road blocks and searched for the stolen oxen, the Fishing Village was devouring the meat from the slaughtered oxen under Ombara's own roof! (p.182)

It is the same kind of humour one gets when Ojuka decides to pay his barber only one shilling instead of two because half of his head is bald, or when he leaves his relations in the lurch after a meal at the Lake Restaurant.

156

The story seems to be constructed on some vague principles of retributive justice. Ojuka does a lot of harm in the village among illiterate people and runs to the town for a better life. He is, however, full of regrets for his past life.

> He was educated well enough to get a good job, lead a respectable life and earn his family a good name as many other educated men had done. Of course, he had secured a well-paid job as a clerk for two months, but he had given it up. It was too boring to be shut up with files all day long. What he has done since that time was to earn money through deceit and give his family a bad name in the land. (p.188)

What one would have expected is that he will now settle down to a purposeful life in town. He makes a good start, gets a satisfactory job and tries to socialise with the people by arranging a party. But this is brought to an abrupt and disgraceful end by robbers. So he is paid in his own coin to atone part of the evil he has done to villagers. We observe here an interplay of different kinds of conflicts – conflict between rich and poor, village and town, honest and dishonest people. To have contained all these within so short a story is no mean achievement on the part of the author.

The Island of Tears

This is the last of Grace Ogot's collections of stories which are treated in this book. There are five stories in this collection and each of them symbolically underlines the theme of loss and national bereavement. It is sufficient to show how the author pursues this theme in two of the stories.

'The Wayward Father' concentrates on how the father brings disgrace to his wife and children by having extra-marital affairs with another woman. The author highlights the damage at personal and family levels which this practice, which is becoming widespread in Africa, does to the fabric of society. In this case not only does it tear husband and wife apart, it also upsets the children and makes the family an object of ridicule in the community.

The author loads the dice too heavily against Mika. The impression given of him is that of an unthinking, reckless and selfish father who cares little about the health and progress of his children. No reason is given why he takes to the streets and decides to desert a home he has worked so hard to make comfortable. Even when in the end the man shows maturity and decides in favour of his family

157

'Anastasia . . . I have made up my mind. I will stick it with you and the children . . . I . . . will find a way of telling the girl that I have changed my mind.' (p.20)

He is given no credit for his action, even though there is an indication that this will lead to reconciliation. The picture of Mika is too bleak to be convincing. The reader might have been given a little of the background against which he acts instead of portraying him as an irresponsible and thoughtless man who goes to his daughter's hostel, of all places, to pick a female student.

The story is told from the point of view of Anastasia, and she is given an advantage which Mika, the other party to the dispute, does not have. She is allowed to sit in judgement over her husband, describe his activities as a playboy and pontificate on the effect this is now having on her and the children. For example, she dwells extensively on the increasing lack of fulfilment and spiritual satisfaction in her family life.

Something was terribly wrong with her and Mika, but she could not put a finger on it. All she knew was that Mika had unusual contentment within him, which seemed to have taken away the hunger he always had for her . . . To a woman this formed the foundation of a joy, dearer to her than material gains. And between them grew an inner and deeper affection, blending into oneness that money, power, or even age could not purchase. (p.8)

And when Mika's affair with the student becomes known, she takes the opportunity of her daughter's reaction to put forward an offensive type of feminist propaganda.

Man was cursed by God, my child even the most loved and most respectable husband will have no shame in dragging the family name in sordid mud. It is the lot of all women however dignified, and you will learn that soon enough when you are married. (p.15)

We do not have enough information about Anastasia for us to accept her as the paragon of virtue she is made out to be. There is no indication that she has been a marvellous housewife and mother, the type that will continue to command her husband's attention and love.

As may well be expected, the author upholds the sanctity of marriage. She considers marriage against the background of Christian doctrine and the traditional beliefs and attitudes of the Luo people. It is for this reason that she pays little attention to the fate of the student who is carrying a child for Mika. This attitude also accounts for the suggestion that the projected marriage between Amondi and Dr Ouma

158

based, as it is, on mutual love and family consent will be successful and fruitful. Again, in avoiding a violent confrontation between Mika and his children the author makes it possible for the family to start a new life and live down the disgrace of the past.

'The Island of Tears' dramatises the sense of bereavement which people all over the world felt at the death of Tom Mboya. The author concentrates activities on Rusinga Island, Mboya's homeland, where the islanders are paralysed by the loss. The people have good reasons for their display of affection. Mboya has been very useful to them. He has built them schools, hospitals and roads. He has encouraged them to embrace modern methods of farming. He has given them electricity and piped water. He has even introduced a ferry service to carry people and vehicles to the mainland. He has been a successful politician on the national and international levels and made his people great before the nation and the world. He has devoted his whole life to doing public good and raised the status of Kenya in international affairs. All these are positive achievements which are appreciated by the people.

To Kenyans, Mboya was one of the greatest men who had ever been born by a woman. To the world beyond the seas, he was a symbol of stability, unity and peace. To the Lake Region people he was a warrior and a hero. But to the Rusinga people Mboya Rateng was a legendary name. Often they only referred to him as 'the son of the sister of Odhiambo'. He appeared to have been blessed by God of the mighty waters, so that he made blades of grass grow where there was nothing before. (p.64)

So the nation mourns, and all roads lead to Rusinga Island where Mboya is to be buried. The author concentrates her narrative energy on the funeral rites and the part played by the islanders and visitors from other parts of Kenya. Even external nature is made to participate in the burial of this national hero. Lake Victoria registers its protest with mighty waves which lash against the walls of the island. Fishes in the water lose their composure and fall on dry land. As a mark of respect for the dead activities of every kind cease for some time and life itself appears to be at standstill. In moving prose the author brings to the reader this scene of desolation and despair.

The little mud huts and the once dignified houses of cement and corrugated iron roofs stood desolate like abandoned ruins. Here hungry dogs barked. Here also chickens pecked aimlessly, now and again tilting their heads as though listening to some sacred words denied to the children of men. There cows heavy with milk roamed

159

about with their calves in their wake, to suck what men had rejected. The fires in these houses had died out the previous night, leaving only the ashes and some stubborn logs which had remained unscathed. The water pots were dry . . . (p.55)

So great is the grief that the tears shed are enough to sink the island. Thanks to the angels who in their benevolence prevent this. Men and the gods combine to pay tributes to the assassinated man of the people.

The author pays close attention to details. Apart from providing a gloomy situation of general lamentation, the parts attributed to the closest relations of the dead are realistic in the circumstance. Mboya's mother, father and wife are understandably broken-hearted and uncommunicative. When the mother finds her voice, she cries out in agony to the gods: 'What did I do among women to deserve this? Who killed my son? Who nipped the flower of my womb in the bud?' (p.60) The father's life, we are told 'had gone with his beloved son, leaving only a shadow that was unaware of its surrounding'. (p.60). The widow, Pamela, introduces an element of mystery into the whole affair.

She pulled out a precious ring from her bosom where it had been kept warm by her own blood, and tenderly put it on her husband's finger. She pulled out a very thick letter from the same place and gave it to her daughter.
'Put this in Daddy's pocket – he will read it when he gets home.' (p.65)

The content of the letter will forever remain a secret between herself and her husband. What is clear for all to see is the open testimony of people of all walks of life that Tom Mboya has lived a good life, brought glory and honour to his fatherland in life and in death and, more importantly, that his assassination is a victory, not a defeat. For, from all available evidence, he has gone to join the saints.

There he would dwell in high places, beyond the reach of darkness, and bathe in the glory of the sun. Neither do people there sow, nor reap the seeds of the earth; and in that land, there would be no wrangling for positions or fight for power. Like the birds of the air, and lilies of the fields, they will need no roofs above their heads, nor log fires for the night. There, Mboya Rateng' would be made an elder among the ancestors, before being permitted to sit with the saints. (p.61)

It is hardly possible for the author to write a greater tribute than this or even achieve the narrative density of this story in another context.

Grace Ogot is one of Africa's most efficient prose writers. She started writing early and has remained in the forefront ever since. She specialises in the short story of which she has been the greatest exponent. She has used this medium to discuss matters of profound human interest like marriage and family life, the role of the woman in the African society, childbearing and mothercare, traditional beliefs, especially as they affect women, and the impact of Western culture on African rural life. In recent years she has written two books of historical fiction in which she delves into the history of the Luo people to show what relevance the past has on the present. Her stories adapted for the stage have proved extremely popular in the cities and rural areas of Kenya.

By her writing Grace Ogot has not only brought pleasure and satisfaction to many readers, she has also set a high standard of artistic performance from which young female writers can benefit. They will find her pre-occupation with the African woman and family edifying, and her style lucid and attractive. She is particularly proficient in the use of verbal art. She integrates oral tradition into the living situations of her stories, especially in those scenes set in the rural areas. This gives her works the necessary authenticity. For as F.B. Welbourn has said,

'... By any standards, Grace Ogot is a very good writer of short stories; and her themes range from traditional occasions, through mission hospitals in colonial days, to the problems of sophisticated Africans at an Egyptian airport and the tragedy of young girls in contemporary Nairobi ... She manages to write from the inside of traditional Luo society, so that it comes to life in a wholly new way.'[7]

Furthermore, her works are capable of reawakening in readers, especially female readers, the memory of the life they lived in infancy, and make them examine how firm their grasp of cultural matters is. Such an assessment is made easy by the fact that most of her heroines are ordinary people, sometimes gifted, but not fighters or revolutionaries. On city life she shows the experience of an observant woman. She puts her finger on items which make city life inferior in quality to rural life – avarice, greed, corruption, sexual laxity. Once she takes a fault she dramatises it in such a way that the danger in that attitude of mind or approach to life becomes obvious. She combines realism with frankness in pointing out the foibles in society. In *The Graduate*, for example, all the difficulties put in the way of Jakoyo by Europeans and fellow Africans are realistic in the context and point to an unpardonable weaknesses in human nature. By consistently calling attention to these faults, she is directly advocating reform.

Grace Ogot's writings have achieved international recognition. Her works are in undergraduate and post-graduate programmes of many universities. An impressive number of theses have been written on them.[8] In an interview granted to Bernth Lindfors in 1976 she points the way forward for the future of East African writing.[9]

'The direction of East African Literature will be guided by the social, economic and political trends in each partner state. I can see the trends of writings in Kenya hitting deep into the economic struggle between the haves and have-nots, the employed and unemployed, the conflict between the youth and the older generation. Again, the desire to dig into the past and resuscitate our treasured oral literature and folktales is strong. Yet Tanzanian Literature will no doubt lean on the Tanzanian brand of socialism and Ujamaa settlements, and Ugandan Literature will lean more towards the country's economic and political situation. But as no society is static, its Literature will no doubt move and change with it.[10]

There can be no doubt that Grace Ogot will be part of this progress and change.

Notes

1 Interview between Grace Ogot and Oladele Taiwo at the New Stanley Hotel, Kimathi Street, Nairobi on 3 February, 1982.
2 Grace Ogot, *The Promised Land* (East African Publishing House, Nairobi, 1966). 1974 Reprint. All page references are to this edition.
3 Grace Ogot, *The Graduate* (Uzima Press Ltd., Nairobi, 1980). All page references are to this edition.
4 Grace Ogot, *Land Without Thunder* (East African Publishing House, Nairobi, 1968). All page references are to this edition.
5 Grace Ogot, *The Other Woman* (Transafrica Publishers Ltd., Nairobi, 1976). All page references are to this edition.
6 Grace Ogot, *The Island of Tears* (Uzima Press Ltd., Nairobi, 1980). All page references are to this edition.
7 F. B. Welbourne in *African Affairs* Vol.69, no.275, April, 1970 quoted in Hans Zell and Helene Silver, *A Reader's Guide to African Literature* (Heinemann, London, 1972), p.49.
8 See, for example, 'The African Woman in Grace Ogot's Work' – a thesis submitted for the degree of M. A. in July, 1978 to the University of Burundi by Miss M. Callixta.
9 Interview in Nairobi on 13 August, 1976 published in *Mazungumzo – Interviews with East African Writers, Publishers, Editors and Scholars*, Bernth Lindfors, ed. Papers in International Studies, Africa series No.41 (Ohio University Centre for International Studies, Africa Programme, 1980, Athens, Ohio) pp.123-133.
10 *Mazungumzo*, pp.131-2.

CHAPTER SEVEN

Miriam Were
and Miriam Tlali

This chapter is devoted to the works of two novelists – Miriam Were from Kenya and Miriam Tlali from South Africa. The novelists write from the standpoint of their social circumstances and orientation to life, and concentrate on problems of immediate concern to their people and community.

Miriam Were is interested in the problems of growth. She analyses in her first two novels those factors which impede or facilitate human development. Her hero's career is traced from the primary to secondary school so that she can provide an insight into the physical and mental strains, the hopes and aspirations, which many boys and girls of his age will encounter at this stage. The emphasis is placed on education which is vital for success in life. The other novels deal with several aspects of life in Kenya's Western Province. The culture of the people is, as it were, put on display. Through the use of conflict between the various clans and religions, between the young and the old, she is able to expose a culture in a state of transition, a situation in which the hold of customary laws and tradition on the people is becoming weak.

Miriam Tlali writes in different circumstances. She displays an incisive knowledge of the application of the vicious doctrine of apartheid to the blacks in South Africa. Her two novels concentrate on the inhumanity and cruelty of this system, the complete denial of human rights to the blacks and the consequences of such a denial as manifested in the Soweto riots of 1976. She describes in detail the institutional arrangements which are designed to make the blacks second-class citizens in their own country and discusses the effectiveness of some of the measures African are taking to fight the obnoxious laws of apartheid.

The Boy in Between

The Boy in Between is a biography which concentrates on the mental and physical development of Namunyu.[1] He finds that he is a boy between two sets of children and decides that 'he was not going to stay forever squeezed between the two camps'. (p.7) What gives him a sense of direction and purpose is that he formulates very early in life an academic ambition to become a Makererean. He makes it a cardinal principle to achieve this ambition. He works extremely hard at home and in school to remove all obstacles in the way. He displays academic brilliance in his school work and he is highly respected by the other boys. Although he is from an economically depressed background, he socialises very easily with boys from poor and rich families, and finally succeeds in bringing the various groups together under his leadership. He turns his position of the boy in between at home into one of enormous advantage at school.

> So thus, even at school, Namunyu became the boy in between; not completely of the Dorm A class yet not of the Dorm B group either. His free movement between the two dormitories, invitations to boys in B to visit him, began to bridge the gap between the two groups. Some of the boys went with him to Dorm B and thus mingling took place. (p.51)

This sets the pattern for his life in school. He brings about solidarity among his classmates at the Mission School and at the Government Secondary School he helps to bring to an end the painful initiation rites for new students by the senior boys. He is bent on using education as a means of overcoming the disadvantages of an unenviable home background and of attaining great social heights.

> 'I am just discovering the funny thing about academic life. It is like climbing a mountain with the top of the peak in sight. And then when you get to that peak, you find that you are at the bottom of another peak!' (p.101)

The novelist puts Namunyu in a situation where he can prove his mettle. The boy attends good schools where he is not only encouraged to pass examinations, but is also given a solid general preparation for life. He is exposed to good and experienced teachers, and a respectable spiritual mentor like Rev. Goodley. He also has the advantage of the direction and supervision of Miss Gleam who is in charge of health and cleanliness. This is a formidable tutorial staff capable of moulding in a purposeful way the life of any boy who is willing to follow instruction. Between them they create an atmosphere in which learning thrives. From this Namunyu derives maximum advantage. He is skilful in playing football, volleyball and tenniquoit. He takes an active part in the provision of manual labour whether as a form of exercise or for monetary reward. He plays a crucial role among the boys, especially in times of crisis. For example, he helps to find a solution to the food crisis in the school and, by siding with Nwanga against Nguri, he becomes the hero of the monos. School activities involve not only classroom work, but other items like plays, parties and visits. In this way all teachers and students have an opportunity of full participation. What emerges of the novelist's portrayal of school life is a credible picture of staff and students attempting to live a happy corporate life in spite of difficulties.

The novelist's approach is on the whole affectionate and sympathetic. There is no attempt to play down the difficulties of running a school or the problems of social adjustment which come with movement up the educational ladder. The author realises that boys will play pranks and that they will often look for easy ways out of difficult situations. Some of these attempts look ridiculous or pathetic while others are seemingly successful. For example, the boys trick their master that they have completed their digging work when, in fact, they have merely covered the plot with soil; the boys make a public outing of the teacher's order that they should carry grass to a private residence, causing great excitement and uproar in the village; to alleviate their hunger some of the boys leave the school premises without permission and go in search of berries which the teacher eventually confiscates and throws into the latrine. Nguri provokes laughter when in desperation he curses the teacher – 'He must die. No one can throw food in a latrine and live.' (p.60) The boys are allowed a lot of freedom of action and credited with a great deal of mental and physical energy which they require to carry out successfully the attractive programme of the school. It is this programme that provides Namunyu with the social and academic background he needs to face the future with confidence.

The High School Gent

The High School Gent is a continuation of the biography of Namunyu.[2] With a great deal of artistic intelligence the novelist dramatises his problem of growth as an adolescent, with all the difficulties and challenges. Practically every area of development is discussed and assessed.

After an initial period of loneliness in the secondary school Namunyu soon begins to play a leadership role in academic and social life. He is a

165

member of the choir, the Readers' Club and and Debating Club; he is a house prefect and scout troop leader. These societies provide the opportunities he requires for close interraction with staff and students. From these interractions he benefits maximally from the facilities offered by the school and is exposed to all kinds of experiences which make him a more useful member of the school, his family and community. For example, as a scout he joins a field trip where he has the opportunity of reacting with girls from Mbulira Girls' School and taking part in discussions, drills and exercises of great educational value. The scouts and guides are left to their own devices during the period of camping and are given a free hand to order their lives together according to agreed principles. This freedom of action in itself poses a challenge to all concerned. The fact that the experiment proves eminently successful does enormous credit to the honesty of purpose of the staff and students of both schools. Another school society which has immediate academic impact on Namunyu is the Readers' Club. Discussions at the Club which are usually held at an intellectual level are extremely beneficial to the boys. Encouraged by the headmaster and the group leader they dwell extensively on the various uses of literature – as a picture of life, as an escape from life, as a medium of transmitting knowledge and as a mode of recreation. They distinguish between developmental and functional kinds of reading. They contra-distinguish between the various literary genres, especially fiction, non-fiction and poetry. With the use of an invisible library technique the students get to read many books in a term and report on them. This has the effect of widening their mental horizon. Little wonder then that Namunyu, notable for his academic brilliance, is 'caught in rapture' about these activities.

> Ideas surged through his mind as he thought over what he heard at the Readers' Club. He felt sorry for those who did not belong to it. They missed so much. He hoped they read these stories for themselves. Some of them were wonderful accounts of human courage – like that one about a Chinese girl who was left out in the snow and her fingers and toes got frozen so that they had to be cut off. And that one, *The Story of my Life*, about a woman who could not hear, see or talk – Helen Keller, yet managed to be so learned that she even got a university degree! (p.25)

With academic growth comes social development. The author sees the two as almost inseparable. She applies to the teenage scene the same kind of humour and sympathy one discovers in her first novel. The boys are exposed to various situations in which they derive social strength and wisdom. They are allowed to mix freely with the girls from Mbulira. They have encounters with female members of staff who are highly qualified professional people and perform their duties creditably. The boys come to realise that being a woman is not a permanent academic disability. A woman can rise to the height of her profession if she displays the necessary talent and determination. As the headmaster says, 'this is a century in which it is brains that count. And anyone can get anywhere if they have the brains'. (p.104) He himself sets an excellent example by his mature relationship with Miss Spark, the head-mistress of Mbulira Girls' School, which ends in marriage and leads to a new and inspiring life for the couple. As a sign of personal growth the boys are already having their own private anxieties about girls. The novelist devotes a lot of space to the social encounter between Namunyu and Sarah. This starts as child play at a camping site and develops gradually into a relationship which affects the happiness of both of them. They begin by exploring the common grounds between them – scouting, guiding, work at youth camps and setbooks – and use these as a launching pad for the consideration of more intimate matters. They soon agree to become friends 'with serious intentions'. All the time Sarah has been deeply suspicious of boys because of her personal experi-ence in the matter. 'Boys are such beasts . . . Why do boys enjoy putting girls in trouble?' (p.118) Clearly this is an association that is intended to succeed. One leaves the novel with the impression that Namunyu and Sarah will overcome their initial difficulties and settle down to a life of marital bliss.

Namunyu exercises a sense of commitment to his family, community and indigenous culture. Fortunately these are areas in which the novelist too shows an infinite interest. The boy takes seriously the observance of age group practices, especially as they relate to cultural matters like wrestling. He prepares hard for an inter-clan wrestling contest in which he does not eventually take part. This wrestling match provides some of the best descriptive passages in the novel and shows the author as a gifted writer of the English prose.

And there they saw the son of Imbitsi still unvanquished. What he had done on being lifted off the ground was to wrap his legs around the back of the son of Liswa. He had then tightened his legs and feet around the man till he was as if compressed, held between crushing boards. He could not move his body.

So there they were, the son of Imbitsi high up in the air with the unflinching arms of the son of Liswa clamped across his back. And the son of Liswa transfixed in his upright position by the paralysing grip of the legs of the son of Imbitsi. The question was which of them would free himself first and get the chance of knocking the other flat. (p.65)

Such a description can only be given by a writer who has an intrinsic interest in the art of wrestling. Namunyu's concern for his circumstances in life is shown in other areas as well. For example, his mother's death increases his responsibility in the family. His older sisters and brothers have left the house for other locations, and he finds himself saddled with the care of the younger ones. He proves equal to the task. 'Even in his grief, Namunyu established himself as a hero in his people's eyes.' (p.91) He regards it as his paramount duty to ensure that the children are comfortable, and constantly contributes his quota to their welfare. He co-operates with a new step-mother to ease his father's burden in order that he may continue to play his role as head of the family effectively. So much practical wisdom has he acquired during his stay at Rasika that at his age he has without much notice become the tower of strength to many members of his family and community. He displays so much humanity and consideration for other people that one feels assured that he will succeed in his inter-personal relationships with friends, colleagues and relations in adult life.

This same attribute makes Namunyu's career prospects extremely bright. But, as usual, there are initial difficulties to overcome. He first has to silence the elders of Ringa who, because of their financial investment in him, want him to become a teacher against his wish. He finds the whole situation unbearable. He communicates his utter disgust to Sarah. 'I find it impossible to believe that they tell you to grow up and make responsible decisions, and then to find that they don't even bother to find out if there is any sense in your point of view . . .' (p.151) Because of the circumstances in which he finds himself he has decided to go straight for a career in the insurance business rather than proceed to a degree course. He soon finds himself working in an insurance office in the same city with Sarah. This is conceived as a personal triumph until he discovers that he has to leave her behind and go to London for a course. Namunyu is confused. He realises, perhaps for the first time, that adult life, like school life, is full of pitfalls and complications, and that the problems of living admit of no permanent solutions.

> Some understanding of life was dawning on the high school gent from Rasika. Life was plagued with complexities and uncertainties. And a man must grapple with them one by one while living within the uncertainty that surrounds him. It wasn't only in school that anxiety existed. The anxiety of passing exams and avoiding being in the headmaster's bad books was replaced by other uncertainties in the life outside school, often much more difficult ones. (p.173)

The novelist touches on matters of global concern. Copious reference is made in this work to the role of the home, school, community and state in the overall education of the child. The home is socially handi-capped from playing its role creditably; so also is the community to some extent. The state fails woefully in any attempt to make adequate provision for education. The educational system is elitist. It allows only a fortunate few, like Namunyu and Ginendwa, to acquire good education and enter lofty professions. Little thought is given to mass education. Inevitably there is a lot of wastage in a system that encourages the survival of the fittest. The few schools available succeed magnificently with the boys and girls sent to them. But they are all the time painfully aware that they are training only a microscopic minority of those anxious to be educated. It is unfortunate in a sense that the novelist appears to condone this situation in the way she lionises the products of these schools. A more broadly-based, humane and just system of education which caters for all levels of ability and intelligence is certainly more acceptable. It is only such a system that can give more people, like Madadi, a sense of social and spiritual fulfilment.

The Eighth Wife

The Eighth Wife highlights matters of great cultural significance.[3] In this work the novelist describes in detail some aspects of the traditional customs and beliefs of the people of Lusui clan of Western Kenya. There is an extensive discussion of circumcision rites. As the boys cross the threshold from boyhood to manhood, they join the work force and the group of eligible bachelors. The spiritual and physical preservation of the village and clan is of supreme importance. Manliness is cherished in this society under focus, and the initiation rites are nothing but a test of endurance. No boy is recognised as a full member of the society until he has 'faced the knife'. He must not be seen to flinch at the sight of the knife, lest he is branded a coward. A boy who exhibits cowardice brings mighty disgrace to his family and is treated as a social reject. Those who show courage and cheerfully pass through their ordeal win the people's admiration and are much sought after as prospective husbands for their girls.

It is against this background that the novelist considers Shalimba's initiation and graduation into adult life. The strain on him as the son of the chief is enormous. As we are told,

It was a big enough ordeal for the ordinary youth to face. And it was even beyond the ordinary run each time a chief's son came forward to present himself. But to be in the position of Shalimba, who must fulfil the cherished dreams of each of his dead brothers in addition to his

169

own . . . would this not be too much for one so young? Would he succeed or would it undo him? The elders crouched waiting as the people discussed the issue endlessly. (p.25)

The people's expectations are not disappointed. Shalimba endures the slashing of the skin with fortitude. Although he falls ill during his period as houseman, he survives this temporary setback and emerges with his honour unstained. He grows in the estimation of his people who begin to appreciate his leadership qualities. They show their loyalty and admiration for him and his father by the enthusiastic reception they give him at the graduation ceremony. The challenge is great, the responsibilities daunting. By this ceremony Shalimba becomes one of 'the guardians of the clan, its warriors'. (p.88) He has fulfilled all requirements and he is virtually installed in his post as the next chief of the clan after his father. It is important to appreciate this point because it is vital for an understanding of the tensions and conflicts which arise later in the work.

The novelist provides a clear picture of the traditional and social framework of society. Chief Malenya as the paramount ruler of his people wields a lot of power and influence. There is a council of elders which deliberates on matters affecting the life and security of the clan. This council derives its authority from the chief who reserves to himself the right to override its decisions. The chief with his elders is the custodian of indigenous culture. His paramount duty is to keep intact the traditional way of life of the people. Polygamy is considered an essential ingredient of this culture. A lot of energy is therefore devoted to the problems created by a polygamous existence. In this connection life in the chief's household is examined in great detail to dramatise the complications which arise from the acquisition of too many wives – the mutual suspicion and envy, the absence of any consideration for others, gloom and despondency, frustration and discord. All these are evident in the chief's family where there are seven wives. His problems become more acute when he attempts to acquire an eighth wife. This further complicates his domestic life which is already in a thorough mess, as he himself confesses.

'If one woman's child meets good fortune and you rejoice with her, the other women remind you of their misfortune. If in your zeal or praise you give a marrying daughter a present, the other women remind you of the insignificant presents you gave their daughters. Woe to me who will never know real peace, me whose joys are marred by the sorrows of one woman after another. Can a man of many wives ever experience the calm of peaceful joy, O, you spirits of my fathers?' (p.30)

Why does he compound his sorrows and frustrations by vying with his son for another wife? How can a man who exercises moral authority over others be so morally chaotic himself? This is one of the puzzles of this novel. The author may not intend an outright condemnation of polygamy. But she does enough to portray the chief's household as an unworthy example of the polygamous system.

Chief Malenya clearly belongs to the past. Hopes for the present reside in the kind of relationship which develops between Kalimonje and Shalimba. The union between the two brings together two ancient families with previous intimate ties. It is because of Malungu's promise to Malenya that Kalimonje is chosen as Shalimba's bride. As is usual in traditional society, the marriage is arranged at the family level, and it is to be conducted according to customary rites. However, Kalimonje is a girl with modern ideas whose bitter experiences of life in a polygamous household have turned her against polygamy. She has seen wives neglected for long periods and then finally discarded. She has witnessed fierce intra-family feuds and controversies with all the attendant dreadful consequences. She resents the way women in polygamous situations are misused by their men.

> Kalimonje began to resent the kind of life a woman led. Look at her mother. She could hardly remember seeing her just sitting and taking it easy. Drawing water, carrying wood, bringing food home, cooking it. All the preparations, the digging, the children. Everything rested on mother. All that the men did was to sit under a tree and talk, waiting for an invasion so that they might guard the clan's boundaries. In Kalimonje's life there had been no such invasion. It seemed to her a rather lazy way of getting out of work. (p.71)

She therefore conceives of a situation where the burden of the family will be equally shared between the man and the woman. She would prefer to be the only wife of her husband. But there are constraints which may compel Shalimba, a future ruler of his people, to take another wife. 'If his wife was visited by an angry ancestor and they had no children at all, would he not have married again? . . . What if she married and became barren?' (p.109) More than any other consideration, the genuine love between the two young people proves to be the deciding factor. They thus introduce a new element into marriage in the clan and show by the way they cling to each other in times of distress that they intend to succeed as man and wife. Ironically, Chief Malenya who should give them support and encouragement becomes the greatest obstacle in their way to a happy life. He is upset by his son's growing popularity and tries to humiliate him by making Kalimonje his eighth wife.

171

The novelist devotes a good deal of narrative energy to the tension which results from the chief's moral turpitude and his insidious attempt to deny his son of the girl who has long been linked with him in the public eye. The chief's desire is in itself a violation of custom. Shalimba and his secret brother Malimu are determined not to let him get away with it. They consider the chief morally diseased. 'When a man is sick both in body and in mind, there is no telling what could happen.' (p.144) They allow the chief to blunder on until the time is ripe for a direct confrontation between him and his son. The climax is reached when Kalimonje takes a last-ditch stand in public against the discredited chief. 'I will not be your wife. I will not stand on the bridal hide. And if the final union rites are carried out, I will be dead upon entering your house . . . You are my father-in-law, never my husband.' (p.163) Shalimba moves forward to embrace his bride to the admiration of all. The chief realises the game is up, and that he has overreached himself. He becomes conciliatory and adopts a face-saving device. 'May the gods bless you, my children. And may the spirits of our forefathers help you to prosper on the earth.' (p.165) Ironically he gives as a defeated enemy the blessing he ought to have given as a father and paramount ruler. Shalimba and Kalimonje assert their individualism and point the way forward to the future. There is clearly a need for change in a situation where a whole community is governed by the dictatorial and corrupt tendencies of an individual. The work proves beyond all doubt that the chief's inordinate desires cannot always prevail, if traditional morality is to be upheld. He is fast becoming a disgrace as an embodiment of the people's culture.

As part of her concern for culture, the author uses songs to authenticate her assessment of people and situations, and enliven the scenes she depicts. Singing and dancing are shown as an integral part of the way of life of the people. Songs are employed for proclamatory and invocatory purposes. They are used as social references and necessary parts of festivals and rituals.[4] Take, for example, the importance of cows to girls, which is reflected in their song during the initiation ceremony.

Solo: What rules our lives, you children of our mother?
Chorus: The cow.
Solo: What makes you leave your home for a strange man?
Chorus: The cow.
Solo: What keeps the floor shining and without dust?
Chorus: The cow.
Solo: O, you children of my mothers, say it over again.
Chorus: The cow. (pp.15-16)

There is also this song of praise and admiration for the bride, Kalimonje,

> Our queen walks on air, sang the soloist.
> Beautiful queen, responded the group.
> Our queen's smile is a magnet.
> Beautiful queen.
> Our queen keeps floors gleaming,
> Beautiful queen, (p.152)

and this lamentation of a heart-stricken mother over the death of her son.

> 'Oh, my child, my son,
> Why did you heap shame on me?
> You departed that I who came first
> Might become the last among them.
> How can a woman that could be my child
> Steal the honours from my wrinkled face?
> Oh, my fathers, fathers of my mother,
> Why did you punish me thus?' (p.28)

The novelist uses the poetic form comfortably and appropriately to reflect the mood of the villagers on every occasion. The poetry is spontaneous and free in form and content. It underlines the people's freedom of action and provides an opportunity for self-expression.

Your Heart is My Altar

Your Heart is My Altar thrives on conflict between pagans and the combined forces of Christians and Moslems, between inherited and foreign culture, between two clans within the same culture.[5] Because of increasing secularisation and the influence of modern ideas many individuals and families find themselves at a cross-roads in religious and cultural matters. Chimoli's family is a case in point. It is made a microcosm of the tribe at large, and shows in its internal divisions and external relations with other groups the type of rift which is already tearing the clan apart. For example, Father and Mother come from two antagonistic clans, and this is a constant source of controversy and embarrassment. Members of the family feel more at ease with ancestral worship, but have embraced Christianity. This brings with it a lot of problems. It sets them apart from the people and denies them the benefits of a culture which has the greatest relevance to the people's way of life. It is this kind of inconvenience that Alumasa is not willing to suffer when he marries his brother's widow and leaves the church. He finds the teachings of Christian converts narrow and unrealistic; they run counter at every point to the tenets of indigenous culture. He therefore decides to throw away the burden which the church represents and regain his freedom of action as an adult member of the clan. Uncle Shivisi, another church-goer who has decamped, puts the whole situation in true perspective when he says: 'I have wide feet . . . How can anyone expect me to walk on that narrow road. I keep hitting my toes on the edges.' (p.106)

The dilemma for the young members of the Christian community is even more acute. They are not allowed to mix freely with the other boys and girls lest they are contaminated with pagan ideas and practices. They are denied any kind of participation in cultural events. 'To dance was sin, and to watch drum-beaters was an even worse sin.' (p.87) They are prevented from having any social intercourse with the vast majority of the people. The result is that they know precious little about the society in which they live. Worse still, they develop a completely erroneous value system and a false method of evaluating character and conduct which shows how limited their mental horizon is.

> We had grown up strangers in our land, always trying to figure out how a Christian should act but never quite sure. The girls from the traditional villages seemed to know so much more than we did. They knew how to handle boys. I just never knew what to say to boys. To want to see or talk to them was lust, I had been told. To speak to them was often rewarded with a beating, and yet family life and marriage were said to be holy. It was always difficult to see how these potential evils in form of boys were supposed to turn into respected husbands. (p.86)

The effect of all this on the family is devastating. Limwenyi is kidnapped and ill-treated because she displays an unnecessary air of superiority to the boys. When Ligami kidnaps a girl, he does not know what custom and tradition require him to do. 'If you want to live by the ways of the devil, then you must learn the rules of that world,' (p.97) his mother tells him. Chimoli is so confused by the situation in which she finds herself that she goes at great personal risk to consult a diviner. Furthermore, because of their complete lack of knowledge of community affairs Ligami and Limwenyi are used, unwittingly, by their more acculturated friends as agents of destruction.

What brings about a violent confrontation in the novel is the attempt of the Moslems and Christians to wipe out ancestral worship and, in the process, destroy the chief, the clan and indigenous culture. The fundamentalists come together under the banner of Believers of the New True

God and blame the traditionalists for all the ills of society, especially the drought which has recently caused widespread hardship. They prepare for a holy war and mobilise the people of another clan in a conspiracy against the chief and his people. Ligami and Limwenyi are unfortunately involved in this treachery against their clan. Ligami plays a leading role as a spy for the enemy. Religious differences are compounded by tribal hatred. This results in a war in which Ligami, his father, the chief and many others lose their lives. The dreadful conflict brings sorrow to many homes. The land is desolate, and the clan is in disarray. The break between the two clans and the various religious groups appears complete.

However, out of this confused and tragic situation comes some hope for the future. The love which gradually develops between Chimoli and Aluvisia is used to bridge the gap between people and religions, and to establish an enduring peace between the two warring clans to which they belong. Their love grows in difficult circumstances and under the shadow of war. Yet they persevere in their attempt, overcome all obstacles and ensure that the unwholesome examples of the adult members of the community do not deter them from pursuing their heart's desire. Aluvisia for a long time remains Chimoli's friend in need. Finally she recognises him as a man with attractive qualities, considerate and bold enough to put his life at risk for her sake. 'Aluvisia had ignited a candle in my heart that had never been lit before. A candle that had never burnt for anyone else. And yet he was my enemy by tradition . . .' (p.138) These two set a high standard of behaviour for others to emulate. They show by their love for each other that ethnic hatred need not be passed from one generation to another, no child is under any obligation to inherit the prejudices of his parents and clan. It is only by the exercise of mutual understanding and tolerance of each other's way of life that the various clans and religions can co-exist in peace and happiness.

Miriam Tlali

Muriel at Metropolitan

Muriel at Metropolitan discusses in great detail the depressing situation in South Africa where the system of apartheid has poisoned relations between the white and black communities, and made the achievement of racial harmony difficult.[6] The policy of separate development for the two races is used as a smokescreen to oppress the blacks and keep them in perpetual bondage. The blacks cannot fend for themselves and have to depend on the whites for their livelihood. They are treated as second-class citizens and are prevented from benefiting from an economy to which they make so much contribution. For the blacks South Africa is a place of physical and mental torture; for the whites it is a paradise. Yet without the sweat and labour of the black proletariat, the Republic cannot survive economically. It is to the hard work and perseverance of the blacks that 'the Republic owes her phenomenal industrial development'. (p.111) A situation in which the white minority oppress the black majority is manifestly unjust. A political arrangement which proclaims the superiority of one culture to another is untenable. An attitude of mind which undermines a black man's ability and performance because of the colour of his skin only helps to produce resentment and discontent. It kills initiative and destroys any sense of loyalty to the state.

In the Republic of South Africa, the colour of your skin alone condemns you to a position of eternal servitude from which you can never escape. You cannot throw away the shackles no matter how hard you try. You are like the doormat. You are a muntu; your place is at the bottom of the ladder and there you must stay. You can never climb higher no matter what you do or what you have achieved. (p.117)

It is to this organised injustice, of which the blacks are the victims, that the author directs her attention in the novel. Attention is focussed on the Metropolitan Radio to show how it reflects in his staff policy, methods of operation and attitude to customers the system of apartheid. Muriel is made to play a substantial part in the work of the company and react with the staff and customers in order to reveal the weaknesses in concept and organisational structure which exist in the establishment. To start with, there is the bureaucratic set-up which leaves no room for the African to rise beyond the level of head-boy or head-girl. The boss, Mr Bloch, is firmly in personal control of every aspect of the work and leaves nothing to the discretion of others. His immediate assistants, Mrs Kuhn, a Jew, and Mrs Stein, an Afrikaner, hate Africans and are even more opposed to African development than the boss. They therefore urge on him brutal repression of Africans, be they workers, salesmen or customers. The African workers are addressed rudely and get only peremptory orders and threats, as those given here to the night watch-boy.

'You must be here every night. If I find you drunk, I'll throw you out. If I find you sleeping, you go. If you miss out one night, I chuck you out, and I don't pay you. Come, give me your pass!' (p.8)

176

At Metropolitan Radio the whites believe that Africans should be put firmly in their proper place at the bottom of the social ladder in order to keep them quiet and disorganised. They therefore help to set up a system which provides for the blacks an abject and subordinate role. They ensure that the policy of apartheid is reflected in the organisation of work in the establishment: the blacks do the menial jobs and exist only to serve the convenience of the whites; steel mesh wires separate the white and black staff in the office; there is a toilet, a rack, a refreshment service reserved only for the whites. Separate ledgers and record cards are kept for white and black customers. The white customers are served only by the white members of staff. They receive prompt and polite attention. Black customers are treated rudely and crudely. 'There was no need to be polite to an African customer.' (p.49) Different systems exist for collecting money from white and black debtors. An African needs a pass to make use of hire purchase facilities. In short, apartheid is applied to every aspect of work at Metropolitan Radio. In this sense, it is a true reflection of the Republic at work.

It is in this situation that Muriel finds herself and struggles to survive. She is subjected to several indignities and treated as any black person will be handled. Initially she is not trusted, and she is given mechanical jobs to do. She is also seated with fellow Africans across the apartheid line from the white workers. Later, when she proves her mettle she is assigned the more respectable job of dealing with ledgers. For this reason she has to sit with the Europeans. This situation poses a dilemma for Muriel. She is only tolerated by her European colleagues and regarded with suspicion by the African workers. To the African customers, with whom she has much dealing, she is a traitor to the African cause, a collaborator with the whites to dupe the blacks, a paid agent of apartheid. This is agonising for Muriel. 'I'm between two fires. My own people on the one hand, and the white staff on the other. I have a lot of trouble with our African customers . . . They think we are just bent on squeezing money out of them to swell the coffers of our white bosses.' (p.81) Muriel derives no satisfaction from her work mainly because of the shabby way she and other African workers are treated. In her situation there is little she can do to improve her lot or that of the numerous Africans who suffer discrimination and oppression at Metropolitan Radio and the country at large. But she can at least avoid a situation where her ability is so grossly underrated, her intentions misunderstood and where she will 'have to remain static, junior, for the rest of my working life, irrespective of my experience and my proficiency, a shock absorber, ready to be used on demand'. (p.140) She decides to stop doing further injury to her conscience and resigns her appointment. Muriel's experiences at Metropolitan Radio highlights the enormous difficulties the African faces in a situation where she is not expected to succeed. Competent and hardworking, she is put in such a state of spiritual depression which makes it impossible for her to perform efficiently. She suffers from the effects of an iniquitous system which starts by weakening a man's resolve to fight evil and ends up destroying his spirit.

An area of achievement in this novel lies in the use of different kinds of characters to expose the weaknesses and cruelties in inter-personal relationships under the apartheid system. In a situation which breeds mutual suspicion and racial hatred, people show little regard and consideration for one another. So one finds that, instead of working as a team for the good of the company, the employees of Metropolitan Radio are dissatisfied and disunited. The boss, Mr Bloch, is autocratic and ruthless in his methods. He trusts no employee, white or black. Not even his sister, Mrs Kuhn, has his full confidence. He therefore tries unsuccessfully to do everything himself. In the process, he clashes with one employee after another and makes a nuisance of himself. In his bid to acquire wealth he drives everybody too hard. He cannot command the respect of his workers because he treats many of them, especially the blacks, as sub-human. As Muriel says: 'We were all under the thumb of a demanding boss, who was unyielding in many ways, giving little consideration to the fact that we had private lives of our own, homes and dependants to look after.' (p.163) This provides the necessary atmosphere for characters like Mrs Stein and Mrs Kuhn to laze away their time, gossiping about the blacks and terrorising black workers and customers. It also encourages inefficiency and fraud on the part of Agrippa and Douglas who, far from showing any loyalty to their employers, appropriate company money and property in a most shameful manner. Lennie, a white mechanic, is a disgrace. He openly supports the system of apartheid but secretly interacts with African girls and goes to bed with them. This hypocritical behaviour is shared by other whites from whom Ben makes money letting his room at night. The only employee who shows any kind of loyalty to his boss is Adam. But he does not profit by it. He works for twenty-six years and he is still on a salary of £7 a week. He is generally regarded as a fool by the other African workers. 'With an empty stomach, he keeps guard over another man's food and doesn't touch it. Why doesn't he pay himself with these goods?' (p.79) Adam is content to be so openly fooled and cheated by his white boss. There is little doubt that he is presented as an object of satire. When a group of people decide to oppress another they deserve neither sympathy nor consideration. The machine of oppression is occasionally turned inwards against some members of their own group. This happens a great deal at Metropolitan Radio and is responsible for the general inefficiency and chaos which prevail in the establishment.

The work highlights the suffering and humiliation which the blacks experience from the mindless application of the principles of apartheid. They have no freedom of speech and movement. They are lumped together in Bantustans as a voiceless majority. They require passes for work and to visit relations in other locations. Workers move from their homelands to work in the cities, leaving behind their families. The system provides cheap labour for the whites. But it disrupts the family life of the black migrant worker who, as a result, is tempted to have illegitimate children all over the place. Muriel denounces this cruel system.

> It is a system based on cheap labour, which undermines all laws of morality and decency, making nonsense of the concept of the family unit. On it the mining industry in the Republic of South Africa has flourished. To my mind, it is comparable only with the slave trade. (pp.60-61)

Blacks are subjected to constant searches and harassment by the security police and are frequently thrown out of their houses. For example, when Muriel's niece is to pay her a short visit she is questioned many times by the police on the necessity for the visit and required to give an undertaking that the child will not constitute a security risk. Again, when Sophiatown is to be acquired for the use of the whites, the town is completely destroyed, thus depriving the blacks of their houses and property. They are moved to a crowded and insanitary new location while Sophiatown is renamed Triomf (triumph), a clear indication that the whites gloat over the suffering of the blacks. The novel provides a catelogue of injustices committed against the blacks who do not feel secure in their homes and places of work. This sense of insecurity, we are told,

> is always there, it haunts you all your life – insecurity. There is nothing firm for you; nothing you can hold on to or fall back on. It is like that with everything you try to build up in every sphere of your life – your home, your work, your future, the future of your children – everything hangs on a thread. At any moment everything about you can be snapped off just like that. Your fate depends entirely on the whims of the white masters! (p.70)

The situation has deteriorated to such an extent that only an organised resistance on the part of the blacks can restore decency and human dignity to the Republic of South Africa.

In *Amandla* the novelist continues her assault on the iniquitous system of apartheid in South Africa.[7] This is a more ample work than the previous novel. She brings in more details and uses these effectively by concentrating them on the Soweto riots of June 16, 1976. The riots are presented as the unavoidable outcome of the flagrant denial of human rights to the blacks. When oppression assumes the monstrous proportions that one reads about in this novel, then the reaction is bound to be violent. What brings matters to a head is the invidious attempt of the minority white government to provide the blacks with an inferior kind of education under the Bantu Education Act and thus perpetuate their servitude. During a student protest against this diabolical design the police open fire, kill many students and set Soweto literally ablaze. In the riots which follow the WRAB buildings and some police posts are burnt down. The police are, as usual, presented as agents of oppression. They harass innocent people, clamp many of them in jail and apply the method of torture to extract information from them. The people who die in jail are denied a decent burial. The police appear particularly hostile to students and display unpardonable moral weakness in the way they often assault girls sexually.

> 'Some say they call them out one by one and promise them their freedom if they agree to have relations with them. Some have had to receive medical attention. Others have had pregnancies terminated. That's the price we have to pay for our liberation. We have to fight hard and free ourselves, otherwise these things will always happen to us. Everybody just tramples on us.' (p.187)

Policemen not only offend against the Immorality Laws, but also help to create a situation which leads to the breakdown of law and order.

On the other hand, the students organise themselves so well that they effectively counter police brutality and outwit the law-enforcement agencies. Their organisation is so efficient that they are able to infiltrate the ranks of the police to collect vital information and free some of their arrested leaders. Under the leadership of Pholoso they establish useful 'contacts' with other sympathetic groups in order to carry forward the spirit of the revolution which they have started. They impress everyone with their deep understanding of the plight of the blacks and their resolve to bring about a change. 'These children... they can be so determined.' (p.23) Their approach is such that can hardly fail. They emphasise the need for regular exercises, self-discipline and wide reading for self-improvement. They stress the importance of educating people on their rights. They establish a method of secret communication by coded messages and get the girls to be completely involved in the struggle. Their high levels of operation and achievement baffle government officials and surprise their own parents. According to a parent, 'their education was really meant to be education for ignorance but now it seems to have boomeranged instead'. (p.25) Those who stand to lose most from this situation are the supporters of apartheid who for long have terrorised the blacks and put them in a state of perpetual fright in their own country. The students are physically and mentally prepared for the fight and are quite conscious of the enormity of the task ahead of them.

> We are up against a formidable, highly-sophisticated enemy whom we must face on equal ground. That our task is a momentous one cannot be denied. The roots of this evil have penetrated deeper than we can speculate. But we dare not give up. If we forget those who laid down their lives, then they will have done so in vain. We the oppressed cannot be expected to think we can go on living as if nothing has ever happened. We cannot sit complacently on this rubbish heap under our seats, laughing and smiling, eating and drinking as if conditions were normal. (pp.289-90)

The conditions are, in fact, not 'normal'. One of the reasons the students continue their agitation is to show the adults how to achieve positive results. The aim is not only to be able to face the enemy 'on equal ground' but also to cleanse their own people of the social impurities which have stood in the way of progress for so long. It is only a disciplined group, acting in concert, that can ever hope to defeat a 'formidable' monster like apartheid. So the students initiate plans to inculcate in the adults habits of self-discipline. They undertake the reform of society so that the blacks may appreciate the need for sacrifice and moderation in their habits. In this they are successful to a great extent. For example, they conduct raids on government liquor houses to ensure that people stop excessive drinking. Through the application of appropriate penalties, they discourage wasteful spending on the part of the people, especially at Christmas and festival periods. The blacks become more ascetic in their habits and accept the need for self-sacrifice. It is a great tribute to the students that they have achieved in a relatively short time what the adults have failed to accomplish in several generations. 'The smile of carefree innocence has disappeared from the faces of our young ones. What we have seen has shocked and sobered the elderly ones, it has transformed our children into adults.' (p.209) The students have helped to lay a firm foundation for a revolution which will sooner or later bring to an end the vicious system of apartheid.

Meanwhile, individuals, families and groups of Africans continue to suffer under the system and from the effects of the Soweto riots. Christmas that year is drab and sorrowful. The usual euphoria connected with the event is nowhere in evidence. Africans are virtually in a state of siege, a situation which increases the social uncertainty they have had to live with. For example, Pholoso for a long time lives the life of a fugitive to escape police arrest. At this time and during the period of his eventual arrest and detention he is separated from his family and his lover, Felleng. This is an unpleasant experience for him. After his miraculous release from prison he decides to flee the country in order to avoid further persecution. His immediate plans for Felleng are not realised, and there is no assurance that they will eventually get married. So uncertain has life become for the African that he is not always in complete control of his actions and movements. For this reason, people like Joseph give up any hope of a decent life and take to drinking. Joseph becomes a nuisance, beating up his wife and causing her bodily harm. Their marriage breaks down, although not irretrievably. There are many other examples of irrational actions which clearly reveal how disturbed people can be in a state of tension. There is the love affair involving Mamabolo, Nicodemus and Teresa which leads to the tragic death of the two men. Teresa's behaviour is reprehensible in the way she encourages Nicodemus to betray his boss. She, like Seapei, is presented as an unworthy example of a Johannesburg woman. 'They won't leave you alone until they have sucked and milked you dry! Johannesburg woman are always demanding more . . . It's sex and money, sex and money all the time.' (p.46) Nothing brings the African woman true happiness. She is either physically paralysed like Gramsy or in a state of uncertainty like Nana and Marta. Soweto has brought in its wake a number of problems which the Africans have to work hard to solve.

The novel discusses in some detail the theoretical arguments for and against apartheid and the various approaches which have been adopted in an attempt to eradicate the evil. Apartheid in theory encourages the separate development of whites and blacks. But in practice the white minority government ensures in all its institutional arrangements that any kind of 'development' for the African is such that gives him a subordinate and humiliating position in society. For example, the African is not allowed to have a sound academic education because he is required to do manual work. 'We should so conduct our schools that the native who attends those schools will know that to a great extent he must be the labourer in the country.' (p.220) It is only for this purpose and not for any reason of academic insufficiency on his part that the African is denied good purposeful education. The denial of equal rights in other areas stems from the same kind of wickedness. The whites are afraid to compete with the blacks on equal terms. They therefore do everything possible to make sure that the two races are never given the same type of recognition. 'If the native in South Africa today . . . is being taught to expect that he will live his adult life under a policy of equal rights he is making a big mistake.' (p.222) The situation is further complicated by the fact that the government has succeeded in making allies of the chiefs and missionaries.

> The priest with the Bible in his hand humbly approaches the chief, then follows the trader with his cheap goods and a bale of Lancashire cotton. Then come the treaties and agreements, by which the chief and his tribe 'agree' to allocate a large piece of their land. Not only from Britain did these Bible-wielding 'men of God' emerge. With the Wesleyans and the Scots came the Moravians, the Rhenish and Berlin Missions – virtually all Europe invaded Southern Africa with their different brands of scriptures. (p.232)

Faced with this formidable strength of the government buttressed by every kind of repressive legislation and secretly encouraged by multi-national corporations and the Western powers, what does the African do? He may adopt a gradualist approach through which he wins concessions piecemeal from the government on the various points in dispute with the aim of ultimately demolishing the structure of apartheid. The novel offers several examples of unsuccessful attempts to adopt this approach. The realistic devices of FIYOH (Freedom in your own hand) with its projects on self-enlightenment campaigns, mass education, Food for Freedom and Know Yourself Lessons stand a chance of succeeding if they are not interfered with by the authorities. However, the most effective answer to white intransigence is provided by the radical stance of the Unity Movement with its ten-point programme. The rationale for this programme is that the whole structure of society is abnormal. Only a ruthless revolutionary change which gets at once to the root of the problem and topples the apartheid monster can bring a lasting benefit to the people. 'Isolated ventures can only result in more and more suffering.' (p.213) The radical programme therefore seeks to demolish the whole edifice of apartheid and destroy its ugly manifestations in the areas of franchise, education, right to privacy, freedom of speech and movement, labour, taxation and, generally speaking, 'full equality of rights for all citizens without distinction of race, colour or sex'. (p.242) It is a comprehensive programme the total realisation of which alone can restore hope and confidence to the African population. It is only such a radical programme that can bring about the dawn of a new day and realise the black man's dream of a happy, prosperous and united Republic of South Africa where no one is oppressed.

That day shall come when all men shall be free to breathe the air of freedom and when that day shall come, no man, no matter how many tanks he has, will reverse the course of events (p.290)

The novelist's achievement in this work lies partly in the unobtrusive manner in which she provides this vision of hope and redemption.

Notes

1 *The Boy in Between* (Nairobi, O.U.P. 1969). Page references are to the 1979 edition.

2 *The High School Gent* (Nairobi, O.U.P. 1972). Page references are to the 1979 edition.

3 *The Eighth Wife* (Nairobi, East African Publishing House, 1972). Page references are to this edition.

4 For a discussion of the various uses of poetry in traditional society see, for example, Oladele Taiwo, *An Introduction to West African Literature* (London, Nelson, 1981) pp.84-104.

5 *Your Heart is My Altar* (Nairobi, East African Publishing House, 1980). Page references are to this edition.

6 *Muriel at Metropolitan* (London, Longman Drumbeat, 1979). Page references are to this edition.

7 *Amandla* (Johannesburg, Ravan Press (Pty) Ltd., 1980). Page references are to this edition.

CHAPTER EIGHT

Bessie Head

Bessie Head's reputation as a writer rests on three novels, a collection of stories and a book on Serowe village. The three novels – *When Rain Clouds Gather, Maru* and *A Question of Power* – form something like a trilogy. In each of them the novelist exhibits strong disapproval for the misuse of power by any individual or group. This dislike is evident in the way she dramatises the process of the abdication of power which gets more complex from the first novel to the last. By the time the reader gets to the end of the third novel the novelist's message is clear: the naked display of power by the racists in South Africa or any other bigots elsewhere can only lead to disaster. There is no way of avoiding the rewards of oppression whether it is of blacks by whites, whites by blacks, whites by fellow whites or blacks by fellow blacks. The wise thing to do is to conceive of power in a progressive evolutionary manner. But, given man's insatiable lust for power, this is hardly possible. The novelist considers at length the psychological basis of power and finds that this has been largely eroded in a world dominated by conflict and the desire for political ascendancy. It is because of this stated position that Bessie Head is, for example, said to express 'an indiscriminate repugnance for *all* political aspirations in *all* races'.[1]

The collection of stories, *The Collector of Treasures* affords the author a chance to display her mastery of the art of storytelling. She understandably concentrates on the position of women and takes every opportunity to project a feminist point of view. She needs all the artistic talents displayed in her previous works to succeed with *Serowe: Village of the Rain Wind*. Here she combines imaginative writing with the fruits of a year's research study to produce work of great distinction. She succeeds magnificently in her reconstruction of the village life of Serowe. The daily occupations, hopes and fears of the ordinary people of the village come alive in the reader's mind mainly because of the opportunity given the inhabitants to tell their own stories. The conception of history here is edifying – history is made out of the preoccupations of the common man, not out of the lofty ideals, cruelty or benevolence of the wealthy and powerful. This reflects the concern for the underprivileged and oppressed masses of the people which is easily discernible in Bessie Head's writings.

When Rains Clouds Gather

In *When Rain Clouds Gather* Bessie Head attempts a reconstruction of Makhaya's gradual disengagement from South African politics and his quest for personal contentment.[2] He has only recently left prison in South Africa and has resolved to cross the border to Botswana to experience 'whatever illusion of freedom lay ahead'. (p.7) From this quotation it seems clear that the author does not expect Makhaya to achieve much by way of personal freedom in Botswana. This is not to deny that he has enough good reasons for wanting to leave his country. The novel in various parts provides a catalogue of atrocities against the blacks by the oppressive regime in South Africa. However, the work is also critical of the blacks in the way they at times easily compromise their human dignity and passively acquiesce in the harsh laws of the rulers. They do not appear to be doing enough to help themselves. For example, why does a man like Makhaya not stay on and fight the system from within, instead of fleeing to another country? South Africa may be 'mentally and spiritually dead through the constant perpetuation of false beliefs'. (p.16) But one does not change these 'false beliefs' by running away from the situation which they have helped to generate. Nor does an intense hatred of apartheid in itself provide an effective solution.

> He hated the white man in a strange way. It was not anything subtle or sly or mean, but a powerful accumulation of years and years and centuries and centuries of silence. It was as though, in all this silence, black men had not lived nor allowed themselves an expression of feeling. But they had watched their lives overrun and everything taken away. They were like Frankenstein monsters, only animated by the white man for his own needs. Otherwise they had no life apart from being servants and slaves. The strain was too much to bear any longer, not when a man was under pressure to assert his own manhood. (p.133)

Makhaya's method of political disengagement is hardly devised to help the African in South Africa to 'assert his own manhood' in the shortest time possible. The impression is clear that he has put his personal safety and comfort before the survival of the group. The black masses in South Africa stand to gain nothing from his escape to Botswana. Nor does he stand the chance of realising his dream of absolute peace of mind and an uninterrupted personal freedom in his new country of abode.

However, once in Botswana, he makes himself useful after an initial period of uncertainties and doubts. He arrives at a time when Gilbert is infusing a new life to the village of Golema Mmidi. These activities come alive in the reader's imagination because of the author's attractive method of presentation. They signal the beginning of a necessary change, a radical departure from the conservative past. Moreover, they seek to provide the necessities of life for a people who are becoming used to hardship, and make available to them the kind of orientation which will certainly result in their future happiness and prosperity. Gilbert by his example imparts dignity to work on the farms and cattle locations, and teaches in a concrete manner the need for cooperation in all fields, if the goal of self-sufficiency is to be attained. This is the philosophy which lies behind the farming and cattle cooperatives. With the tobacco cooperatives he brings out the women to play a leading role for the first time in the commercial life of the village, thus directly raising the status of women in the community. Makhaya takes charge of this aspect of the programme and, through his efficiency, wins the admiration of the women and the villagers at large. The building of dams, the intro- duction of farming under irrigation, the propagation of millet as a cash crop, the establishment of the thrift and loan club – all different aspects of a well co-ordinated masterplan – result in a meaningful and bene- ficial development. They create in the villagers a sense of belonging. They satisfy their physical needs and provide them with a great deal of spiritual satisfaction. Such is the originality displayed by Gilbert, and the loyal and competent support given by Makhaya, that the villagers come to regard both men as local heroes.

Gilbert and Makhaya succeed mainly because they have the unflinching support of eminent villagers who, ordinarily, would have regarded them with suspicion. These powerful individuals soon discover that Golema Mmidi is fast becoming a place of pastoral elegance, a centre of intense creativity which deserves the respect and sympathy of all responsible people. This situation they owe to two outsiders who have introduced to the village laudable programmes of self-fulfilment for every villager wise enough to take advantage of the new ventures. In these circumstances, the only reasonable thing to do is to encourage their efforts. So we find Dinorego not only adopting Gilbert and

Makhaya as his children, but also giving them all necessary help and protection. He is a highly respectable man, well-known for his determination to stand against evil and do good. For this reason he is popular with his people who admire the way he continues to resist the evil machinations of Chief Matenge. His support for Gilbert is important in the way it rallies opinion in favour of the agrarian revolution. What gives Gilbert a firm local base is the fact that he eventually marries Maria, Dinorego's daughter. Mma-Millipede for her part uses Christianity to win people to her side. This method is gainfully employed on several occasions in this novel. As we are told, 'she was able to grasp the religion of the missionaries and use its message to adorn and enrich her own originality of thought and expand the natural kindness of her heart'. (p.68) In a disputation with Makhaya she does not only succeed in purging him of part of his violent hatred for South Africa, but also in turning his mind to the personal good qualities of Paulina. Paulina later plays a prominent role in the self-sufficient agricultural economy which Gilbert helps to set up and ends up marrying Makhaya. These individuals who have in one form or another experienced griefs and disappointments in the past are able to start a new, respectable life because they agree to join hands with others in an exciting cooperative venture.

Meaningful progress is achieved only after the threats posed by the old corrupt chiefs and the new self-seeking politicians have been overcome. Chief Matenge is a nuisance. He is unpopular because of 'an overwhelming avariciousness and unpleasant personality'. (p.23) He is a terror to his people and places every kind of obstacle in the way of Gilbert and Makhaya. He relies on the outdated provisions of the land tenure system to obstruct the wishes of the villagers and stand in the way of progress. He oppresses Dinorego for supporting Gilbert and unsuccessfully attempts to deport Makhaya. His attempt to humiliate Paulina leads to his death. His brother, Chief Sekoto is apparently not against progress. But he is too absorbed by his personal pleasures to be effective as a ruler. These two are a disgrace to custom and tradition. They rely on the antiquity of their positions and reckon that the villagers will continue to obey them, however badly they behave. 'The chiefs were unable to see that people could not go on being children forever and their humble servants.' (p.58) Matenge and Sekoto are largely responsible for the erosion of traditional authority. Perhaps this would have come in any case with the increasing secularisation taking place in the village, the creative activities initiated by Gilbert and the rowdy politics introduced by Joas Tsepe. Tsepe and his gang disturb the smooth surface of village life, violently oppose Gilbert and Makhaya and, in the name of African nationalism, harass people, claiming that they are 'in the grip of the force and direction of the law of change'. (p.63) Once it becomes known that Tsepe has been acting as Matenge's secret agent, he is rejected by the people. So it is the case that both traditional authority and the new nationalism are discredited. The greatest hope for the people lies in Gilbert's good works which they now embrace more fervently than ever.

Herein lies the value of Bessie Head's assertion in this work. Golema Mmidi is presented as a place which offers its people with a number of alternative routes to their prosperity and happiness. The uncertainty and conservatism of the past, as represented by the chiefs, are unhelpful and must be discarded in the interests of progress and good government. So also is the wasteful radicalism of the young nationalists. The ruthlessness of Matenge has brought enormous hardship to the people, and the illusion of grandeur which Sekoto consistently entertains has proved deceptive. In what then does the salvation of Africa lie? The novelist keeps her vision of Africa constantly alive throughout the work in the activities of Makhaya. Makhaya leaves South Africa as part of a move towards the abdication of his political responsibility to his people. When he arrives at Golema Mmidi he reckons that he can live a self-contained, self-sufficient life and remain aloof from public affairs. He soon gets involved in the co-operative efforts initiated by Gilbert and marries Paulina. His involvement with the community is complete. He develops an ambition for his new community which he cannot entertain for the old one.

> He liked the idea that the whole of Golema Mmidi would be full of future millionaires. It blended in with his own dreams about Africa because he could not see it other than as a continent of future millionaires, which would compensate for all the centuries of browbeating, hatred, humiliation, and worldwide derision that had been directed to the person of the African man. And communal systems of development which imposed co-operation and sharing of wealth were much better than the dog-eat-dog policies, take-over bids, and grab-what-you-can of big finance. Therefore, in Makhaya's mind, the poverty and tribalism of Africa were a blessing if people could develop sharing everything with each other. (p.156)

Makhaya has certainly matured. Because of his accumulated experience his vision of Africa is now deeper than it was. His thoughts cover a wider spectrum of life and bring under focus the whole of Africa. Given the right atmosphere, there is hardly any need now for individuals to leave South Africa for another part of Africa since every part of the continent can benefit from his new ideas. His attempt at political disengagement in South Africa has resulted in the awareness of the need for greater social and spiritual involvement with the people of Golema Mmidi. It is these laudable activities that the novelist invests with an aura of universal acceptance.

Maru

Bessie Head pursues her interest in the theme of the abdication of political power in *Maru*.[3] The statement here is more powerful than that of her first novel. In *When Rain Clouds Gather* Makhaya abandons all political responsibility for the struggle of the masses in South Africa and flees to Botswana. But, as has been pointed out, he merely throws away one kind of yoke to take on a heavier and more permanent one. His responsibility to his people has been largely notional – he is not earmarked for a particular role or given any specific assignment. What he has been obliged to forego is therefore, to some extent, an intangible duty or privilege. This is not the case with Maru. Maru is a candidate for high office, a paramount chief elect, only waiting to step into the shoes of his predecessor. He is already deeply involved in the administration of his kingdom and plays a leading role in the social and political life of his people. However, his close interaction with the villagers has only succeeded in impressing on him their personal and group inadequacies. He therefore resolves to bring about a change.

> Three quarters of the people on this continent are like Morafi, Seth and Pete – greedy, grasping, back-stabbing, a betrayal of all the good in mankind. I was not born to rule this mess. If I have a place it is to pull down the old structures and create the new. Not for me any sovereignty over my fellow men. I'd remove the blood money, the cruelty and crookery from the top, but that's all. There's a section of my life they will never claim or own. (p.68)

Maru is a visionary who would have preferred to remain behind to reform his society. But he is also a man who 'never doubted the voices of the gods in his heart'. (p.8) The reader is invited to believe that it is these gods which move him against his people, against his bosom friend, Moleka; these gods enjoin him to marry a Masarwa and, for her sake, abandon his people and head 'straight for a home, a thousand miles away where the sun rose, new and new and new each day'. (p.125)

It is in the context in which Maru's activities eventually lead to the freedom of Margaret and, by extension, to the liberation of all subjugated people everywhere that the novelist provides her readers the greatest hope and joy. For throughout the work Margaret is portrayed as a symbol of oppression. She is the representative of a rejected and despised race of people, and is often publicly and privately treated as such. On her arrival at Dilepe village she is humiliated in several ways by the people and the Administration. Little consideration is given to the fact that she is highly qualified for her work as a teacher and deserves to be treated with respect. Once she announces that she is a Masarwa everybody is seized with great panic, and every kind of prejudice is brought into play. The Batswana people direct to a fellow black woman, a so-called Bushman, the type of prejudice and hatred they experience from the whites – 'How universal was the language of oppression! They had said of the Masarwa what every white man had said of every black man.' (p.109) It is from such authorial comments that we know where the sympathy of the novelist lies. If the blacks in South Africa want their complaints against the whites to be taken seriously, they have no right to treat the Masarwa as second-class citizens. The people of Dilepe ought to have accorded Margaret a great deal of respect and treated her as the professional equal of any other teacher in Leseding School. The prejudice against the Masarwa is so much a part of life in Botswana that not even Margaret's early con-nections with Moleka and Dikeledi are enough to save her from dis-grace. It may well be that Margaret's sad experiences are essential for her to be able to fulfil the 'purpose and burden' imposed on her from childhood by her foster mother: 'One day, you will help your people.' (p.17) So we find that, like Maru, she too is destined to become an instrument of change and rejuvenation.

The clash between Maru and Moleka helps to accelerate this process of change. The rivalry between the two is used to highlight the ruthless-ness which close friends can sometimes display when vying for the love of a woman, even when the woman involved is a Masarwa. Maru and Moleka are notorious in the village for their disgraceful love affairs, for the way they often share the same women and rejoice over their conquests. As we are told, 'Maru always fell in love with his women'. (p.35) But to Moleka women are no more than toys to be used and discarded. So we see that although the two look outwardly equally irresponsible, their purpose and method are different. This individual attitude is reflected in their relationship with Margaret. Moleka capitalises on the fact that he is the first to meet Margaret who falls in love with him at first sight. He is kind to her, but is unable to make her happy. He plays to the gallery by appearing to admit all Masarwa to an artificial type of brotherhood. His motives are suspect. Maru is convinced that Moleka will, as usual, eventually disappoint Margaret, that he will do nothing conclusive to remove her social stigma. He there-fore decides to move against his friend partly because of his love for Margaret and partly to contain Moleka's infinite capacity to do evil. He

191

realises from the beginning that the task is not going to be an easy one and that he has to tread cautiously.

> Perhaps he had seriously miscalculated Moleka's power, that Moleka possessed some superior quality over which he had little control. Was it a superior kind of love? Or was it a superior kind of power? He'd trust the love but not the power because power could parade as anything. He'd weep too, if he really believed that Moleka had a greater love than his own. What his heart said was that Moleka had a greater power than he had, and he had felt no remorse at what he had done to the only person he loved as he loved his wife. This brooding and uncertainty made him malicious. (pp.9-10)

After a short period of doubt Maru becomes openly 'malicious' and plans to dislodge his friend from his position of strength with Margaret.

Maru shows superior intelligence and greater ability at scheming by getting Moleka to renew his love affair with Dikeledi. He feels that Moleka has toyed with his sister for too long and decides to use this situation against his friend.

> 'Why must Moleka have everything? He's always touched gold and handled it carelessly. I've always touched straw. This time I'm stealing the gold because I've grown tired of the straw.' (p.84)

Moleka falls into Maru's trap, marries Dikeledi and leave Maru free to make advances to Margaret. This leads to a complete breakdown in the relationship between the two friends. When Maru finally leaves his kingdom with Margaret the position of the two rivals becomes irreconcilable. They become sworn enemies, one would imagine, for life. In this way the novelist resolves the complex love tangle she has dextrously created among the contending lovers, Maru and Moleka on the one hand, Dikeledi and Margaret on the other. Dikeledi and Margaret are deeply in love with Moleka who loves only Margaret. Maru watches from the sidelines until he is ready to act. He eventually intervenes in order to prevent Moleka from marrying Margaret and merely retaining his sister as one of his many concubines. The decisive action of Maru helps to clarify the various issues at stake and throws some light on why he falls out finally with a bosom friend to fulfil a divine mission which enjoins him to live by 'the standards of the soul'. (p.126)

Maru's marriage to Margaret is presented not only as a personal act of enlightened self-interest. It is also a major political achievement. By it the novelist makes an important statement of hope and redemption for all oppressed people in Africa and elsewhere. The concluding passage of the novel puts this beyond all resonable doubt.

When people of the Masarwa tribe heard about Maru's marriage to one of their own, a door silently opened on the small, dark airless room in which their souls had been shut for a long time. The wind of freedom, which was blowing throughout the world for all people, turned and flowed into the room. As they breathed in the fresh, clear air their humanity awakened. They examined their condition. There was the fetid air, the excreta and the horror of being an oddity of the human race, with half the head of a man and half the body of a donkey. They laughed in an embarrassed way, scratching their heads. How had they fallen into this condition when, indeed, they were as human as everyone else? They started to run out into the sunlight, then they turned and looked at the dark, small room. They said: 'We are not going back there.'

People like the Batswana, who did not know that the wind of freedom had also reached people of the Masarwa tribe, were in for an unpleasant surprise because it would be no longer possible to treat Masarwa people in an inhuman way without getting killed yourself. (pp.126-7)

The message is for all those who treat others 'in an inhuman way'. The racists in South Africa stand a good chance of 'getting killed' unless they change their vicious apartheid laws before it is too late. Maru abandons his political responsibility in order to demonstrate his belief in freedom of action for the individual and help extend that freedom to people of all races.

A Question of Power

A Question of Power is as yet Bessie Head's most complex work.[4] In it she combines the richness of material with depth of analysis to produce a powerful novel. The complexity of the work is reflected in the way it progresses almost imperceptibly from the theme of alienation to that of commitment. Elizabeth moves in and out of sanity and, on every such occasion, advances the overall objective of the author who uses her deranged mind as a symbol of the activities of a deranged society. For this reason the probing of the interior personal experiences of the chief character goes much further here than in any of the previous novels so that her sufferings and hallucinations may reproduce in full the sufferings of rejected humanity.

In this work the abdication of political kingship reaches its climax. The novelist not only criticises the questionable use of power by the present South African government and other oppressive regimes, she also looks ahead to the future to the ultimate survival of the oppressed.

193

Hence the emphasis on commitment. With dedication and commitment the oppressed will survive the greatest atrocities and re-establish themselves in dignity and honour. It is for this purpose that Elizabeth is endowed with a great capacity for self-control and an unlimited power of endurance so that she may contribute maximally to the work of rehabilitation which takes place at Motabeng. This work is undertaken by a number of local and foreign groups. The villagers are encouraged to take an active part in turning the village into a new world. The youth-development work-groups give impetus to the ideals of social transformation. However, the attempt to which the novelist seems to attach the greatest importance is that of Elizabeth who succeeds in finding a new home for the Cape Gooseberry in Botswana.

> The work had a melody like that – a complete stranger like the Cape Gooseberry settled down and became a part of the village life of Motabeng. It loved the hot, dry Botswana summers as they were a replica of the Mediterranean summers of its home in the Cape. (p.153)

The author symbolically gives approval to an exile's sense of commitment to her new environment and indicates the need for sacrifice and hard work, if new ideals are to flourish in strange surroundings.

These ideals of self-reliance and self-sufficiency succeed through well-coordinated local and international agencies. Individuals and organisations play significant roles. Eugene occupies a prominent position. He discovers and utilises local talents, mobilises opinion in favour of team work, develops in the people the urge to create, sets up local-industries, projects and cooperative groups to produce and market goods. Why is an Afrikaner refugee allowed to take so much credit for the work of social transformation at Motabeng? Ordinarily, he will be unacceptable to the people. But he has shared the fate of the blacks in South Africa and has been kicked out of the country. Like Elizabeth, he has developed a sense of commitment to his new home and decided to make it a comfortable place to live in. The author may be emphasising the equality in suffering between Eugene and the black man in much the same way that Margaret, the Masarwa, becomes equal to Dikeledi, a girl of royal blood, at a stage in *Maru*. In both cases political power has slipped from the hands of those born to wield it and is now being shared by others. The author shows clearly that she believes only in 'a power that belongs to all of mankind and in which all mankind can share'. (p.135) The agricultural experiments at Motabeng succeed only in a situation of power-sharing in which the people exercise a sense of belonging. The Danes and several other individuals – Tom, Thoko, Mrs

Jones, Mrs Stanley – who vigorously contribute to this effort do so as members of a team, not as overseers or overlords. This is the secret of the success story of Motabeng. This is the concept of power Bessie Head seems to approve of in this novel.

The work devotes a lot of space to Elizabeth's interior personal experiences and her connection with Sello and Dan. The novelist, as it were, opens a window into Elizabeth's tortured mind for the reader to see. What the reader perceives during her periods of insanity is thoroughly disturbing. Many factors contribute to this state of affairs – her torment by Sello and Dan, the frightening role of Medusa, her experiences of apartheid in South Africa where 'a black man or woman was just born to be hated' (p.19), her long periods of solitary confinements. The author's treatment of Elizabeth's mental breakdown has some autobiographical significance. Compare, for example, what the mission school principal tells Elizabeth about her origins,

'We have a full docket on you. You must be very careful. Your mother was insane. If you're not careful you'll get insane just like your mother. Your mother was a white woman. They had to lock her up, as she was having a child by the stable boy, who was a native,' (p.16)

with what the author says of her own mother.

'I feel with a situation like we have in South Africa, there must be a lot of people who have tragic circumstances surrounding their birth.

'When there are so many artificial barriers set up between the races, people being people are going to try to break through those artificial barriers.

'As far as my mother was concerned, she was from a Scottish family but born in South Africa. The family owned race horses . . . and they kept Black men in the stables to groom, exercise and clean the horses.

'My mother, for some reason of her own, was attracted to one of the grooms . . . and in that way she acquired me.

'After she had taken association with him, her family had her committed (to a mental hospital). I was initially handed over to a White family for adoption, that is an Afrikaner Boer family. After a week I was returned since they said the baby appeared to be Black and they could not accept a baby like this.'[5]

The novelist handles this aspect of Elizabeth's life with the knowledge of one who has had similar experiences or can at least put herself mentally in Elizabeth's situation. Physical and mental isolation is used as a principal weapon of making the victim a prisoner of her own thoughts. On such occasions she lives in a fantasy world of her own, dreams dreams and sees visions which, however frightening, the novelist projects before the reader's eyes in a cinematographic fashion. The novelist's achievement in this connection should not be underestimated. The method is entirely successful as a means of communication and of revealing Elizabeth's anguish. It exposes the community of feeling between the novelist and character, even though Bessie Head takes extreme care to keep the two personalities separate. This method also gives the reader an insight into how the iniquitous system of apartheid not only tries to weaken the body but also to destroy the soul of its victim. For Elizabeth 'the dividing line between dream perceptions and waking reality was to become confused'. (p.22) This results in uncertainty. But it is out of this situation that she ultimately acquires the sense of commitment to do positive good to the village of Motabeng.

Elizabeth's mental breakdown is caused mainly by two characters, Sello and Dan. The two are in different ways agents of evil, even though at various times Sello displays a certain capacity to do good. The book is structured in a way that devotes the first part mainly to Sello and the second part to Dan. Even so, it is not easy to apportion tragic responsibility for Elizabeth's insanity and anguish in this neat way. Sello, the white-robed monk, appears in Elizabeth's room at night to throw her into a state of mental torment. If, in this way, he starts her insanity, Dan certainly aggravates the situation by the obscene display of his exploits with women of insatiable sexual appetite. His depth of depravity with women like Madame Loose-Bottom is intended to highlight the social obscenity and political viciousness which dominate interpersonal relationships in racially disturbed areas like South Africa. His greater responsibility in the matter of Elizabeth's mental breakdown is acknowledged by the victim herself.

'I am not a tribal African. If I had been, I would have known the exact truth about Sello, whether he was good or bad. There aren't any secrets among tribal Africans. I was shut out from the everyday affairs of this world. Dan knew and traded on my ignorance. He did more. He struck me such terrible blows, the pain made me lose my mind.' (p.145)

This partly exonerates Sello, but certainly not his accomplice, Medusa, who 'was simply given a wide, free field to display her major preoccupations, the main priority of which was the elimination of Elizabeth'. (p.62) She is a symbol of obscenity and destruction, and does more to torment Elizabeth than any of the other figures, from Buddha to Jesus Christ, which appear to the victim in her hallucinations. The author cleverly brings these forces together as a monumental evil and shows how they combine to oppress Elizabeth and alienate her from the Batswana villagers.

It is by a display of strong will-power that Elizabeth extricates herself from these evils and stops her soul from remaining an 'open territory easily invaded by devils'. (p.192) The work is so superbly executed that at the end the local and universal significance of Elizabeth's experiences becomes obvious for all to see. She recovers spiritually from the mental confusion she has been in for a long period, feeling 'this time infinitely more powerful and secure'. (p.202) The economic recovery is even more spectacular with the money she makes from the sale of gooseberry jam. She feels generally triumphant and hopeful; her confidence in man and the supremacy of reason have been restored – 'There is only one God and his name is Man. And Elizabeth is his prophet.' (p.206) She is now at peace with herself and has put behind her the harassment and uncertainties of the recent past. She feels strong enough to commit herself, body and soul, to her country of sojourn.

> She put Shorty to bed and, for the first time in three years, embraced the solitude of the night with joy . . . As she fell asleep, she placed one soft hand over her land. It was a gesture of belonging. (p.206)

It is this commitment which makes it possible for her to join the group of foreign volunteers and local talents who bring lasting benefit to Botswana.

Again, Elizabeth's enormous capacity for suffering and her ability to overcome evil in the long run are put in the context of the struggle for equality by the oppressed people of South Africa and other parts of the world.

> The victim of a racial attitude cannot think of the most coherent and correct thing to do to change the heart of evil. He can scare them with violence. He can slaughter them; but he isn't the origin of the poison. It's like two separate minds at work. The victim is really the most flexible, the most free person on earth. He doesn't have to think up endless laws and endless falsehoods. His jailer does that. His jailer creates the chains and the oppression. He is merely presented with it. He is presented with a thousand and one hells to live through, and he usually lives through them all. The faces of oppressed people are not ugly. They are scarred with suffering. But the torturers become more hideous day by day. There are no limits to the excesses of evil they indulge in. There's no end to the darkness and death of the soul. The victim who sits in jail always sees a bit of the sunlight shining through. He sits there and dreams of beautiful wonders. He loses his children, his wife, his everything. What happens to all those tears? Who is the greater man – the man who cries, broken by anguish, or his scoffing, mocking, jeering oppressor?' (p.84)

We have here the kind of profound, universal political statement which the author provides at the end of *Maru*. The warning to the oppressor this time is, however, more subtle. If the victim of a racial attitude is 'the most free person on earth', then the oppressor has gained nothing by his oppression. He only succeeds in making life more difficult for himself and others. The resilience of the exile which Elizabeth's life symbolises in this work and the profitable cultivation of the Cape Gooseberry in a foreign land are intended to dramatise the fact that the spirit of freedom cannot be permanently suppressed, even by the most brutal dictatorship.

The Collector of Treasures

The Collector of Treasures is a collection of stories set in a Botswana village.[6] Some of these stories recreate the myths connected with the origin of the village and espouse communal life and togetherness. Different aspects of traditional African customs and practices are touched upon – tribal migration, witchcraft, traditional religion as opposed to Christianity. Other stories deal with the breakdown of tribal or village life which results from the introduction of a monetary economy, western ideas, foreign religion and education. The sequence of the stories recognises the gradual deterioration in the quality of rural life and the decline in moral values.

In each of these stories a woman plays a leading role and provides the focus from which all other characters are considered and evaluated. Many of the stories are used to make social and political comments, especially as they relate to the status of women in a modern African society – the village under focus is used as a microcosm of traditional Africa at large. The work is valuable for the human interest it encompasses, its exciting literary style and the imaginative skill displayed by the author. There are thirteen stories in the collection. But only eight of them are discussed below.

'The Deep River: A Story of Ancient Tribal Migration'

The story puts Sebembele and Rankwana right in the centre of the activities which eventually lead to the migration of some of the people of the kingdom of Monemapee to the south. Sebembele relinquishes his right to the throne because of his love for Rankwana, throws the kingdom into great confusion and creates a problem of succession to the throne. His two brothers, Ntema and Mosemme, capitalise on the situation and attempt to make him unpopular with the people by emphasising what they consider his weakness for a woman. Sebembele shows his unbending resolve and deep attachment to Rankwana by leaving with her and some loyal subjects to establish a new settlement elsewhere.

To this day there is a separate Botalaote ward in the capital village of the Bamangwato, and the people refer to themselves still as the people of Talaote. The old men there keep on giving confused and contradictory accounts of their origins, but they say they lost their place of birth over a woman. They shake their heads and say that women have always caused a lot of trouble in the world. They say that the child of their chief was named, Talaote, to commemorate their expulsion from the kingdom of Monemapee. (p.6)

Most of Sebembele's problems arise from the social context in which he finds himself – his royal blood, the customs and beliefs of his people, his position in the family. The situation is complicated by his secret love affair with Rankwana which results in the birth of Makobi. Apart from all else, Makobi is a strong bond which holds Sebembele and Rankwana together, making for Sebembele the choice between Rankwana and the throne an intolerable dilemma. 'At one moment his heart would urge him to renounce the woman and child, but each time he saw Rankwana it abruptly said the opposite. He could come to no decision.' (p.4) Sebembele tries to please himself at the expense of tradition and, in the process, does a great deal of damage to society. Indigenous culture usually leaves little room for the display of personal choice – group loyalty comes first. In traditional society any assertion of individualism, such as we have here, tends to undermine the whole structure of society and results in social instability.

The whole story is constructed on two sustained metaphors, those involving 'a deep river' and 'a face' – 'the people lived together like a deep river', 'the people lived without faces, except for their chief, whose face was the face of all the people'. (p.1). A deep river is still and peaceful; so is the land under Monemapee. When the land shows only one face under a ruler, there is harmony. When his children reveal individual faces, they bring chaos and partisanship to the land. It is hardly possible for the people to speak with one voice for all time. One has to recognise the effects of social changes on people. With the passage of time come increased secularisation and the need for greater public enlightenment. These are unavoidable changes which often disturb the serenity of village life. They encourage man to experiment with new ideas, try to attain new heights and, if necessary, make a new beginning. The migration here is presented as one of such attempts.

199

'The Village Saint'

'The Village Saint' deals with the fate of Mma-Mompati who imposes herself on the villagers of Bamangwato as a saint for a long time. She earns her reputation by outwardly ministering to the sick, helping the needy and taking care of the young and old. She courts cheap popularity by appearing to be gentle and pious.

No villager could die without being buried by Mma-Mompati: she attended the funerals of rich and poor. No one could fall ill without receiving the prayers of Mma-Mompati. Two days a week she set aside for visits to the hospital and in the afternoon, during visiting hours, she made the rounds of the hospital ward, Bible in hand. She would stop at each bed and enquire solicitously:

'And what may ail you, my daughter? And what may ail you, my son?'

At which, of course, the grateful ailing one would break out with a long list of woes. She had a professional smile and a professional frown of concern for everything, just like the priests. But topping it all was the fluidity and ease with which she could pray. (pp.14-15)

The approach of the author is to dwell extensively at the beginning of the story on the various ways in which Mma-Mompati tries to fool the people and the measure of public recognition she has achieved locally. In a typical Bessie Head irony we are told 'she has had a long reign of twenty-six years, and a fool-proof facade'. (p.13) The method is effective because it helps to highlight the tragedy of her fall from the great social heights she is supposed to have attained.

Her son, Mompati, and her daughter-in-law, Mary, are used as the instrument of Mma-Mompati's downfall. To start with, her husband deserts her and leaves the villagers guessing how really good she is. At this stage the truth is not completely out yet. There is still the tendency to give her the benefit of the doubt. So long as her son remains 'overwhelmingly devoted' to her and satisfies all her financial needs, all is well. Once he gets married and behaves as a faithful husband, he gets into trouble with his mother. Because of his mother's excesses and greed Mompati becomes more attached to Mary and keeps his pay packet to himself. This infuriates the mother who applies various sanctions against Mary in order to make her uncomfortable. The facade is removed and the people are given their first opportunity to look behind it at the real person. As we are told, 'the pose of God and Jesus were blown to the winds and the demented vampire behind it was too terrible to behold'. (p.18) Mma-Mompati is recognised for the cheat and liar she has been all the time. Far from being a village saint she becomes a notorious villain.

'Jacob: The Story of a Faith-Healing Priest'

This is one of the longest stories in the collection. It therefore gives the author an opportunity to demonstrate her mastery of the techniques of storytelling and her ability to turn storytelling into an event of great social and cultural significance. We find many of the qualities of a good story to which reference is made in chapter six – a beginning which arrests attention, attractive narrative skill, lively descriptions, a strong story line. Flashbacks are effectively used to give information about the previous lives of the main characters. In this way the author is able to avoid unnecessary details in the body of the work and concentrate attention on the impact which the activities of selected individuals have on the social life of Makaleng.

The work contra-distinguishes between the orientations and attitudes to life of two prophets – Jacob and Lebojang. One is honest, the other is thoroughly dishonest. One is poor, the other is abnormally rich. The people initially despise Jacob and follow Lebojang in large numbers. The approaches of the priests to the ministry are also different. Lebojang adopts the method of a soothsayer and presents himself as possessing vast magical powers. He exploits the gullibility of the people and makes a lot of money for himself by handing out false prophecies to those who come 'to make use of his stunning powers'. (p.28) This prophet is an embodiment of evil. But it takes the people some time to discover his devilish intentions.

> Such was the power of Lebojang; he would come out with names and dates and prophecies. His charges for these services were very high. It did not matter to him that people were secretly poisoned or driven mad by his prophecies; he simply took his money and that was that. But at least these prophecies of names and dates could bear the light of day. Once his other deeds became known people were to ponder deeply on the nature of evil. (p.28)

In the same way it takes the villagers a great deal of effort to come to appreciate Jacob's goodness. Given Lebojang's example, they are inclined to feel that a prophet must be rich and prosperous to be effective. Little do they realise that a poor and honest man may become the vehicle for the transmission of God's words. Jacob develops true fellowship among members of his congregation and wins more people to his flock through the use of practical help.

A man in that gathering would have no work for a year and his family would be destitute. After seeing Jacob and participating in the worship of his church, the man would strike a job in two or three days; not anything spectacular, but his poverty would be eased. There was something else too that developed in a quite natural way – an exchange of gifts system. No one ever left Jacob's hut without a parcel. Many grateful seekers of help brought gifts to Jacob: a bag of corn, a bag of sugar, a box of eggs, and so on. These gifts in turn filled many destitute people with good things so that they did not leave Jacob's home hungry. (p.29)

In this work Lebojang is used as a foil to Jacob. It is through his nefarious activities that the good works of Jacob are appreciated. While Lebojang ends up in jail as a murderer, Jacob eventually settles down to a life of marital bliss. The author quite rightly devotes a lot of attention to Jacob who obeys the voice of his God at every point and carries out his every injunction. He is a man who has himself experienced poverty and has been defrauded of his rightful inheritance through the evil machinations of an uncle – 'Those who are born to suffer, experience suffering to its abysmal depths.' (p.24) Jacob's sad experiences of the past are a necessary part of his preparation for the glorious task which is now assigned to him. Children are made to play a crucial role in his ministry in order to give a sense of continuity and emphasise how different his priesthood is from that of Lebojang. Furthermore, Johannah brings a fresh inspiration to Jacob and opens up new avenues of faithful evangelical work. He is exposed to a kind of domestic happiness that has always seemed beyond his reach.

As for Jacob, a whole new world of learning and living opened up for him. He soon found that his home was run peacefully with clockwork precision, by a woman full of the traditions and customs of the country. Jacob had no full knowledge of these customs as his upbringing had been that of an outcast living apart from the household and it was as though he was transported back into a childhood he might have had had his mother lived. His first wife had been a very different type of woman from Johannah, very modern and daring and very de-tribalised. If there were such things as customs which governed the behaviour of children and adults, she knew nothing about this. Now, from Johannah, he was to learn that there were strict, hard-and-fast laws, governing the conduct of family life. (p.34)

It is a measure of the author's achievement that the reader has been well prepared for this glorious end to Jacob's domestic and religious activities.

'Witchcraft'

'Witchcraft' thrives on the conflict which arises when a traditional society comes in contact with Christianity. The reader is presented with a society which initially fervently believes in witchcraft and the enormous evil and uncertainty which go with its devilish practices. This belief governs the way of life of the people and influences their relationship with other groups or sects – 'If a whole society creates a belief in something, that something is likely to become real.' (p.47) It is usual for cheats, liars and quack doctors to attempt to profit from such massive ignorance and backwardness. Again, belief in witchcraft is likely to leave a moral void which, in this case, manifests itself in the display of jealousy, lack of confidence in one's self, moral laxity and social decadence. These are faults which must be uprooted if society is to survive. The quickest way out is to remove the root cause, which is the villagers' unhealthy reliance on superstitious beliefs and practices.

The conflict between Christianity and superstition takes the form of an encounter between Lekena, the Tswana doctor, and Mma-Mabele who comes from a more enlightened part of the village – 'I know I can be poisoned and so meet my end, but I cannot be bewitched. I don't believe in it.' (p.48) She is one of the first few to embrace Christianity. Lekena takes every opportunity to test her faith. When she is in trouble, he offers her traditional medicine, claiming that Christianity cannot save her. She pulls through in difficult circumstances and thus shames her tormentor.

'I know we have Tswana custom as well as Christian custom, Lekena. But all the people respect Christian custom. There is no one who would laugh when a person mentions the name of the Lord. This thing which I see now laughs when I pray to the Lord.' (p.55)

Modernity triumphs over tradition and superstition and paves the way for the people to live a new purposeful life.

'The Wind and a Boy'

The story tells of the extraordinary life and death of Friedman. He is born in peculiar circumstances and is reared by his grandmother who 'was one of the old churchgoers'. (p.71) This ensures a fairly comfortable upbringing in an atmosphere which emphasises high moral standards. Like the grandmother he has a 'flaming youth' and participates fully with other boys in outdoor activities. Indoors, especially at bedtime, he is told stories which fire his imagination and urge him to great achievements. To the villagers he is an impressive lad who is given to gainful pursuits. 'All his movements were neat, compact, decisive, and for his age he was a boy who knew his own mind.' (p.70)

As in 'The Village Saint', the author here contrasts deceptive outward appearances with the choatic private behaviour of an individual. While mothers in the village hold Friedman up to their children as a paragon of virtue, the boy is, in fact, an accomplished thief and a leader of an armed robbery gang. He has been inspired by his grandmother's version of the story of Robinson Crusoe and decides to play that role. 'One day, I'm going to be like that. I'm going to be a hunter like Robinson Crusoe and bring meat to all the people.' (p.73) He brings upon himself unnecessary responsibility and uses this as an excuse for his disappointing behaviour. It is surprising that he is able to maintain this facade for such a long time. However, it is clear that the author does not approve of his nefarious activities, whatever superficial reasons are invented for them. He can fool the villagers for as long as he wishes, but he soon finds out that city dwellers have their own way of eliminating crooks.

> In this timeless, sleepy village, the goats stood and suckled their young ones on the main road or lay down and took their afternoon naps there. The motorists either stopped for them or gave way. But it appeared that the driver of the truck had neither brakes on his car nor a driving licence. He belonged to the new, rich civil-servant class whose salaries had become fantastically high since independence. They had to have cars in keeping with their new status; they had to have any car, as long as it was a car; they were in such a hurry about everything that they couldn't be bothered to take driving lessons. And thus progress, development, and a pre-occupation with status and living-standards first announced themselves to the village. It looked like being an ugly story with many decapitated bodies on the main road. (p.75)

The author dramatises the conflict between town and country, between old and new, with an implied adverse criticism of town life, especially the attitude of the new middle class in their haste for material progress. The criminality of the truck driver has on this occasion helped to eliminate a boy who has had an 'enchanted wind' blowing for him for too long. The weeding out of such undesirable elements is presented as a necessary step to the peaceful 'development' of the cities.

'Snapshots of a Wedding'

'Snapshots of a Wedding' is an account of the conflict situation in which Kegoletile finds himself when he has to choose between Neo and Mathata for a wife. The choice is made particularly difficult for him because the two girls are vastly different in temperament and orientation. Neo is educated, but proud and ungovernable while Mathata is humble, submissive but illiterate. Kegoletile's relatives naturally prefer Mathata, but he is concerned about the economic reality of the situation – the only work Mathata 'would ever do was that of a housemaid, while Neo had endless opportunities before her – typist, book-keeper, or secretary'. (p.77) So he decides for Neo, but not before he has had a child by Mathata.

The wedding between Kegoletile and Neo is used to dramatise some of the changes which are affecting village life as far as wedding ceremonies are concerned. An important factor in this case is the arrogant attitude of Neo which reduces enthusiasm for the wedding from both families. For this reason the maternal aunts play their crucial roles in a perfunctory manner and other participants act merely to satisfy formalities. What the reader is presented with is not the usual traditional wedding in which a whole village is emotionally involved and in which friends, relations and well-wishers participate energetically. This is the measure of the change which the author intends to com-municate. The villagers seem to accept this change and go along passively with what they consider to be 'a modern wedding' – 'If the times are changing, we keep up with them.' (p.77) In the conflict between tradition and modern experience the latter is allowed to prevail. Kegoletile exercises a personal choice against the prevailing mood of the villagers and is allowed to get away with it.

'The Special One'

This story is an opposite social commentary on married life in a given society. The 'special one' is Gaenametse who seeks to gain respectability, as it were, through the back door. She starts off as a 'wild and wayward' woman who tries to work her husband to death sexually. The man runs away; she becomes miserable and blames every other person but herself for her fate. The author leaves no one in doubt that she is a morally chaotic person and that the man is justified in deserting her. It is difficult to believe her profession of love for her husband – 'No one could have loved my husband as much as I did. I loved him too much.' (p.84) – considering the way she attempts to re-establish herself in society after her divorce. She shows an inordinate desire to make love with young boys after the alleged practice of Mrs Maleboge. But while Mrs Maleboge apparently succeeds, she fails woefully because she 'could not keep her emotions within bounds'. (p.85) She is a special one only in an ironical and ridiculous sense.

The author puts a twist to the story at the end by linking it with the problems of polygamy.

> And as I walked on alone I thought that the old days of polygamy are gone and done with, but the men haven't yet accepted that the women want them to be monogamists. (p.86)

At this point Bessie Head's feminism is suddenly brought to the fore. Polygamy is an accepted way of life in the traditional society where her story is set. But she intentionally creates female characters who display strong monogamous tendencies which bring them into clash with their husbands or their relatives. For example, Mrs Maleboge wants to monopolise all her husband's property on his death. This results in a dreadful conflict between her and her brothers-in-law, which is resolved in their favour in a court of law. Again, it is because Gaenametse is so possessive that her husband deserts her. The impression is clear that if these women have allowed themselves to be guided in their actions by traditional customs and practices, the outcome for them may have been happier. The women suffer in each case because they attempt to impose on society 'modern' ideas which it is not yet prepared to embrace. The days of polygamy are not 'gone and done with'. True, women may, out of enlightened self-interest, want their men to become monogamists. But the time has not come for women to have their way in this matter. The need for change which the author indicates here is part of the whole pre-occupation of the feminist movement and the advocates of equal rights for women.

'The Collector of Treasures'

The title story, like most of the other stories, is written with a bias for a woman's point of view. The story is built around Dikeledi's personality – her thoughts, actions, orientation to life, hopes and fears. She is at the centre of affairs, and it is in her relationship with other people that they fail or come alive. The picture which emerges is that of a talented woman, devoted mother and dutiful housewife who gets into trouble because she is misused and discarded by a heartless man. In the midst of her domestic unhappiness Dikeledi finds time to make friends, and derives enormous pleasure in doing good – 'She had always found gold amidst the ash, deep loves that had joined her heart to the hearts of others . . . she was the collector of such treasures'. (p.91) These noble qualities are ably demonstrated in her relationship with her neighbours, Paul Thebolo and his wife, Kenalepe. The author devotes so much attention to this friendship because of the crucial role which the couple play in the events of the story and the fact that, in their apparent marital bliss, they provide a contrast to the bitter experiences of Dikeledi and Garesego. The intimacy which develops between the two women is particularly useful in the amount of comfort and inspiration it provides Dikeledi and the way it allows her to exercise a sense of fulfilment.

I am the woman whose thatch does not leak. Whenever my friends wanted to thatch their huts, I was there. They would never do it without me. I was always busy and employed because it was with these hands that I fed and reared my children. My husband left me after four years of marriage but I managed well enough to feed those mouths. If people did not pay me in money for my work, they paid me with gifts of food.' (p.90)

While Dikeledi is portrayed almost as an embodiment of goodness, Garesego is presented as an odious, vicious and irresponsible man who by his activities exposes his wife and children to physical and moral danger. He exploits mercilessly the situation which 'relegated to men a superior position in the tribe, while women were regarded, in a congenial sense, as being an inferior form of human life'. (p.92) He deserts his wife and children, keeps several concubines outside his matrimonial home, refuses to pay his children's school fees and becomes an alcoholic. His encounter with Paul Thebolo on the suspicion that he is having an affair with his wife is intended to show how credulous and restless he has become. The portrait may have been overdrawn in order to provide extenuating reasons for his murder by Dikeledi. He certainly provokes her when, after a prolonged absence, he suddenly returns to her hut only to demand sex and lord it over her. The author exposes Dikeledi's thoughts and reflections for the reader to assess. Her mind has become a battleground where she tries to fight back desperate suggestions.

Her thought processes were not very clear to her. There was something she could not immediately touch upon. Her life had become holy to her during all those years she had struggled to maintain herself and the children. She had filled her life with treasures of kindness and love she had gathered from others and it was all this that she wanted to protect from defilement by an evil man. Her first panic-stricken thought was to gather up the children and flee the village. But where to go? Garesego did not want a divorce, she had left him to approach her about the matter, she had desisted from taking any other man. She turned her thoughts this way and that and could find no way out except to face him. If she wrote back, don't you dare put foot in the yard I don't want to see you, he would ignore it. Black women didn't have that kind of power. A thoughtful, brooding look came over her face. (p.101)

Dikeledi is not a mindless criminal, but she is a murderer all the same. No amount of irresponsibility on the part of a man can be used as justification for murdering him. Dikeledi ought to have applied some of the other remedies open to her to achieve redress and maintain her financial and social independence. Paul's promise of help to Dikeledi at the end – 'You don't have to worry about the children, Mma-Banabothe. I'll take them as my own and give them all a secondary school education.' (p.103) – may be intended as some compensation for the help she has rendered his family. But it tends to confirm Garesego's suspicions and provides an obnoxious reward for murder. However, the author's sentimentalism is redeemed somewhat by the fact that Dikeledi is sent to jail where she experiences hardship.

The story is used to discuss important aspects of Botswana life. The author is particularly interested in the condition of man in the society. There are two kinds of men – the destructive kind which Garesego Mokopi represents, and the kind which creates himself 'anew' which Paul Thebolo represents. All the characters appear to fall neatly into one camp or other. Care is taken to ensure that all the important female characters fall into the first camp. Even so, the author is not satisfied with the role assigned to women – 'Women still suffered from all the calamities that befall an inferior form of human life.' (p.92) During the difficult days of slavery and colonialism they have given their menfolk strong logistic support. They now deserve better treatment. The author reflects on the rewards of independence which for Botswana has so far been elusive and throws a searchlight on the conditions of the prisons which are mainly punitive institutions. Even in the difficult conditions of a prison Dikeledi is still able to display her talent and resourcefulness. So intimately is the author attached to her female characters. So remarkable is her contribution to the feminine literary tradition.

Serowe: Village of the Rain Wind

In this book Bessie Head uses her imaginative skill as a novelist to reconstruct the history of Serowe in a favourable light.[7] She relies mainly on oral tradition and the recollections of many villagers in different spheres of life to highlight changes which have taken place in the village over a period of time. Her emphasis is on social reforms, educational progress and self-help projects. She describes the confusion which these efforts bring to the previously smooth surface of village life. Serowe is gradually transformed from a conservative traditional village into a progressive one, and this necessarily has great social and political repercussion for the people. The period unhappily coincides with the establishment, glorification and termination of British imperialism. The result is that several stages of Serowe's development are inextricably linked with the humanitarian or authoritarian aspects of the colonial regime. As a result of these events the people's mental horizon widens, and they cultivate a world view which transcends the village. Tradition comes to play an insignificant role – 'Tradition, with its narrow outlook, does not combine happily with common sense, humanity and a broad outlook.' (p.xiii) By going into minute details of life the author portrays Serowe as a village rooted in reality, small but complete and attractive. It is blessed with great personalities who want 'to change the world' and 'have an oceanic effect on society'. (p.xv) For greater effectiveness the story is woven around three of such prominent personages – Khama the Great, Tshekedi Khama and Patrick van Rensburg. Each in his time plays a crucial role and becomes a source of communal happiness and pride.

Khama the Great lays the foundation of true greatness for his people. The author's comments supported by historical evidence and the oral testimony of a variety of people attest to this. He is a dynamic leader who moves his people in difficult stages from the era of darkness and ignorance to that of true enlightenment and freedom. He embraces the new values which come with Christianity and therefore rejects polygamy as a way of life. He accepts British protection, encourages the work of the London Missionary Society and increases the provision for primary education. The faith-healing churches which mushroom all over the place alongside the established Christian churches pose a problem. They operate more like business concerns than places of worship and capitalise on the people's belief in magic and supernatural forces. Evidence is adduced to confirm their waywardness, extortionist policies and tendency to exploit the people. Khama's high reputation is partly owed to the way he removes this unnecessary threat and strongly supports the established churches.

Khama exercises tremendous authority over his people who, fortunately, have great faith in him. For them his is a time of prosperity acquired through self-sufficient skills like pot-making, farming, tanning, hut-building. The villagers produce most of what they need. He is liberal enough to allow trade between his people and foreigners. To ensure that the villagers are not cheated he personally supervises foreign trade and initiates commercial activities beneficial to the tribe. His benevolent grip on the population often reveals itself in the orders which he often imposes. For example, the work includes an 'Exhortation' in which Khama, in his urge for social reform and self-reliance, upbraids his people for violating his 'laws and regulations'. These relate to drinking, divorce, sale of cows, and the habit of disposing of cattle in unauthorised places. These laws are intended to promote the welfare of the people, and emanate from the reformist zeal which Khama shows throughout his reign. He succeeds in infecting others with his enthusiasm and in creating for himself an important place in the history of the Bamangwato people. Many of them in their evidence refer to him with love and affection.

> Wherever there is a spark of genius or true greatness in a man, mankind pays its homage. And so it is with Khama. All the missionaries, travellers and administrators who passed through his town took due note of his striking personality and achievements and there are innumerable such records of his life. Unfortunately, all this material is as yet uncollected in one complete biography. Unfortunately too, according to the language and values of the Victorian era, he is treated as an exception to the rule and hailed from all sides as the one 'kaffir' or 'native' who somehow made it straight to God amidst the general 'savagery', 'abominations' and 'heathendom' of his land. Overlooked is the fact that all men are products of their environment and that only a basically humane society could have produced Khama. (p.3)

Khama is so important in the social and political landscape of Botswana that his death is said to have left 'a gaping hole in the fabric of society'. (p.59) There has been a complete breakdown of family life which individuals attribute to various causes – Khama's reforms, insecurity in marriage and family life, the abolition of bride price, family feuds resulting from polygamy, and church marriage which puts the man under immense strain. Other factors are identified: the new evils which have come with independence, family planning, the fact that 'women no longer regard themselves as a prize that has to be won' (p.62), shortage of men, the economic independence of women. Whatever the reason, Khama's death marks the end of an era. Many traditional historians recall with pleasure the glorious age of Khama and painfully regret the social degeneration which follows his death. The distinction is made between the dignified behaviour of those who benefit from Khama's rule and the moral laxity of those who do not.

> The older people all look like Khama. They move around quietly, Bible in hand. They are absolutely sure of the existence of God. The young live in complete chaos. Nowhere is this more evident than in

the breakdown of family life in Serowe. This breakdown affects men and women of the age groups from forty to fift and all the young people who follow on after them, so much so that most mothers are unmarried mothers with children who will never know who their real father is. Out of every one hundred children born in Serowe, three on the average are legitimate; the rest are illegitimate. (p.58)

White historians are blamed for glossing over the heroic struggles of pioneers like Khama and for 'denying for a long time that black men were a dignified part of the human race'. (p.67) Even so, Khama is remembered as a man of great personal magnificence. It is left for other public-spirited people to carry forward his ideas and improve on his various attempts at reform.

Tshekedi Khama follows in his father's footsteps and makes contributions in the areas of social reforms, the provision of welfare services, the modernisation of the people's thoughts and way of life. His era is linked with remarkable educational progress and widespread adoption of the system of self-help. For example, most of the primary schools started by his father were held under the shade of trees. It is during his time that school buildings are erected and the schools are put on proper footing. The founding of the Moeng College is a major educational achievement. It provides the necessary basis for self-confidence and tolerance in the relationship between whites and blacks. For the first time in the history of the country an opportunity is provided for white and black teachers to live together as professional equals in the same kinds of houses. As an experiment in education Moeng College combines academic activities with manual work so that pupils leave college well prepared for the challenges of life – 'They stamped corn, worked in the gardens, baked their own bread, milked their own cows – all the food they ate, except sugar and tea, was grown on the school farm.' (p.85) This is a new conception of the role of education for which Moeng College becomes famous through the illustrious support of Chief Tshekedi. It is mainly because of his achievement in the educational field and the constructive use he makes of the 'work regiments' (the 'age regiments' of the previous administration) that his era is considered one of the most eventful in Serowe's history.

In Tshekedi's time, work regiments were a part of everyday village life and he had a terrific amount of projects going on all at the same time. It's so different today where no single man is an initiator of projects, but then, he was the sole initiator of all the work projects. He concentrated mainly on schools and the water supply, and the use of regiment labour was the only means of self-help. His method of mobilising people into work regiments spread from Serowe to all the outlying villages in Bamangwato country. And unlike today, there was no aid money to build schools – the regiment labour people offered was free, and apart from that he asked for donations of cattle – Moeng College was entirely built on cattle donations from the tribe and regiment labour. He also levied new taxes such as cattle sales commission and site rents; this mostly affected the white traders. It was just done by the word of Tshekedi, even though it was discussed in a most democratic manner at the kgotla. Today, when we levy new taxes in the council, we have to get legal authority to do so. (pp.80-81)

Oral testimony speaks of achievements in other directions. Chief Tshekedi takes steps to found Pilikwe Village in circumstances which would have daunted a man of inferior calibre. The social viability of the new village is a tribute to his administrative efficiency and managerial ability. He is a fierce believer in the democratic process, which frequently results in conflict between him and the colonial authority. Having democratised the Kgotla system, he expects the British to follow his good example in their dealings with their African subjects. The colonial power only succeeds in making him more popular with his people by sending him into exile twice on flimsy excuses. He is remembered as an affable gentleman, capable of treating everybody, rich or poor, as equals, one who 'could live with kings and commoners with equal ease'. (p.86) His rule is connected with the massive expansion of medical services, the establishment of antenatal clinics, the introduction of family planning and help from the International Planned Parenthood Federation. The 'minor war' between the Tswana traditional doctor and modern medicine is resolved in favour of modern science. Traditional magic gives way to scientific proof as more people become disillusioned with traditional medicine. Furthermore, Tshekedi, like his father, encourages local and foreign trade and ensures that the benefit of this is enjoyed by the people. History records the co-operation of white traders in this matter, especially those of them like Billy Woodford and Sonny Pretorius who have come to regard themselves as 'tribesmen'. Through the affiliation of traders in the Chamber of Commerce, they promote the objective of social reform and help to ensure for Tshekedi Khama a place of great honour in the history of Botswana.

Patrick van Rensburg continues Chief Tshekedi's good work. His particular achievements are in the areas of new educational theories, project work and rural development. His popularity derives from the founding of the Swaneng Hill School through which he develops his new educational ideas. He believes education should not be used 'to provide a new elite for white collar jobs'. (p.136) It should be a means of raising the quality of life of the whole community. For this reason the school is turned into a village development workshop where academic and technical training are combined to the pupil's advantage. This new concept is further developed in the idea of the 'Brigades' which provide vocational training for those who cannot have secondary education. The emphasis is on individuals acquiring skills relevant to the needs of the community.

The minimum that is required of us is that we should make each of our pupils an agent of progress. To do that, it might be enough simply to awaken in each a desire to better himself. But in fact, we would like to go further. We hope that when our pupils leave us, they will consciously recognise their role as agents for progress. Most of all, we would like them to feel under some compulsion to fight hunger, poverty and ignorance in their country. At Swaneng Hill School, we will certainly discourage any notion that education is just a ladder on which ambition climbs to privilege. (p.137)

The Brigades are designed to contribute maximally to public welfare. During the period of training the pupils learn to support themselves financially. Hence the slogan 'Earn While You Learn'. The skills imparted reflect societal needs and aspirations – farming, building, carpentry, engineering, weaving, printing and tanning. Some of these — for example, the printing and engineering Brigades – become so successful that they 'rose quite rapidly to the position of business establishments and directly employed their trainees'. (p.146) Furthermore, at Boiteko van Rensburg develops a village self-help project to produce articles which the villagers initially exchange for other articles and later sell for cash. The aim is for the villagers to become self-sufficient and take their destiny, industrially and commercially, in their own hands instead of relying on help from outside groups and agencies. The Swaneng Consumer's Co-operative Society, another project initiated by van Rensburg, is intended to teach the people how to pool their resources. It makes it possible for them to buy cheaper goods at wholesale prices. All these projects reflect van Rensburg's humanity, his concern for the villagers' progress and freedom of choice, the type of concern which leads him to relinquish his diplomatic appointment with the South African government when that regime becomes too oppressive. His various projects impart self-confidence to the people and, given the number of foreign volunteers involved, help to turn Serowe into an international village. One cannot therefore but agree with the author that the Swaneng project means 'respect for man, no matter who he is'. (p.138) This is an appropriate tribute not only to van

213

Rensburg, but also to Khama the Great and Tshekedi Khama through whose ingenuity, resourcefulness and dedication Serowe has achieved its greatness. It is to Bessie Head's literary ingenuity that we owe the fact that this greatness is vividly implanted in the reader's imagination.

Notes

1 Nadine Gordimer, 'English-Language Literature and Politics in South Africa' in Christopher Heywood, ed., *Aspects of South African Literature* (London, Heinemann, 1976), p.114.

2 *When Rain Clouds Gather* (London, Victor Gollancz Ltd., 1968). Page references are to the Heinemann New Windmill Series, 1981 edition.

3 *Maru* (London, Victor Gollancz Ltd., 1971). Page references are to Heinemann, African Writers Series edition, 1980 Reprint.

4 *A Question of Power* (London, Davis – Poynter Ltd., 1974). Page references are to Heinemann, African Writers Series edition, 1981 Reprint.

5 Book Review of *A Question of Power*, *Daily Nation*, Nairobi, 28 January, 1982.

6 *The Collector of Treasures* (London, Heinemann, A.W.S., 1977) Page references are to this edition.

7 *Serowe: Village of the Rain Wind* (London, Heinemann, A.W.S. 1981) Page references are to this edition.

Conclusion

The novels and short stories considered in this book betray an amazing variety in content and approach. The attempt to establish a link between tradition and modern experience poses problems which each novelist has tried to solve in her own way. Some solutions are more attractive than others. All are, however, worthy of attention, and a few have resulted in interesting experiments which deserve close literary scrutiny. These novelists have written under vastly different conditions and with varying motivations. Yet each in turn has produced works which, whatever their quality, have made a contribution towards the achievement of the social aspirations of women and the formulation of the ideals of a feminine literary tradition.

The success of a novel often depends on the type of material used and the mode of communication employed. A concern that is basically traditional may become exciting if it is made relevant to modern life. Relevance in most cases is heightened by conflict or some other unusual events. So we have, for example, in *Honeymoon for Three* a conflict between the old and new, between traditional religion and Christianity, all intricately interwoven into the love affair between Naiga and Nuwa. The same can be said of the relationship between Gikere and Selina in *Ripples in the Pool* and that between Cy and Hima in *Black Night of Quiloa*. *The Eigth Wife* and *Your Heart is My Altar* also belong to this group of novels. The success of these works lies in the way the authors use the intimate relationship between two individuals to reveal the strengths and weaknesses of man in society and to make statements of cardinal importance. Where the relationship succeeds, such as in the case of Nuwa and Naiga, the author dramatises the conditions which lead to success and happiness in marital life. Where it fails, as in some of the other cases, the circumstances which lead to failure are made obvious for all to see. At times there is the element of tragic inevitability surrounding a relationship, as we have in the case of Cy and Hima. Hazel Mugot gives the impression that whatever the two lovers do or fail to do, their love affair will fail. However hard they try, the social gulf which divides them gets wider. Not only are they socially incompatible, there are also racial differences to contend with. The reader is invited to conclude that, given the same conditions at any other time, in any other circumstances, the result is likely to be the same. It is usually by such intelligent artistic use of material that these writers establish a link between tradition and modern life.

These novels highlight many other areas of conflict in contemporary society. There is, for example, the problem of growth in which Miriam Were takes particular interest. What are the appropriate roles of the home and the school in the upbringing of the child? What is the best method of making these agencies complement each other? How can the school best discharge its obligation to promote indigenous culture? These are some of the questions to which Miriam Were addresses herself in her works. It is wholly inappropriate for the school to regard itself as the instrument of modernity and, for that reason, act in total disregard of the social necessities of the home and the community. As the children grow in knowledge and wisdom, so they must develop a sense of belonging and be completely integrated into their cultural environment. Conflict situations are also developed on sensitive topics like mothercare, breastfeeding, childlessness in marriage, racial prejudice, bride price and slavery. In some of these cases tensions arise mainly from the impulse of the individual to attempt to live by a code of personal conduct, while at the same time he recognises that he cannot do this successfully without reference to others and the rules and conventions which govern their lives. Many of the novels uphold traditional ideas and expect conformity. In most cases characters who assert their individualism and deviate from societal norms come to grief. However, there are a few instances where individuals defy society and get away with it. Naiga and Nuwa in *Honeymoon for Three* and Chiyei and Echi in *The Moonlight Bride* are outstanding examples of this. There are also cases where societal expectations are not realised. Take, for example, the issues raised, and only partly resolved, in *The Joys of Motherhood*. The work is constructed on a sustained irony which turns Nnu Ego's 'joys' into sorrow. She is the victim of the need for women in traditional society to have children. She is expected to take delight in these children and work hard to train and please them. All these she does. Unfortunately they disappoint her in old age, and she dies a miserable person. She reaps a sour harvest after a life of extreme devotion to her children. At her death her fortunes are no better than those of a childless woman. The novelist may be suggesting that there should be loftier ambitions for women than the mere fact of having children.

Attempts at experimentation with material abound in these novels. This necessarily leads to a variety of approaches. There is, for example, the autobiograpical novel, *Daughter of Mumbi*, where a conscientious effort is made to develop the aspirations of an individual in the context of national history. It is through the eyes of Mumbi that the reader comes to appreciate the difficulties and trials a nation experiences. There is also Bessie Head's extraordinary work, *Serowe: Village of the Rain Wind*, in which she imaginatively embodies the achievements and failings of selected individuals into the success story of Serowe. Practically every kind of prose writing is attempted, from historical fiction in *In The Beginning* and *Pricess Nyilaak* to novels providing comments on social and cultural life like *The Graduate, A Call at Midnight, Second-Class Citizen* and *The Beggars' Strike*.[1] The last novel takes the form of a dilemma tale in which a mediocre politician, Mour Ndiaye, finds himself in dreadful conflict with city beggars. He drives them off the street only to discover later that he needs them to climb up the political ladder. These beggars, who ordinarily will be considered inconsequential, bring about his defeat and fall. Into this theme the novelist cleverly weaves other matters of social and political relevance, which makes this novel, originally published in French, one of the most powerful by a female African novelist.

> Aminata Fall Sow's theme of dignity is interlaced with the popular controversial themes of polygamy, the women's liberation movement, and the generation gap, all of which stem from the widening chasm between tradition and Western ideologies.
>
> Polygamy and women's liberation are often two sides of the same problem. Mour Ndiaye's wife, for example, after years of obedience, speaks out against her stunned husband when the latter decides to take on a second wife. Traditional societal and peer pressures, however, force her to submit in order to avoid the shameful consequences. Tradition has become too much a part of her life for her to change now.[2]

The success of the novel lies in the way it provokes thought on several issues of enormous interest to other writers.

These concerns at times become obvious in the novelist's critical attitude to events around her. The war novels like *Destination Biafra, Never Again* and *One is Enough* imply criticism of both sides of the

Nigerian civil war. So also are the works on apartheid which painfully focus on the atrocities perpetrated against the blacks in South Africa. The message of a female African novelist in these circumstances is to the whites who commit these outrageous acts. She describes a society divided against itself. Instead of employing a language of violence, she presents her works in a way that brings out their distinctive features, as arising from the African mode of imagination and embodying the African aesthetics. Herein lies the strength of the works of writers like Miriam Tlali and Bessie Head. To do otherwise is to betray the African cause, play into the hands of the enemy and give the impression that the writer has nothing new to offer.

> To accept the white aesthetic is to accept and validate a society that will not allow him to live. The Black artist must create new forms and new values, sing new songs (or purify old ones); and along with other Black authorities, he must create a new history, new symbols, myths and legends (and purify old ones by fire). And the Black Artist, in creating his own aesthetic, must be accountable for it only to Black people. [3]

For virtually the same reasons Adaora Ulasi's novels are critical of the social order. Her targets are usually the colonial authority, government officials and the gullible masses of the people. The fact that her jibes are embodied in detective and mystery novels makes them all the more pungent once her message is unravelled. However, the level of criticism is raised to that of bitter satire in works like *Our Sister Killjoy* and *Naira Power*. The latter is a bitter sarcastic commentary on the complete lack of social amenities in Lagos, and how the apparent inactivity of the government and the chaotic behaviour of the people have combined to make life intolerable for the citizens. The picture of life painted by female novelists is usually not as bleak as this. But nowhere on these pages does one find an uncritical total acceptance of the political authority, the programmes of the government or the attitude of the people. These writers, perhaps because they are women, show great sensitivity for what is necessary and proper for the moral health of the nation and the material well-being of the people.

These novels are conceived as a major contribution to the feminist ideals – the woman's point of view is made prominent at every stage. The woman is often put in the centre of affairs, leaving the man free to accept or reject his subordinate role. It is from these circumstances that women derive their confidence. These pages are full of instances of the display of such confidence. Reference has already been made to the attempt to establish a lesbian relationship between Sissie and Marija, to which most of *Our Sister Killjoy* is devoted. The attempt fails only because of the need to emphasise the interdependence of the sexes. It is, however, noteworthy in the way it helps to lay the foundation of an aspect of a possible feminine literary tradition.

It is not only in the realm of ideas but also in the form and mode of expression that these novels are important. The novelists, like their male counterparts, have benefited from the traditional modes of expression – riddles, proverbs, folktales, songs and chants – and have used these to adorn their works and make them more acceptable, culturally and linguistically. This is not altogether surprising, given the role of women in formulating and codifying these modes of expression in traditional society. It is to the credit of these writers that a large-scale transfer of knowledge and skill has taken place in the second language and has been so well utilised. When one adds to this the experiment with ideas such as we have in *The Beggars' Strike* and *The Night Harry Died*, the experiment with form such as is attempted in *So Long a Letter*, and the experiment with language and style such as we have observed in *Our Sister Killjoy*, it becomes obvious how particularly enterprising these authors have been. In their novels and short stories they have almost invariably, in content and style, adopted a refreshing approach to creativity and, to a large extent, succeeded in establishing for the African female novelist a place of high esteem in the literary field.

Notes

1 Aminata Sow Fall, *The Beggars' Strike* (translated from the French original by Dorothy Blair) Longmans, London, 1981.

2 D.H. Diop, Review of *The Beggars' Strike* in *Ufahamu*, Regents of the University of California, Los Angeles, Vol.xi, No.2 (Fall 1981 – Winter 1982), p.180.

3 Ezekiel Mphahlele, *Voices in the Whirlwind* (London, 1973), p.65.

Bibliography

Basic Texts

Aidoo, Ama Ata, *Our Sister Killjoy* (London, Longman, 1977)

Ba, Mariama, *So Long a Letter* (London, Heinemann, AWS, 1981)

Bakaluba, Jane, *Honeymoon for Three* (Nairobi, East African Publishing House [EAPH], 1975)

Emecheta, Buchi, *In the Ditch* (London, Allison & Busby Ltd, 1972)

—— *Second-Class Citizen* (London, Allison & Busby Ltd, 1974)

—— *The Bride Price* (London, Allison & Busby Ltd, 1976)

—— *The Slave Girl* (London, Allison & Busby Ltd, 1977)

—— *The Joys of Motherhood* (London, Allison & Busby Ltd, 1979)

—— *The Moonlight Bride* (London, O.U.P., 1980)

—— *Destination Biafra* (London, Allison & Busby Ltd, 1982)

—— *Naira Power* (London, Macmillan, Pacesetters Series, 1982)

Fall, Aminata Sow, *The Beggars' Strike*, trans. by Dorothy Blair (London, Longmans, 1981)

Head, Bessie, *When Rain Clouds Gather* (London, Victor Gollancz Ltd., 1968)

—— *Maru* (London, Victor Gollancz Ltd., 1971)

—— *A Question of Power* (London, Davis-Poynter Ltd., 1974)

—— *The Collector of Treasures* (London, Heinemann, AWS, 1977)

—— *Serowe: Village of the Rain Wind* (London, Heinemann, AWS, 1981)

Mugot, Hazel, *Black Night of Quiloa* (Nairobi, EAPH, 1971)

Njau, Rebeka, *Ripples in the Pool* (London, Heinemann, AWS, 1978)

Nwapa, Flora, *Efuru* (London, Heinemann, AWS, 1966)

—— *Idu* (London, Heinemann, AWS, 1966)

—— *Never Again* (Enugu, Nwamife Publishers Ltd., 1975)

—— *One is Enough* (Enugu, Tana Press Ltd., 1981)

—— *This is Lagos and Other Stories* (Enugu, Nwankwo – Ifejika & Co Publishers Ltd., 1971)

220

—— *Wives at War and Other Stories* (Enugu, Flora Nwapa & Co., 1980)

Ogot, Grace, *The Promised Land* (Nairobi, EAPH, 1966)

—— *Land Without Thunder* (Nairobi, EAPH, 1968)

—— *The Other Woman* (Nairobi, Transafrica Publishers Ltd., 1976)

—— *The Island of Tears* (Nairobi, Uzima Press Ltd., 1980)

—— *The Graduate* (Nairobi, Uzima Press Ltd., 1980)

Tlali, Miriam, *Muriel at Metropolitan* (London, Longman Drumbeat, 1979)

—— *Amandla* (Johannesburg, Ravan Press (Pty) Ltd., 1980)

Ulasi, Adaora Lily, *Many Thing You No Understand* (London, Michael Joseph, 1970)

—— *Many Thing Begin for Change* (London, Michael Joseph, 1971)

—— *The Night Harry Died* (Lagos, Research Institute Nigeria Ltd., 1974)

—— *The Man from Sagamu* (Fontana Books, 1979)

Waciuma, Charity, *Daughter of Mumbi* (Nairobi, EAPH, 1969)

Were, Miriam, *The Boy in Between* (Nairobi, O.U.P., 1969)

—— *The High School Gent* (Nairobi, O.U.P., 1972)

—— *The Eighth Wife* (Nairobi, EAPH, 1972)

—— *Your Heart is My Altar* (Nairobi, EAPH, 1980)

Books

Abrash, Barbara, *Black African Literature in English since 1952* (Johnson Reprint Corporation, New York, 1967)

Altenbernd, Lynn and Lewis, Leslie, *A Handbook for the Study of Fiction* (London, Macmillan, 1969)

Ferguson, Mary Anne, *Images of Women in Literature* (University of Massachusetts, Houghton Mifflin, Boston, 1973)

Gilbert, Sandra and Gubar, Susan, *The Madwoman in the Attic* (New Haven and London, Yale University Press, 1980)

Gordimer, Nadine, *The Black Interpreters: Notes on African Writing*. (Spro-Cas/Ravan Press, Johannesburg, 1973)

Hafkin Nancy and Bay, Edna, *Women in Africa* (Stanford University Press, Stanford, California, 1976)

Hedges, Elaine and Wendt, Ingrid, *In Her Own Image: Women Working in the Arts* (The McGraw Hill Book Co., New York, 1977)

Heywood, Christopher, ed., *Aspects of South African Literature* (London, Heinemann, 1976)

Jahn, Janheinz, *Who's Who in African Literature* (Tubigen, Horst Erdmann Verlag, 1972)

Leith-Ross, Sylvia, *African Women* (London, Routledge and Kegan Paul, 1965)

Lindfors, Bernth, *Black African Literature in English* (Detroit, Gale Research Company, 1979)

—— *Mazungumzo-Interviews with East African Writers, Publishers, Editors & Scholars* (Athens, Ohio, Africa Programme, 1980)

Moers, Ellen, *Literary Women* (London, The Women's Press Ltd., 1978)

Mphahlele, Ezekiel, *The African Image* (London, Faber, 1962)

Obiechina, E.N., *Culture, Tradition and Society in the West African Novel*

221

(Cambridge, CUP, African Studies Series, 1975)

—— *An African Popular Literature* (Cambridge, CUP, 1973)

Omotosho, Kole, *The Form of the African Novel: A Critical Essay* (Akure, Olaiya Fagbamigbe, 1977)

Palmer, Eustace, *An Introduction to the African Novel* (London, Heinemann, 1972)

Roscoe, African, *Uhuru's Fire-African Literature East to South* (Cambridge, CUP, 1977)

Showalter, Elaine, *A Literature of Their Own* (London, Virago Press Ltd., 1978)

Taiwo, Oladele, *An Introduction to West African Literature* (London, Nelson, 1967)

—— *Culture and the Nigerian Novel* (London, Macmillan, 1976)

—— *Agencies of Education* (London, Macmillan, 1966)

Uchendu, U.C., *The Igbo of Southeast Nigeria* (New York, Holt Rinehart and Winston, 1965)

Zell, Hans and Silver, Helene (eds), *A Reader's Guide to African Literature* (London, Heinemann, 1972)

Articles

Adewoye, S. A., 'The Role of the African Women in Traditional Literature', Paper presented at a conference of the Literary Society of Nigeria.

Awoonor, Kofi, 'Tradition and Continuity in African Literature' in Rowland Smith, ed. *Exile and Tradition*, (London, Longman, 1976)

Brown, L.N., 'Ama Ata Aidoo: The Art of the Short Story and Sexual Roles in Africa', *World Literature Written in English* 13, Arlington, Texas

Callixta M., 'The African Woman in Grace Ogot's Work', M.A. thesis for the University of Burundi.

Conde, Maryse, 'Three Female Writers in Modern Africa: Flora Nwapa, Ama Ata Aidoo and Grace Ogot', *Presence Africaine*, no.82 2e trimestre, 1972.

Cook, David, Review of *The Promised Land* in *Journal of Commonwealth Literature*, No.6, January 1969.

Dathorne, O.R., 'Grace Ogot: Role of the Black Woman', *African Literature in the Twentieth Century* (Minneapolis, University of Minnesota Press, 1974).

Emenyonu, Ernest N., 'Who does Flora Nwapa Write for?' *African Literature Today*, No.7 (London, Heinemann, 1975)

Fleming, Victoria, 'Women and Development', *West Africa*, 7 December, 1981.

Gowda, H.H. Anniah, 'The Colonial Encounter: Criticism', *Literary Half-Yearly* 21, ii, 1980 (Mysore)

James, Adeola, Review of *Idu* in Jones ed., *African Literature Today*, No.5, 1971.

Marquard, Jean, 'In Exile and Community in Southern Africa: The Novels of Bessie Head', Times Literary Supplement 18 ix-x, 1978.

Masolo, Dismas A., 'Towards Authentic African Literature: Luo Oral Literature', *Africa* (Rome) Vol.31, No.1, Marzo 1976.

Mazrui, Ali A., 'Identity and the Novelist: An Iron Law of Individualism', in

Nursey-Bray, Paul E. ed., *Aspects of Africa's Identity: Five Essays*. (Kampala, Makerere Institute of Social Research, Makerere University, 1973)

Moore, Gerald, 'The Language of Literature in East Africa.' Halifax, Dalhousie Review, Vol 53, No.4, Winter 1973-74.

Mphahlele, Ezekiel, 'African Literature: What Tradition?' Colorado, *Denver Quarterly* 11, Summer, 1967.

—— 'The New Mood in African Literature' *Africa Today* xix, 4, Fall 1972.

New York Times (New York) Book Review of *The Bride Price* on 27 January, 1980.

—— Book Review of *The Joys of Motherhood* on 11 November, 1979.

Nwankwo, Nkem, 'The Artist's Place in Modern African Society', Los Angeles, *Ufahamu* iv, 1, Spring 1973.

Obadina, Tunde, 'A Worshipper from Afar', interview with Buchi Emecheta in *Punch* (Lagos), May 17, 1979.

Ogungbesan, Kola, 'The Cape Gooseberry also grows in Botswana: Alienation and Commitment in the Writings of Bessie Head', *Presence Africaine*, No.109, first quarter, 1979.

Okai, Atukwei, 'Literary Criticism and Culture', *West Africa*, 14 July, 1980.

Rubadiri, D, 'The Development of Writing in East Africa', *Perspectives on African Literature*, Christopher Heywood, ed. (London, Heinemann, 1971)

Shoga, Yinka, 'Women Writers and African Literature', *Afriscope*, Lagos, Vol.3, No.10, October, 1973.

Taiwo, Oladele, 'Junior Poetry in English – Orientation, Content, Language and Methodology', *Junior Literature in English*, S.O. Unoh, ed. (Ibadan, A.U.P., 1981)

Times Literary Supplement (London), Review of *Second-Class* Citizen, 31 January, 1975.

Umeh, Marie, 'African Women in Transition in the Novels of Buchi Emecheta', *Presence Africaine*, 116, 1980.

Wanjala, Chris., 'Roadside Drama', *The Weekly Review* (Nairobi) No.84, September 20, 1976.

Welbourn, F.B., Book Review of *Land Without Thunder* in *African Affairs* (London) Vol.69, No.275 April, 1970.

West Africa, Book Reviews of *Destination Biafra* on 14 March 1982 and of *The Beggars' Strike* on 17 May, 1982.

World Literature Written in English (Arlington, Texas) Book Review of *Second-Class Citizen* on 15 January, 1976.

Index